America in Peril

Other Titles by Author

The Counterforce Syndrome: A Guide to U.S. Nuclear Weapons and Strategic Doctrine (Washington, DC: Inst. for Policy Studies, 1978; Tokyo, Iwanami Shoten, 1978).

First Strike: The Pentagon's Strategy for Nuclear War (Tokyo: TBS-Britannica, 1979; Boston: South End Press, 1983; London: Pluto Press, 1983; Munich: Werkhaus Verlag, 1984; Speracedes, France: Alternative et Culture, 1988; Denmark: Claus Eric Hamle, 1989).

Nuclear Empire (Vancouver: New Star Books, 1989).

Titles Co-authored by Author

Accidental Nuclear War: The Growing Peril (Ontario: Peace Research Inst.–Dundas, 1984).

Children And Nonviolence (Pasadena, CA, Hope Publishing, 1987).

Resisting the Serpent: Palau's Struggle for Self-determination (Baltimore: Fortkamp, 1990).

Co-edited by Author

The Nuclear Time Bomb: Assessing Accidental Nuclear War Dangers Through the Use of Analytical Models (Ontario: Peace Research Inst.–Dundas, 1986).

America in Peril

by

Bob Aldridge

Foreword by

David Ray Griffin

Hope Publishing House
Pasadena, California

For information address:

Hope Publishing House
P.O. Box 60008
Pasadena, CA 91116 - U.S.A.
Tel: (626) 792-6123 / Fax: (626) 792-2121
E-mail: hopepub@sbcglobal.net
Web site: http://www.hope-pub.com

Printed on acid-free paper
Cover design – Michael McClary/The Workshop
Cover art – Robin Aldridge

Library of Congress Cataloging-in-Publication Data

Aldridge, Robert C.
    America in peril : / by Bob Aldridge ; foreword by David Ray
Griffin. -- 1st. ed.
        p. cm.
Includes appendices.
ISBN 978-1-932717-15-0 (alk. paper)
    1. Civil rights--United States. 2. Democracy--United States. 3.
Conservatism--United States. 4. Authoritarianism--United States.
5. Political corruption--United States. 6. United States--Politics
and government--2001- 7. United States--Foreign relations--2001-
8. September 11 Terrorist Attacks, 2001--Influence. 9. September
11 Terrorist Attacks, 2001--Causes. I. Title.
JC599.U5A49855 2008
973.931--dc22

                                            2007052003

Contents

Written with love
for
my grandchildren
and
great-grandchildren
and
all the children in America,
now and in the future.

Acknowledgements

Two very good people whom I have had the honor to call friends for over a quarter century provided the critical evaluation so direly needed to organize and focus this work. They got me started on the right track and helped me sort out the chaff to get down to the bare message. For that help I am grateful to George Kent and Jim Douglass. Thank you, George and Jim.

Glitches invariably appear in the computer mystique, and the software used for preparing *America in Peril* was no exception. My son-in-law David Grabel and my son Mark Aldridge were of invaluable assistance in sleuthing out those stealthy little bugs that tend to invade my computer and paralyze the products generated. Thank you, David and Mark.

My granddaughter-in-law Mika Aono and daughter Jane Johansen generously shared their expertise to offer suggestions which went into the cover design. Thank you, Mika and Jane.

In preparing this book I was most fortunate to have Faith Sand as my editor and publisher. She patiently steered me to assemble a jumble of words in a fashion that is readable and understandable. It was fun working with her on this project. Thank you, Faith, for your diligent guidance.

I owe so much to Janet, my wife and partner for 60 years. First and foremost I had her encouragement and support to carry me through this project. Then there was all the assistance she provided in everything from searching the internet and brainstorming ideas to the mundane tasks of proofreading and critiquing the content. Thank you, my darling.

Thank you also to all the other family and friends who provided encouragement, ideas and so much more. It was wonderful having your love and support.

Earlier versions of some portions of this book appeared in my Pacific Life Research Center papers, available at http://www.plrc.org

Foreword

Bob Aldridge's *America in Peril* is a wake-up call for Americans. Several such wake-up calls have been published recently, but this book is different.

Aldridge not only points out that many developments since 9/11 have moved us toward fascism; he also discusses in detail these post-9/11 developments—such as secret detentions, military commissions, extraordinary renditions, torture, the loss of *habeas corpus,* the PATRIOT Act, extraordinary military spending, unprecedented government secrecy and unprecedented claims for presidential authority—all in the name of "national security." He also shows how the invasions of Iraq as well as of Afghanistan have been justified on the basis of 9/11 and demonstrates how these wars and most of the other recent developments are in line with neoconservative ideology, which 9/11 allowed the administration to turn into official policy.

Aldridge's book is distinctive because, besides highlighting all these things, he resists the standard explanation, even among left-leaning thinkers, according to which the Bush-Cheney administration simply took advantage of the shock created by the 9/11 attacks. Rather than portraying these attacks as merely good fortune from the point of view of the Bush-Cheney administration, Aldridge comes right out and says what millions of Americans—including growing numbers of architects, engineers, pilots, scientists and former military and intelligence officers (see the Patriots Question 9/11 website) believe—namely, that the 9/11 attacks were planned and carried out by this administration, precisely for the sake of putting its preëstablished agenda into effect.

Then, bringing this analysis to bear on our present peril—which is the imminent danger of martial law—he says: "All that is needed is a 'catastrophic emergency' to set the wheels of martial law in motion. 9/11 illustrates how easily such an emergency can be orchestrated."

If Aldridge is right about this, and I believe he is, then America truly is in peril. Aldridge suggests that the remedy, in the first place, is simply truth. Another great American patriot who believed this was the Reverend William Sloane Coffin Jr., who said shortly before his death in 2006: "9/11 truth is a very important issue with the power to bring lasting change to our country."

As Aldridge's book shows, the idea of "9/11 truth" needs to be understood broadly as including not only the truth about 9/11 itself, but also the truth about its not unintended consequences, which we can call 9/11 Wars and 9/11 Social Policy.

A more inclusive remedy, Aldridge then adds, will require a spiritual perception of life. And by this Aldridge means something quite different from the kinds of American pseudo-spirituality that either remain indifferent to social-political issues or else support the imperialist drive toward a *Pax America*. This genuine spirituality will be needed to counter the bogus spirituality of neoconservatives inspired by Leo Strauss (see Shadia Drury's two insightful books, *The Political Ideas of Leo Strauss* and *Leo Strauss and the American Right*). Strauss, having accepted Nietzsche's dictum, "God is dead," said that Nietzsche's only mistake was to utter it out loud. Rather, Strauss counseled, religion should be used to control and mobilize the masses behind the policies of their rulers.

A genuine spirituality, one that engenders respect for all peoples and hence mobilizes us to work for the common good, will be needed to reverse the developments that have brought us to our present peril.

—David Ray Griffin, author
9/11 Contradictions: An Open Letter to Congress and the Press

Introduction

We hold these truths to be self-evident, that all men are created equal, that they are endowed by their Creator with certain inalienable rights, that among these are life, liberty, and the pursuit of happiness. That to secure these rights, governments are instituted among men, deriving their just powers from the consent of the governed, that whenever any form of government becomes destructive of these ends, it is the right of the people to alter or abolish it, and to institute a new government, laying its foundation on such principles and organizing its powers in such forms, as to them will seem most likely to effect their safety and happiness. —The Declaration of Independence
Adopted by Congress July 4, 1776

Those inspiring words announced a colony's determination not to be exploited by a ruler in England named George. They rallied a higgledy-piggledy assortment of farmers and tradespeople into a resistance movement that won this country's independence from one of the strongest powers on earth at that time. Those words metamorphosed into a constitutional democracy in which exploitation of human and civil rights could never happen again.

Or so our forebears thought. Time has taken its toll. Our Declaration of Independence has been relegated to something students learn about in history courses. Our inalienable rights to life, liberty and the pursuit of happiness are taken for granted. The distinction between government and country has become blurred. The irresponsible notion of an invincible America has corrupted our motivations and jaded our thinking.

There are certain people who recognize this mass complacency and exploit it. Such a group recently obtained power in America under another ruler named George. Life became cheap, liberties fell away, and any perceived pursuit of happiness became a desire for the future, at least for many. America, as a democratic and free nation, is in peril.

Amid this ideological transposition we citizens are like the proverbial frog in a pot of water on the stove. As the temperature rises the frog doesn't notice. But when the boiling point is reached the frog is no more. Under the guise of a "war on terror" and "national security," our government under George is scrapping constitutional rights and privileges in a systematic manner. Most citizens aren't paying attention to the water temperature in this cauldron of state. The flame must be doused quickly if democracy is to survive. To save our country we need to heed the advice of our forebears regarding government – it is time *"to alter or abolish it, and to institute a new government, laying its foundation on such principles and organizing its powers in such forms, as to them will seem most likely to effect their safety and happiness."* This will take more than another election. It will require a collective change in attitude.

That is why I am writing *America in Peril.* As this drama unfolds the reader will see a steady pattern of intrigue and deception. When one assault on our Constitution falters, another comes from a different direction under a new name and by a fresh sponsoring agency. Putting it all together, as I have tried to do in this book, the total picture is overwhelming – a composite the reader may not have previously recognized.

In the first chapter I will lay out the background on the cast of characters, how they wiggled their way into the White House and how they conjured up a crisis to rally the country behind a wartime president. Then I will delve into how democracy has been undermined following the attack on Sept. 11, 2001 and how the infrastructure has been put in place for authoritarian rule (chapters 2-4). Following that I will show how the government is attempting to keep tabs on the populace while simultaneously keeping them ignorant (chapters 5-7). Next I explain the gradual erosion of civil rights, the hoaxing and brainwashing of the populace, the trickery to bypass the judicial process and the attempts to scrap humanitarian law (chapters 8-9). I end this discussion by suggesting two possible outcomes to America's present path. Chapter 10 outlines the path to dictatorship if we citizens do not take corrective action. Chapter 11 suggests a worldview that can save this country if enough perceptive people see its potential and put it in motion.

America is indeed in peril. The test we face is profound. It will take an aroused and indignant public to save this country. By all that is human I am not optimistic. I pray that a higher power will arouse Americans to the necessary indignation that will get us out of this mess. —*Bob Aldridge,* Santa Clara, California

We will not recognize it as it rises. It will wear no black shirts here. It will probably have no marching songs. It will rise out of a congealing of a group of elements that exist here and that are the essential components of Fascism.

...

It will be at first decorous, humane, glowing with homely American sentiment. But a dictatorship cannot remain benevolent. To continue, it must become ruthless. When this stage is reached we shall see that appeal by radio, movies and government-controlled newspapers to all the worst instincts and emotions of our people. The rough, the violent, the lawless men will come to the surface and into power. This is the terrifying prospect as we move along our present course.

– John T. Flynn
American Mercury, February 1941

1

The Neoconservatives Launch Their Agenda

Constant reference to a war on terror did accomplish one major objective: It stimulated the emergence of a culture of fear. Fear obscures reason, intensifies emotions and makes it easier for demagogic politicians to mobilize the public on behalf of the policies they want to pursue.
—Zbigniew Brzezinski[1]

Pax Americana literally means "American Peace," or peace on America's terms. It is derived from the term *Pax Romana* which refers to the terms of peace imposed by Rome on the people in its empire. Many observers have appropriately translated this term as "American Empire." That is the goal of the neoconservative agenda.

The Neoconservative Agenda

The image of big business, tarnished during the depression years, regained some of its luster because of its participation in the World War II effort when the military-industrial complex was born. During the 1940s it flexed its muscles to become the dominant player in our political drama as we entered the nuclear age and engaged in the cold war. Later came computer technology and space exploration. Mass communication took giant strides through the mediums of television, the internet and cellular phones.

A significant change after World War II was the disenchantment of certain liberal Democrats who reversed themselves to become the most right wing of Republicans who now tout themselves as the new breed of conservatives–"neoconservatives" or "neocons." This group crafted an ambitious agenda to achieve world domination in the 21st century. Many believe the foreign activities of the George W. Bush administration were reactions to world events. They were not. Rather these were meticulously planned and are the unfolding of *Pax Americana*.

What Is A Neoconservative?

Irving Kristol, who refers to himself as the "godfather" of all neocons, wrote in *The Weekly Standard* that "the historical task and political purpose of neoconservatism would seem to be this: to convert the Republican party, and American conservatism in general, against their respective wills, into a new kind of conservative politics suitable to governing a modern democracy."[2]

Kristol believes patriotism is a natural and healthy sentiment, that world government is a bad idea, that politicians must be able to distinguish friends from foes, and that "national interests" go beyond geographical definition to include ideological and material concerns. He also champions overall military superiority and says that with "power come responsibilities, whether sought or not, whether welcome or not.... [E]ither you will find opportunities to use it, or the world will discover them for you."

A neoconservative website that touts itself as "the far right lane on the information highway" provides a similar definition, categorizing the three aspects of American conservatism as social, fiscal and foreign-policy conservatism. The first cherishes traditional family values, the second works to limit government intrusion on economic matters, and the third wants a strong military to spread democracy around the world. The website claims traditional conservatives can believe in any of these three categories, but a neoconservative believes in all three. "Neoconservatism is the intersection of economic, social and foreign policy conservatism. We are true conservatives in that we believe in all aspects of conservatism..."[3]

The *Christian Science Monitor* describes neoconservatives in more forthright language: "Neocons envision a world in which the United States is the unchallenged superpower, immune to threats. They believe that the US has a responsibility to act as a 'benevolent global hegemon.' In this capacity, the US would maintain an empire of sorts by helping to create democratic, economically liberal governments in place of 'failed states' or oppressive regimes they deem threatening to the US or its interests."[4] The article describes the neocon dream as spreading democracy over the entire Middle East to eliminate a breeding ground for terrorists. It also states that neocons believe only strong US leadership backed by a strong military will bring world peace, and they have little respect for what they consider weak treaties. This is *Pax Americana* in its most profound sense.

The *Christian Science Monitor* article then explained that neoconservatives would meet hostile regimes with force—not through appeasement or containment—and would reconfigure America's global military force to be mean, lean and agile to contain hot spots quickly in the Middle East, Central Asia, Southeast Asia or other regions. They support increased US military spending, particularly on high-tech weaponry adaptable to preëmptive strikes. Although they would make an apparent effort to work with the United Nations and other countries, they would always be ready to act unilaterally to satisfy America's interests.

Neoconservatives, who were mostly Democrats disenchanted with their party's excess in social programs and its reluctance to improve military strength, first emerged in the 1960s. Most had become Republicans by the 1980s and found the Reagan administration favorable to promoting their agenda. The end of the cold war coupled with the Bush Sr. and Clinton administrations slowed their progress. They spent the 1990s perfecting their ideas and regrouping. The first surfacing of the neoconservatives' post-cold war agenda occurred in 1992 in the initial draft of the "Defense Planning Guidance."

Defense Planning Guidance

After the Soviet Union collapsed and the Persian Gulf War came to an inconclusive end, President George H.W. Bush announced a "New World Order" in which the US was the sole remaining superpower. Then Defense Secretary Dick Cheney had a new "Defense Planning Guidance" drawn up. Directing preparation of this document were Cheney's Undersecretary of Defense for Policy, Paul Wolfowitz (later deputy defense secretary under Rumsfeld), and his Deputy Undersecretary of Defense for Policy, I. Lewis Libby (later Vice President Cheney's chief of staff). Others involved were Richard Perle and Zalmay Khalilzad. This classified 46-page February 18th draft was leaked to *The New York Times* and the *Washington Post*, creating such an uproar, that Cheney was told to rewrite it.

Barton Gellman, the *Washington Post* journalist to whom the draft document was leaked, quoted a revealing passage: "Our number one mission in the world, now that we are the sole superpower, is to make sure we stay that way."[5] That Feb. 18th draft was our first glimpse of *Pax Americana*. Senator Robert Byrd stated cynically: "We love being the sole remaining superpower in the world and we want so much to remain that way that we are willing to put at risk the basic health of our economy and well-being of our people to do so."[6] The saga that unfolds throughout this book will show how prophetic that statement was.

It is wise to note that the original draft was replaced only after its content became public knowledge. That earlier draft was quite indicative and followed the theme that the US "must maintain the mechanism for deterring potential competitors from even aspiring to a larger regional or global role."[7] For instance, the draft document said:

- "Our first objective is to prevent the reëmergence of a new rival" to replace the former Soviet Union. "This is a dominant consideration underlying the new regional defense strategy and requires that we endeavor to prevent any hostile power from dominating a region whose resources" would allow it to wield global power.
- "The US must show the leadership necessary to establish and protect a new order...convincing potential competitors that they need not aspire to a greater role or pursue a more aggressive posture to protect their legitimate interests."
- "In non-defense areas, we must account sufficiently for the interests of the advanced industrial nations to discourage them from challenging our leadership or seeking to overturn the established political and economic order."
- "In the Middle East and Southwest Asia, our overall objective is to remain the predominant outside power in the region and preserve the US and Western access to the region's oil."

Reading that carefully, one notes it demands peace on America's terms or no peace at all. This draft arrogantly asserts that "the sense that the world order is ultimately backed by the US will be an important stabilizing factor" and that "we will retain the preëminent responsibility for addressing selectively those wrongs which threaten not only our interests, but those of our allies and friends..."

That was in 1992. Pentagon plans were toned down during the Clinton administration but neoconservative thinking behind that document continued to expand. Then they wrote to President Clinton.

The 1998 Letter to President Bill Clinton

In January of 1998 some 18 neoconservatives signed a letter to President Bill Clinton, just days before his state of the union message. It urged him "to enunciate a new strategy that would secure the interests of the US and our friends around the world.

That strategy should aim, above all, at the removal of Saddam Hussein's regime from power." This letter asserted that containment was not working so that sanctions were losing credibility. It claimed Iraq's lack of coöperation with weapons inspectors "has substantially reduced" our ability to assure that Saddam is not building weapons of mass destruction and that it's "difficult if not impossible" to monitor chemical and biological weapons production.

The letter blatantly stated: "The only acceptable strategy is one that eliminates the possibility that Iraq will be able to use or threaten to use weapons of mass destruction. In the near term, this means a willingness to undertake military action as diplomacy is clearly failing. In the long term, it means removing Saddam Hussein and his regime from power. That needs to become the aim of American foreign policy." Of the signatories to that letter, eleven held key positions in the Bush administration. All the signers are listed in Appendix A, along with their past and present government positions and their organizational membership.

When Saddam Hussein evicted the UN weapons inspectors in December 1998, Clinton unleashed a four-day barrage on Iraq code-named Desert Fox. But this was suspected to be more a ploy to mitigate his impeachment vote than a response to the letter. The next step was to characterize the neoconservative agenda.

The September 2000 Report—Rebuilding America's Defenses

The Project for the New American Century (PNAC) was founded in the spring of 1997 with the goal of promoting America as the global leader. Co-founders Robert Kagan and William Kristol later signed the 1998 letter to Clinton. PNAC's "Statement of Principles" asks: "Does the United States have the resolve to shape a new century favorable to American principles and interests?" It claimed what was needed is "a military that is strong and ready to meet both present and future chal-

America in Peril

lenges, a foreign policy that boldly and purposefully promotes American principles abroad, and national leadership that accepts the United States' global responsibilities." It warned that "the United States must be prudent in how it exercises its power. But we cannot safely avoid the responsibilities of global leadership or the costs that are associated with its exercise."[8]

That sounds noble but let us look at the details. Distressed by the flat-line military spending of the 1990s, PNAC began a study of defense plans and resource requirements in the spring of 1998 which built on the 1992 draft "Defense Planning Guidance" and culminated in a September 2000 report entitled "Rebuilding America's Defenses: Strategy, Forces and Resources for a New Century." Thomas Donnelly, the principal author, plus 27 others from a wide spectrum of specialties contributed to this 76-page document which addressed everything from strategy and policy to deployment and procurement – and is a dream list for unlimited resources that would bankrupt America. The proponents and their interests, of course, would become very rich. It was released a year before the 9/11 attacks, during an election year, and as the Pentagon was gearing up for the second Quadrennial Defense Review due in 2001.

Probably the first public awareness of "Rebuilding America's Defenses" came from Scotland's *Sunday Herald* on Sept. 15, 2002, when investigative reporter Neil Mackay outlined how Bush and his cabinet had planned "regime change" in Iraq even before he was elected president.[9] He pointed out this plan for US global domination calls for "maintaining global US preëminence, precluding the rise of a great power rival, and shaping the international security order in line with American principles and interests." It also points out the need for a US military presence in the Middle East that transcends just ousting Saddam and says the unresolved issues with Iraq provide immediate justification for the buildup of forces. Beyond the Middle East, this secret plan calls for the US capability to "fight and win as rapidly and decisively as possible, multiple, nearly simultaneous major theater wars."

Such blatancy is astounding. "Rebuilding America's Defenses" refers to US forces abroad as "the cavalry on the new American frontier" and supports an earlier document by Wolfowitz and Libby which posited the US must "discourage advanced industrial nations from challenging our leadership or even aspiring to a larger regional or global role."[10] Mackay listed other issues addressed in the report:

- Rely on key allies like the UK to achieve global leadership.
- Put peacekeeping missions under US rather than the UN.
- Warns of rivalry by the European Union.
- Keep all US bases in the Middle East indefinitely regardless of indigenous opposition.
- Warns that Iran may become a threat to US interests.
- Increased US military presence in Southeast Asia.
- US must totally dominate space and cyberspace.
- Suggests that US development of biological weapons "that can 'target' specific genotypes may transform biological warfare from the realm of terror to a politically useful tool."
- Labels North Korea, Libya, Syria, and Iran as dangerous regimes.

Mackay quotes British Parliamentarian Tam Dalyell who blasted the PNAC report as "a blueprint for US world domination—a new world order of their making. These are the thought processes of fanatic Americans who want to control the world."

The National Security Strategy of the United States of America

This report calling for the US to be top gun was devious but only suggestive. When such ideas work their way into official policy, the world becomes more dangerous—which is what happened when Bush released the 2002 "National Security Strategy of the United States of America."[11]

Ostensibly because of the "war on terror," this 23-page document departs markedly from any strategy of the past, but

America in Peril

relies heavily on the PNAC report. It says "US national security strategy will be based on a distinctly American internationalism that reflects the union of our values and our national interests." To dismiss international opinion the strategy states "we will be prepared to act apart when our interests and unique responsibilities require."

Under the guise of fighting terrorism, Bush's national security strategy takes on a more aggressive tone, saying "we recognize that our best defense is a good offense.... As a matter of common sense and self-defense, America will act against such emerging threats before they are formed."

Later it gets more specific: "While the United States will constantly strive to enlist the support of the international community, we will not hesitate to act alone, if necessary, to exercise our right of self-defense by acting preëmptively against such terrorists, to prevent them from doing harm against our people and our country." Addressing weapons of mass destruction, the document reads: "We must deter and defend against the threat before it is released.... [T]he United States can no longer rely on a reactive posture as we have in the past.... We cannot let our enemies strike first."

There is more: "The greater the threat, the greater the risk of inaction – and the more compelling the case for taking anticipatory action to defend ourselves, even if uncertainty remains as to the time and place of the enemy's attack. To forestall or prevent such hostile acts by our adversaries, the United States will, if necessary, act preëmptively." Preëmption is woven throughout the strategy. It is quite clear the administration has an announced first-strike policy. Shortly after the national security strategy was released, its full ramifications became apparent with "shock and awe" in Iraq.

I must now back up a bit. Before the neoconservative agenda could be implemented, they first had to grab control of government, and then hold onto it. Here is how that happened.

Political Conquest Through Rigged Elections

The 2000 presidential election gave neocons their opportunity to actually implement their agenda. First objective: capture the White House. George W. Bush – governor of Texas, brother of Florida governor Jeb Bush and son of former president G.H.W. Bush – was chosen as the Republican candidate. His Democrat opponent was Vice President Al Gore.

Election 2000: The Florida Coup

First reports on Election Day evening indicated Gore was leading. Then something unprecedented happened in Florida. Although exit polls showed Gore winning, the official count favored Bush. If Gore won Florida's 25 electoral votes, he would lead with 291 electoral votes to Bush's 246 (270 needed to win), but if Bush got Florida's 25 electoral votes he would squeak through with a one-vote margin: 271 to 266. Two important factors influenced how this drama played out: 1) Bush's brother was governor of Florida and 2) Florida Secretary of State Katherine Harris was co-chairperson of Bush's presidential election campaign for the state. Both pressed their influence to insure a Bush victory.

Bush won by a mere 537 popular votes. However, the events leading to that victory were so suspicious that the US Commission on Civil Rights (USCCR – established in 1967 to address voting rights issues) looked into the matter. Its preliminary investigation found widespread allegations. A more extensive investigation discovered that: "Potential voters confronted inexperienced poll workers, antiquated machinery, inaccessible polling locations, and other barriers to being able to exercise their right to vote...widespread voter disenfranchisement – not the dead-heat contest – was the extraordinary feature in the Florida election."[12]

Many who registered simply had their registration cards thrown out. "Millions of minority citizens registered to vote using what are called motor-voter forms.... [T]he Commission on Civil Rights found widespread failures to add these voters to the registers. My sources report piles of dust-covered applications stacked up in election offices."[13] These were mainly poor and Black applicants of which some 90% would have voted for Gore, thus handily overcoming Bush's 537 popular vote lead.

Even getting registered doesn't mean you can vote–90.2% of those on Florida's purge list of ex-felons were innocent of any felony, causing 57,700 voters to be removed from the voting roster. Some 31% of them were Black. The USCCR Report stated: "The purge system in Florida proceeded on the premise of guilty until proven innocent.... Once on the list, the process places the burden on the eligible voter to justify remaining on the voter rolls." The report attributed the resulting widespread disenfranchisement to "encouraging an error-laden strategy that resulted in the removal of a disproportionate number of eligible African American voters from the rolls."

So you voted, but that didn't mean your vote was counted. There were 179,855 "spoiled ballots" which Florida refused to count. A vote can be "spoiled" for many irregularities–a stray mark, a ballot punched twice, a machine malfunction, or writing in a candidate's name instead of checking it. The USCCR estimated that 54% (97,121) of these were cast by Blacks, of whom some 90% would have been for Gore. Of the remaining 82,855 spoiled votes, the USCCR estimated that half (41,400) would have been for Democrats. The final estimate through all these mishaps was that Gore lost 138,521 votes but Bush only lost 41,334. Remember, Bush only had a 537 popular-vote lead.

The USCCR concluded the "problems Florida had during the 2000 presidential election were serious and not isolated. In many cases they were foreseeable and should have been prevented. The failure to do so resulted in an extraordinarily high and inexcusable level of disenfranchisement, with a significantly disproportionate impact on African-American voters," over 90% of whom vote Democratic.

From here proceeded the sensational events that led to Bush

being appointed president by the US Supreme Court. The infamous butterfly ballot, the hanging chads, long lines and inadequate handicapped assistance, absentee ballot disputes, the on-again, off-again recounts, riots that prevented poll workers from recount, and much more are all well-recorded history.

Assassinations and the 2002 Midterm Election

After the 2000 election, the Republicans had a lead of 223 to 211 in the House with the Senate split 50-50. Vice President Cheney weighing in where there was a tie gave the Republicans control of the Senate. That precarious lead vanished when Senator James Jeffords, Republican from Vermont, announced on May 24, 2001, he was switching to an Independent. The resulting upset put the Democrats in control – 49 Republicans, 50 Democrats, and 1 Independent who became more aligned with the Democrats.

Control went back to the Republicans after the 2002 midterm elections. But two mysterious events involving too many suspicious circumstances contributed to that Republican victory. The first happened late evening on 16 October 2000, three weeks prior to the presidential election. A twin-engine Cessna crashed in a wooded area near Goldman, Missouri killing Missouri Gov. Mel Carnahan and others. Carnahan was running for the Senate seat held by John Ashcroft. He had established himself as a traditional Democrat – raising taxes to pay for public school improvements, proposing legislation regulating insurance companies, pushing for better children's health insurance and getting 26,000 people off of welfare.

Missouri election law would not allow Carnahan's name to be removed from the ballot. Lt. Gov. Roger G. Wilson succeeded Carnahan as governor and said he would appoint the governor's widow if Carnahan won the election. He won and Jean Carnahan became the junior senator from Missouri until the mid-term 2002 election.

The second mysterious event occurred nine days later, just

before the election. A Beechcraft King Air A-100 approached Eveleth-Virginia Municipal Airport, landing gear down and wing flaps extended. At 10:21 AM it lost radio contact with the tower and crashed two miles short of the runway, killing Minnesota Senator Paul Wellstone and others.[14] Wellstone was probably the foremost liberal senator on Capitol Hill and had voted against the bill that would allow the use of force in Iraq. He advocated help for the disadvantaged, crusaded for homeless veterans and opposed bankruptcy reforms which benefited banks, credit card issuers, automobile finance companies and retailers at the expense of the people. He fearlessly took solitary stands for the poor and hapless putting him pretty much on the opposite end of what the Bush administration stood for.

Wellstone was running against former St. Paul Mayor Norm Coleman who then won. Jean Carnahan, Mel Carnahan's widow, subsequently lost her seat to Republican James Tenet. This changed the Senate lineup to 51 Republicans, 48 Democrats and 1 Independent. Of course if Paul Wellstone had lived, he would undoubtedly have been a very strong obstacle to the Bush administrations ambitions for Iraq and had both he and Mel Carnahan survived, they would undoubtedly be occupying the seats that gave the Republicans control of the Senate.

Stealing Ohio in 2004

About 23% of the voters cast ballots on touch-screen or other direct-reading-electronics (DRE) machines. Problems with these machines surfaced during the 2002 midterm election but were more pronounced in 2004 after states scurried to install DRE machines with federal Help America Vote Act (HAVA) funds. Problems ranged from improperly trained poll workers through computer hacking to outright malicious programming. Voting machine manufacturers operated in secret with their software zealously guarded. Nevertheless, independent computer experts obtained and analyzed the code and correctly predicted fraud.

Two days after Election Day, unofficial vote tallies showed Bush ahead with 266 electoral votes and Senator John F. Kerry trailing with 252 with 270 needed to win. Ohio, with 20 electoral votes, was still a wild card. Like Florida in 2000, Ohio was the swing state. If Kerry had won he would have had 272. And also like Florida in 2000, Ohio's secretary of state was co-chair of Bush's Ohio reëlection campaign.

There were thousands of complaints in Ohio about voting irregularities and fraud. Investigations and legal actions ensued. Again, exit poll predictions and official vote tallies differed. Exit polls, conducted on Election Day, derive from representative samplings of voters asked how they voted as they leave polling stations. Adjustments are made using scientifically determined variables in voting patterns for demographic groups (gender, age, race, religion, income, political affiliation, etc.) which are then statistically adjusted to be representative of the entire population. Exit polls have been so refined they are used to detect election fraud in Third World countries.

The 2004 exit polls, taken by a pooled effort of news organizations, were designed to be the most accurate in history. On election night the exit polls showed Kerry had won Ohio by 52.2% of the vote with Bush getting 47.9%. Yet when the votes were certified, the official tally gave Bush the lead with 51% and Kerry trailing at 48.5%. Kerry's predicted popular vote lead of 4.2% switched to Bush's certified 2.5% win.[15]

That is an enormous margin of error for an exit poll. Exit polls in Germany for the 1994, 1998 and 2002 elections averaged only a 0.27% error. In the German part of the 2004 European Parliament elections the differential shift was only 0.42%. Exit polls detected fraud in the 2003 presidential election in the former Soviet republic of Georgia and the 2004 presidential election in the Ukraine. Yet when fraud is indicated in the US, the exit polls are "calibrated" to agree with official tallies. Hardly anyone today is aware that exit polls have been altered to agree with the "official" tally.

The DRE voting machine problems, manipulation and malicious programming did not account for all of the percentage shifts in favor of Republican candidates. Voter disenfranchisement and ballot disqualifications experienced in the 2000 election were still very prevalent.

Election 2006: Hacked but Not Quite Enough

Election Day 2006 was expected to be rife with fraud. All 435 seats in the House and 33 in the Senate were up for reëlection. Democrats had to gain 15 in the House and 6 in the Senate to get control. Again, voters would be facing understaffed polls with improperly trained workers and inadequate numbers of voting machines. About a dozen states had passed voter ID laws which discriminate against poor and minority voters who usually vote Democratic. Absentee voting gained popularity and faced the usual mixup of deadlines, delayed mail and postal damage. New military rules for using e-mails and faxes to cast absentee ballots raised the potential for tampering. Voter databases mandated by HAVA were inaccurate and sloppily maintained. Provisional ballots cast when there was doubt about a voter's legitimacy had no assurance of being counted. Aside from all this, there were still long lines, voter intimidation, fake sample ballots, false information about polling station relocations and distributing inaccurate voting regulations. Deceptive telemarketing techniques were stepped up ten-fold in the last days. Provisions for handicapped people and minority language groups fell far short of that required by the federal Voting Rights Act. Naturally these problems occurred in poor and minority precincts that favored Democrats.

Some 32% of registered voters cast their ballots on machines added since the 2004 election. Almost half of the voters used some form of paper ballot which was then scanned and tallied on an electronic optical scanner; 38% used touchscreen machines, many without a voter-verified paper audit trail. Election 2006 was a high-tech ball game with new rules and a different playing field. Problems were recognized for tens of thousands of voters in at least 25 states but since this was a mid-term election with no nationally elected candidates, the problems may have been more widespread but were simply overlooked.

Since all the voting glitches in the past favored the Republicans, why worry? Just because the election favored the Democrats doesn't mean it wasn't rigged. It was. The glitches and "isolated incidents" are what poll workers were able to observe. What went on prior to the election and inside the computers was another matter. These came to light on November 16th when the Election Defense Alliance (EDA), a national election integrity organization, released its report on exit polls which was an indictment of the vote-counting process in the United States. EDA co-founder Jonathan Simon elaborated, "We found evidence of pervasive fraud, but apparently calibrated to political conditions existing before recent developments shifted the political landscape, so the 'fix' turned out not to be sufficient for the actual circumstances.... What was plenty to win on October 1st fell short on November 7th."

Sally Castleman, another co-founder of EDA and its chairperson, added: "It looks for all the world that they'd already figured out the percentage they needed to rig, when the programming for the vote rigging software was distributed weeks before the election."[16]

So Simon and Castleman are explaining that computerized voting machines had to be programmed in September by just enough for a Republican win and not enough to appear suspicious. The margin of success was determined by the political climate at that time, but then the scandal of Florida Republican Mark Foley's sexually-explicit e-mail messages to teenage House pages broke into the news, immediately followed by the shame of Republican Bob Ney taking bribes in exchange for legislative failures. Compounding all that was Bush's plunging confidence ratings on his handling of the Iraq war. The political climate shifted drastically in October to favor Democrats—but too late to change the election-rigging programming.

The "unadjusted" exit polls at 7:07 PM election night showed 55% voted Democratic and 43.5% Republican in the House races–a Democratic edge of 11.5%. By 1:00 PM the next day exit polls had been "adjusted" to exactly mirror the reported vote tally. Democrats were shown with 52.6% of the total House vote and the Republicans with 45%–now only a 7.6% lead. If we are to believe the more representative "unadjusted" exit-poll data, the Democratic victory would have been 3.9%, or 3 million votes higher than what we read in the media.

Those who defend the official vote count say the "unadjusted" exit polls reflect a higher Democratic victory because Republicans were more reluctant to answer exit polls than Democrats, suggesting more Democrats were sampled which would naturally reflect a higher Democratic vote. This is the same reluctant-Republican-responder theory put forth after the 2004 election when exit polls showed Kerry had won.

The same explanation was again advanced because it is the only argument with any perceived credibility in explaining the discrepancy. But "this time there is an objective yardstick ... which establishes the validity of the exit polls and challenges the accuracy of election returns."[17] This objective yardstick was a background question asking all respondents who they voted for in the 2004 presidential election. The answers provided clear proof that Democrats and Republicans were sampled in correct proportions. Here's how it worked:

Bush's "official" victory in 2004 was by a 2.8% margin. Answers to the who-did-you-vote-for question in the "unadjusted" 2006 exit poll at 7:07 PM election night recorded 45% for Kerry and 47% for Bush. That gave Bush a 2% lead which compares to the 2.8% actual–within the margin of error of the poll. The "adjusted" 2006 exit poll was another story. When a poll is adjusted to agree with one area, every question in that poll must be adjusted in the same proportion. After being adjusted, that same question about who the respondents voted for in 2004 showed 43% for Kerry and 49% for Bush. That moved Bush's winning margin to 6%, which is a great distortion of his official lead of 2.8%. "In order to match the results of the official tally, the 2006 exit poll adjustment was so extensive that it finally depicted an electorate that voted for Bush over Kerry by a 6% margin—very clearly an under-sampling of Democrats and an over-sampling of Republicans."[18] So much for the reluctant-Republican-responder theory.

This means the Democratic margin of victory in 2006 should have shown 11.5% ± 1% lead, not the 7.6% in reported vote tallies. However, there is even more that should be considered. In a footnote to their EDA paper, Simon and O'Dell qualified their methodology. By taking Bush's 2.8% margin of victory in 2004 at face value, they point out that the same distortion in vote tallies was also shown by the 2004 unadjusted exit polls. If the "2.5% margin for Kerry in 2004 is taken as the appropriate baseline, a correctly weighted sample in 2006 would have included even more Kerry voters and even fewer Bush voters than even the 7:07 PM unadjusted poll indicated, with a substantial consequent up-tick in the Democratic margin."

That up-tick in the Democratic margin would have been 5.3%—the difference between Kerry's polled win and Bush's reported win in 2004. This changes the Democratic win margin in 2006 from the 11.5% to 16.8%—a landslide. Furthermore, had so many Democratic voters not been prevented by various means from casting a ballot, this landslide would have been considerably larger. No wonder that the EDA report concluded that "the degree of statistical distortion now required to force exit polls to match the official tally is the clearest possible warning that the ever-growing catalog of reported vulnerabilities in America's electronic vote counting systems are not only possible to exploit, they are actually being exploited."

So the rigged 2006 election still helped the Republicans considerably since the Democrats have a majority to pass responsible legislation but not the super majority needed to override a subsequent presidential veto. Thus the standoff. Had the election in 2006 been fair, there would undoubtedly have been enough of a Democratic majority to override vetoes. Had the elections in 2000 and 2004 been fair, Bush wouldn't have ever been in the White House.

Elections aren't the only events that are rigged. History has shown international events are sometimes manipulated to gain public support for a desired plan. The emotional impact of Pearl Harbor rallied the American people to enter World War II. That support continued for the duration of the war but quickly reverted to a peaceful atmosphere when the war ended. The neoconservative plan for *Pax Americana* needed a longer lasting war. September 11, 2001, was designed to provide that.

September 11, 2001 – Pearl Harbor of the 21st Century

The PNAC report *Rebuilding America's Defenses* defined a specific chain of events America should follow in this new century. Its strategy guidelines detailed how military forces should be transformed into a "dominant force," along with the resources and increased budget needed to complete that transformation.

The neoconservatives knew this called for sweeping changes and a new commitment to military buildup, to say nothing of a more aggressive foreign policy, all of which had to be sold to the American people. The report stated: "Any serious effort at [dominant military] transformation must occur within the larger framework of US national security strategy, military missions and defense budgets.... The process of transformation, even if it brings revolutionary change, is likely to be a long one, *absent some catastrophic and catalyzing event – like a new Pearl Harbor*"[19] (emphasis added). With those words the neocons defined the first link in their planned chain of events.

9/11 – Disrupting America's Continuity of Life

The official story claims 19 Arabs, directed by Osama bin Laden from a cave in Afghanistan, learned the rudiments of controlling large jet aircraft and hijacked four of them. Then, due to a parade of errors and bureaucratic bungling those four hijacked aircraft, out of radio contact, with their identifying transponders turned off, wandered around the eastern US skies until they crashed into the World Trade Center towers, the Pentagon, and a field in Pennsylvania. We have all heard the story *ad infinitum* and I will not repeat it here.

Nor will I delve into rebutting the official story of why interceptor planes weren't scrambled, why procedures and warnings weren't heeded, why intelligence prior to 9/11 was disregarded, or why the Congressional Joint Investigation and the 9/11 Commission were hampered in their work with most of their findings covered up. All those areas have been profusely discussed and anyone interested in further study can refer to books and articles listed in the References noted below. Here I want to address the preponderance of evidence indicating the 9/11 attack was planned and executed by people in the United States and their co-conspirators, including those in government.

Decades ago a historian named John Toland undertook an investigation of the Pearl Harbor attack with the intention of once and for all putting to rest the "conspiracy theories." As he gathered information he underwent a change in thinking. In 1982 he published a book, *Infamy: Pearl Harbor and its Aftermath,* which was, up to that time, the most damning indictment of the Roosevelt administration's actions and inactions that allowed and even provoked the Japanese attack on America.

Theology professor David Ray Griffin followed a similar pattern after 9/11. He admits he initially scoffed at 9/11 "conspiracy theories," but his investigations brought him to write *The New Pearl Harbor* which catalogs all the questions and evidence that should be investigated to determine how and why 9/11 happened. In his book Griffin doesn't offer his personal opinion, but merely presents evidence and asks "Why?" In the foreword to that book, renowned international law professor Richard Falk states:

[G]etting 9/11 right, even belatedly, matters desperately. The layer upon layer of unexplained facts, the multiple efforts by those in power to foreclose independent inquiry, and the evidence of a pre-9/11 blueprint by Bush insiders to do exactly what they are now doing on the basis of a 9/11 mandate is why the Griffin assessment does not even require a reader with a normally open mind. As suggested, 30-percent receptivity will do, which means that all but the most dogmatically blinded adherents of the Bush presidency should be convinced by the basic argument of this book.[20]

Griffin published another book in 2006 entitled *Christian Faith and the Truth Behind 9/11*. One remarkable bit of new information was a collection of oral histories provided by on-the-scene firefighters and officials. They were barred from public disclosure until a New York Court of Appeals ordered their release, so these became available to the public on August 12, 2005. These testimonies by 503 firefighters and medical workers, extremely damaging to the "official story," are included in the following brief summary of unanswered questions.

Why Were Hijacked Planes Not Intercepted?

The official timeline for 9/11 has been flexible. The first version, presented on the day of the attacks, implied White House complicity. Within a week NORAD made adjustments but other unanswered questions popped up. The 9/11 Commission then took its turn at tweaking in a still-unsuccessful attempt to make the timeline appear credible.

Griffin deals with that timeline for each hijacked plane, and with the well-established procedures that should have been followed by both the FAA and NORAD at each stage of each hijacking. Why weren't those procedures followed? Why has there been no meaningful investigation into why they weren't? Why was no one fired for such gross incompetence?

How Did the World Trade Center Towers Collapse?

When I first saw the twin towers collapse live on TV, my first thought was that it was a controlled demolition. Then I was deceived by the official story. Now after reading scientific facts about their construction and about how controlled demolition works, I have returned to my original impression.

The Federal Emergency Management Agency (FEMA) was charged with investigating that collapse. Griffin also points out the FEMA's report admitted that "the sequence of events leading to the collapse of each tower could not be definitely determined." Although it does speculate on what might have happened, it is geared toward reinforcing the official story. Experts in the field of building construction and fire investigation rejected the FEMA report early on, but that rejection was not widely published. Griffin details specific factors that dispute the official account these buildings collapsed from impact and fire:

- The difference in time and timing when each tower started to collapse is not consistent with the damage to each.
- The combined collision force and explosive ignition of jet fuel as each plane struck the tower was insufficient to cause collapse.
- The burning fuel did not burn hot enough to significantly weaken the *entire* steel structure.
- The simultaneous failure of each steel structural member which allowed the buildings to fall almost in their own footprint is not a mode of failure from fire and collision.
- The 10-second time for an entire 1,300-foot-tall building to collapse is almost free fall speed—a mode of failure not possible from fire or collision.
- The urgency to clear away and dispose of the structural steel, while ignoring objections that it was necessary to examine the debris, prevented scientific investigation regarding cause of failure.

A detailed exploration into these events strongly suggest collapse due to controlled demolition from the top down.

What Caused WTC Building 7 to Collapse?

Few people know that a third building in the World Trade Center complex also collapsed. Building 7, a 47-story structure located two blocks from the nearest of the twin towers, was not hit by an airplane or significant debris but it collapsed many hours later, at 5:20 PM. The official story says enough debris reached Building 7 to start a small fire which ignited 1,000 gallons of diesel fuel stored on the ground floor. The diesel fuel in turn, the official story goes, generated enough heat to weaken the steel structure and cause the building to collapse.

Griffin also points out that the sprinkler system failed to work. Why? The fire chief refused to let his men enter the building. Why? All photos of the building showed flames in just a few windows primarily on the 7th and 12th floors. No official explanation has been given for the collapse. The FEMA report also admits "the specifics of the fires in WTC 7 and how they caused the building to collapse remain unknown at this time. Although the total diesel fuel on the premises contained massive potential energy, the best hypothesis [collapse from the diesel fuel fire] has only a low probability of occurrence."

Fire investigation evidence suggests controlled demolition from the bottom but, again, the steel rubble was disposed of before forensic examination could take place. Andreas von Bulow, a German parliamentarian for over 25 years, says that the 9/11 attack was run by the highest levels of the US intelligence apparatus using WTC Building 7 as a command bunker which was later demolished in order to destroy the crime scene."[21]

What Hit the Pentagon's West Wing?

The official story says American Airlines Flight 77 crashed into the Pentagon's west wing. Physical evidence belies that story. Photos of the west wing façade, taken before it collapsed and before fire crews got to it, shows a hole less than 20 feet in diameter – not even large enough for a 757 fuselage let alone its wings and tail. There was no visible damage around the hole – no wings or tail or engines that may have been sheared off.

Barbara Honegger, a senior military affairs journalist at the Naval Post Graduate School and special assistant for policy analysis during the Reagan administration, provides compelling evidence that a bomb did massive damage to the Pentagon at 9:32 AM, five minutes before it was hit by an aircraft or missile.

She further shows that whatever did hit the Pentagon after the bomb attack was significantly smaller than a Boeing 757.[22]

Honegger relates how the front hub assembly of the front compressor of a JT8D jet engine was found in the wreckage. JT8D engines are not used on 757s, but are used on earlier jet passenger liners and a few existing old Douglas A-3 Sky Warrior planes. Honegger discloses how the A-3s were secretly retrofitted as Ft. Collins-Loveland Municipal Airport in Colorado to be flown by remote control and carry a missile. Tom Flocco substantiates this retrofit and explains in detail how remote control systems from Raytheon's Global Hawk unmanned aerial vehicle were used on the A-3s, as well as on air-to-ground missiles made by Hughes.[23] Hughes and Raytheon have now merged.

Another disturbing bit of information comes from Jim Hanson of Columbus, Ohio – a 70-year-old retired attorney and 50-year Republican who was district campaign manager for Richard Nixon. Three years of researching 9/11 convinced him the government was not innocent. A photo claimed to be of Flight 77 wreckage made Hanson suspicious. "After blowing up the photo and matching rivets to those of the 757 that supposedly crashed into the Pentagon, I found there wasn't a match."

Hanson also noticed "a curious piece of wood, or what I have determined to be a liana vine, imbedded in the aluminum piece of wreckage." Unable to understand how that could be when the aircraft hit bricks, he investigated other crashes. "I found out that another 757 went down in the South American jungle in 1995 where liana vines (similar to wicker) grow abundantly." The National Transportation Safety Board told him "the wreckage of the 757 that crashed into the jungle was being held in a military disposal site for investigation," but the location was unknown. Hanson concluded that "the military substituted this piece of wreckage in an attempt to deceive the public, in an attempt to make them believe Flight 77 hit the Pentagon when it didn't."[24]

Was Flight 93 Shot Down?

The official story has it that Flight 93 passengers overcame the hijackers and then the plane crashed. The flight was 41 minutes late taking off and some on board allegedly learned of the twin towers and Pentagon crashes via cell phone conversations. Realizing they, too, were on a suicide mission the passengers thought they had nothing to lose.

That could be true. But if so, why did it crash when there was a professional pilot on board as one of the passengers? Suspicious signs indicate the plane may have been shot down to prevent the world from knowing what really took place.

Comparing times of the cockpit voice recorder and the seismic signal recorded of the crash indicate that the last three or four minutes on the voice recorder tape are missing. In addition, transcripts of the flight control recorder tapes (not to be confused with the cockpit voice recorder) for all hijacked planes except Flight 93 have been released. Flight control recorders monitor, among other things, the planes flight path and attitude. Cockpit voice recorders monitor conversations of the flight crew.

Various reports indicate that F-16 jets were ordered to engage Flight 93 and eyewitnesses on the ground report seeing a plane following Flight 93 just before it crashed. Other witnesses report hearing loud bangs just as the plane went out of control. Locations of scattered wreckage also indicate Flight 93 may have been shot down. One engine was found over a mile from the main wreckage. The type of debris that would have been blown out of the cabin during rapid decompression was strewn along the flight path for eight miles before the crash.

The Precautionary Principle

Col. George Nelson (USAF, ret.) introduced the "precautionary principle" into 9/11 which claims you can't prove a false claim, but at the same time just because a claim is not proven does not make it false. With an event as serious and world-changing as

9/11, we should definitely be cautious. Since the Bush administration has shown not one shred of evidence "that the terror attacks were the work of Muslim extremists or even that the aircraft that struck their respective targets on September 11 were as advertised," we should not dismiss the possibility that "the 9/11 hijackings were part of a black flag operation carried out with the coöperation of elements in our government."[25]

Nelson, a professional aircraft accident investigator who reviewed countless accident investigation reports for the Air Force inspector general at Pacific headquarters during the Vietnam conflict, says it would be simple to prove the aircraft were as claimed in the official story. Every aircraft has a special registration number. In each aircraft there are hundreds of parts critical to flight safety. For planes that carry passengers, whether civilian or military, each of these special parts is identified by a unique serial number. When the part is installed on a plane, its serial number is recorded in the aircraft's logbook with a paper trail showing what part is on which aircraft. With that degree of control in mind, Nelson comments on each of the four aircraft involved in 9/11.

United Airlines Flight 93 is reported to be a Boeing 757, registration number N591UA, which crashed into a Pennsylvania field. Although there was a huge hole, private investigators were barred from the scene. Nelson said hundreds of serially-controlled parts would have been available to support the government's story. Instead, according to Nelson, an aircraft with that same registration number is still in operation.

American Airlines Flight 11 reported to be a Boeing 767, registration number N334AA, crashed into the north tower of the World Trade Center. Nelson said, again, serially-controlled could have been found. An engine or a landing gear would have survived the catastrophe.

United Airlines Flight 175 is reported to be a Boeing 767, registration number N612UA, which crashed into the south tower of the World Trade Center. The same thing applies about serially-controlled parts which would have proven the aircraft's identity.

American Airlines Flight 77 is reported to be a Boeing 757 with registration number N644AA. Nelson said it would have been easy to find enough serially controlled parts to prove the aircraft's identity. That was not done, although some aircraft parts were apparently found but were hidden from view. He concludes: "That is the trouble with the government's 9/11 story. It is time to apply the 'precautionary principle'."

The Government's Attempts to Debunk "Conspiracy Theories"

The rising number of people disputing the government's 9/11 story has disturbed the Bush administration. A May 2006 Zogby International poll showed 42% of Americans believe the 9/11 Commission "concealed or refused to investigate critical evidence" in the terrorist attacks.[26] A Scripps Howard/Ohio University poll at about the same time yielded more disturbing results – 36% of Americans consider it "very likely" or "somewhat likely" that "federal officials assisted in the 9/11 terrorist attacks or took no action to stop them so the United States could go to war in the Middle East."[27]

That's a good chunk of the US population, prompting the administration to take the unusual step of responding to "conspiracy theories" to bolster its own official story. During August 2006 two federal documents were released: The National Institute of Standards and Technology (NIST), charged with conducting the official investigation of World Trade Center building collapses, released a fact sheet of frequently asked questions regarding World Trade Center buildings collapsing[28] and the US State Department issued a rebuttal to the top 9/11 conspiracy theories.[29]

These reports were long on words but short on facts. They also misconstrued known facts to reach a desired but erroneous conclusion which most people would likely accept as true. That may be why NIST spokesman Michael E. Newman stated: "We realize that this fact sheet won't convince those who hold to the alternative theories that our findings are sound. In fact, the fact sheet was never intended for them. It is for the masses who have seen or heard the alternative theory claims and want balance."[30] Yes, it is intended for the non-technical masses – the people of the polls that gave approval percentages so damaging to the administration.

Here are a few examples of the deception presented in the NIST and State Department documents: In refuting the controlled demolition theory the government states: "Cleanup crews found none of the telltale signs of controlled demolitions that would have existed if explosive charges had been used." Well, cleanup crews aren't the ones who look for those things so you wouldn't expect them to notice. It is the NIST that was charged with the technical examination and its document says in answer to the question about the steel being tested for thermite residue from explosives: "NIST did not test for the residue of these compounds in the steel." By its own admission the controlled demolition theory has not been disproved.

The NIST statement is also wrong. Cleanup crews did find evidence of controlled demolition – molten steel, a tell-tale sign explosives were used to cut the steel columns. Among the witnesses to this sign were Peter Tully, president of Tully Construction, and Mark Loizeaux, president of Controlled Demolition, Inc. "Tully said that he saw 'pools of literally molten steel' at the site. Loizeaux said that several weeks after 9/11, when the rubble was being removed, 'hot spots of molten steel' were found 'at the bottoms of elevator shafts of the main towers, down seven [basement] levels'" (Griffin 2006:43). The steel columns having been sliced into manageable lengths was, itself, evidence of controlled demolition.

Another indication noticed during cleanup was the condition of the steel-support members. The FEMA report noted some of the steel was "rapidly corroded by sulfidation," which is an effect from explosives. Related to that, Dr. Jonathan Barnett, a professor of fire protection engineering at Worcester Polytechnic Institute said "that 'fire and the structural damage... would *not* explain steel members in the debris pile that appear to have been partly evaporated.' But the NIST Report, in its section headed 'Learning from the Recovered Steel,' fails even to mention either evaporation or sulfidation."

The government claimed: "Demolition professionals always blow the bottom floors of a structure first, but the WTC tower collapses began at the upper levels, where the planes hit the buildings." That statement is obviously intended to lead to the conclusion that because the WTC collapse started at the top it could not be a controlled demolition. Other experts have shown that a controlled demolition could have started at the top and worked down. Furthermore, oral history reports by firefighters and other witnesses at the scene, released to the public in August 2005 by court order, indicate other evidence of a controlled demolition starting at the top.

The government says: "Non-experts claim that debris seen blowing out of windows [of the WTC towers] was evidence of explosive charges, but experts identify this as air and light office contents (papers, pulverized concrete, etc.) being forced out of windows as floors collapsed on each other." Pitting experts against non-experts makes an impressive but inaccurate argument. Experts in the New York Fire Department, plus other witnesses, testified in favor of explosive charges. Oral history from such witnesses indicated events characteristic of controlled demolition: seeing and hearing an explosion high up on the building, and then a creaking noise, or rumbling like twisted metal, as the building started to collapse; hearing multiple explosions and then a groaning and grinding sound as the building started to come down; hearing many sequential pops, like TV coverage of buildings being demolished; seeing what looked like the building blowing out on all four sides and shooting chunks of metal and concrete dust out hundreds of feet; seeing the collapse start below the strike zone and fire, not above as would happen if the collapse was from heat as postulated in the official story; the appearance of implosion[31] as the building collapsed; an explosion ring of popping and orange/red flashes that proceeded all around the building like a belt; and other phenomena characteristic of controlled demolition.

The government declares: "Demolition firms had very sensitive seismographs operating at other sites in Manhattan on September 11. None recorded any explosions during the tower collapses." Perhaps that was not possible amid the rumbling and shaking *during* the collapse, but how about just *before* the collapse? Oral history accounts testify to the ground shaking just before each tower collapsed, then seeing debris blowing out and the start of collapse.

When asked why the NIST did not consider a controlled demolition hypothesis with computer modeling, it answered: "NIST conducted an extremely thorough three-year investigation into what caused the WTC towers to collapse." Then after a long description of its activity the NIST concluded; "In summary, NIST found no corroborating evidence for alternative hypotheses suggesting that the WTC towers were brought down by controlled demolition." Summing up, the NIST said, "This hypothesis may be supported or modified, or new hypotheses may be developed, through the course of the continuing investigation. *NIST also is considering whether hypothetical blast events could have played a role in initiating the collapse*"(emphasis added). In other words, NIST hasn't yet studied a controlled demolition hypothesis which is why they found no corroborating evidence indicating controlled demolition. Furthermore, the steel was removed so fast and sold overseas that NIST could only examine 3% of the perimeter columns and 1% of the core columns – and that not for forensic evidence.

To bolster their conclusions, the State Department refers to the March 2005 *Popular Mechanics* article attempting to debunk embarrassing questions about 9/11. After summarizing the eleven features of a controlled demolition, this article completely ignored evidence of key features and how witnesses observed many of these aspects.[32]

The government reports go on and on in this same vein of insinuations and leading statements, all of which sounds technical and professional, and thus believable to the layperson. At the same time they try to assuage critical questions concerning the WTC, the Pentagon strike and what happened to Flight 93.

★ ★ ★ ★ ★

What that black Tuesday in September did provide was the "catastrophic and catalyzing event" – the "new Pearl Harbor" – which neoconservatives saw as needed to sell the American people on their agenda. 9/11 was indeed an overt act which greatly interrupted the continuity of life in America and provided the vicious enemy image that was needed to unify the public behind Bush's "War on Terror." It produced the emotions of fear and anger – the *crowd* mentality that allowed the Bush government to invade Afghanistan and execute its preplanned takeover of Iraq. While lawmakers and the people were in this frenzied state of mind, the Bush administration rushed through Congress the Patriot Act which curtailed civil liberties and constitutional rights. That was followed by other legislation to construct a barrier of secrecy and administrative unaccountability which drastically reorganized the government to control every aspect of domestic activity and foreign policy. Then followed a string of executive initiatives that preëmpted legislative and judicial oversight.

This steady erosion of the US Constitution, American values and human rights has led to an authoritarian government which is fast approaching fascism. That is the peril America faces – the steady decay of our democratic nation. That is the scope of chapters to follow.

Notes for Chapter 1

1. Brzezinski, Zbigniew, "'War on Terror' is the wrong slogan," *San Jose Mercury News*, 29 Apr 2007.

2. Kristol, Irving, "The Neoconservative Persuasion: What it Was and What it Is," *Weekly Standard*, 25 Aug 2003.

3. neoconservatism.net; "Neoconservatism Defined," at http://www.neoconservative.net/about_neoconservatism.htm.

4. "Neocon 101," *The Christian Science Monitor* website at http://www.csmonitor.com/specials/neocon/neocon101.html

5. Gellman, Barton; interview with "Frontline" (PBS), 20 Feb 2003, at http://inner-outerpeaceproject.net/BartonGellman.htm

6. Griffin, David Ray, *Christian Faith and the Truth Behind 9/11* (Louisville: Westminster Press, 2006) p. 88

7. "Defense Planning Guidance," 18 Feb 1992 draft. Published on Yale Univ. website at http://www.yale.edu/strattech/92dpg.html

8. "Rebuilding America's Defenses: Strategy, Forces and Resources for a New Century," a report of The Project for the New American Century, Sept 2000.

9. Mackay, Neil, "Why the CIA Thinks Bush is Wrong," *Sunday Herald* (Glasgow, Scotland), 13 Oct 2002.

10. Mackay, Neil, "Bush Planned Iraq 'Regime Change' Before Becoming President," *Sunday Herald* (Glasgow, Scotland), 15 Sep 2002.

11. "The National Security Strategy of the United States of America," (released 20 Sep 2002), p. 3.

12. USCCR Report—"Voting Irregularities in Florida During the 2000 Presidential Election," report of the US Commission on Civil Rights, Jun 2001, Executive Summary.

13. Palast, Greg; "Vanishing Votes," *The Nation*, 17 May 2004.

14. For incontrovertible evidence that Wellstone's death was not an accident see *American Assassination: The Strange Death of Senator Paul Wellstone* by Four Arrows and Jim Fetzer (Brooklyn, NY: Vox Pop, 2004).

15. Percentages from Freeman, Steven F., "The Unexplained Exit Poll Discrepancy: Part I," Univ of Pennsylvania, Graduate Division, School of Arts & Sciences, Center for Organizational Dynamics, Working Paper #04-10, 21 Nov 2004.

16. Simon and Castleman quotations from Rob Kall's "Clear Evidence 2006 Congressional Elections Hacked," *OpEdNews.com*, 17 Nov 2006.

17. EDA Press Release—"Major Miscount of Vote in 2006 Election: Reported Results Skewed by 4 Percent, 3 Million Votes," 16 Nov 2006.

18. Simon, Jonathan and O'Dell, Bruce, "Landslide Denied: Exit Polls vs. Vote Count 2006," a research paper for the Election Defense Alliance, 16 Nov 2006.

19. "Rebuilding America's Defenses," op cit, p. 51.

20. Griffin, David Ray, *The New Pearl Harbor: Disturbing Questions About the Bush Administration and 9/11* (Northampton, MA; Olive Branch Press, 2004), page viii.

21. Watson, Joseph and Alex Jones, "Former German Minister Says Building 7 Used To Run 9/11 Attack," *Prison Planet*, 21 Apr 2006. At http://www.prisonplanet.com/articles/april2006/210406runattack.htm

22. See Barbara Honegger, "Seven Hours in September: The Clock That Broke the Lie," appendix to *The Terror Conspiracy* by Jim Marrs, (NY: Disinformation Co. 2006).

23. Flocco, Tom, "Witnesses Link Missile to Small Military Jet Parts Found at Pentagon on 9/11," *TomFlocco.com*, 26 May 2005.

24. Szymanski, Greg; "Life-long Republican Believes Only Piece of Flight 77 Wreckage Was Planted at Pentagon on 9/11," *Idaho Observer*, February 2005.

25. Nelson, George, "9/11 and the Precautionary Principle: Aircraft Parts as a Clue to Their Identity," *Physics 911*, n.d., available at http://www.physics911.net/ georgenelson.htm

26. Olson, Geoff, "Doubt about Official Version of 9/11 Widespread," *The Vancouver Courier*, 25 Aug 2006.

27. Hargrove, Thomas, "Third of Americans Suspect 9/11 Government Conspiracy," Scripps Howard News Service, 2 Aug 2006; available at http://www.scrippsnews.com/ 911poll and Grossman, Lev; "Why 9/11 Conspiracy Theories Won't Go Away," *Time*, 11 Sept 2006.

28. See "NIST and the World Trade Center," Aug 2006; available at http://wtc.nist. gov/pubs/factsheets/faqs_8_2006.htm

29. "The Top September 11 Conspiracy Theories," 28 Aug 2006; available at http:// usinfo.state.gov/utils/printpage.html

30. Dwyer, Jim, "2 US Reports Seek to Counter Conspiracy Theories About 9/11," *NY Times*, 2 Sep 2006.

31. Implosion as a characteristic of controlled demolition is caused by destroying the center critical supports of a building first so the walls will collapse inward. This causes the building to fall straight downwards.

32. The eleven features of a controlled demolition are: sudden onset, collapsing straight down (due to implosion), falling at almost free-fall speed, total collapse of the structure, sliced steel (resulting in molten metal, evaporation of metal, and sulfidation), pulverization of concrete and other materials to dust, dust clouds, horizontal ejections, demolition rings of smoke and flame, molten steel and sounds produced by explosions.

2

Sabotaging Democracy

[W]hen [Woodrow] Wilson reached for a word—indeed for a methodology of social engineering—to move the Congress and the nation, he chose "democracy." He did not select the word because of its dictionary definitions of universal suffrage and popular government. He used it because it was charged with emotional meaning for millions of Americans in ways that went way beyond any rigorous definition of "democracy" as opposed to "autocracy." He used it because "democracy" had been an American religion.
—William Graebner[1]

Democracy is all too often worn as a badge rather than practiced as a way of life. Wearers have long forgotten that democracy has its moral basis in truth, tolerance, freedom and respect for human dignity; and requires participation, awareness and willingness to invoke necessary changes. Rather, those badge wearers exhibit behavior stemming from what Canadian psychologist Dr. Daniel Burston calls "irrational authority"—succumbing to the coaxing and enticement of an authority "which routinely resorts to violence, deception and secrecy to achieve its ends." Burston notes that "Crowds can be persuaded through specific formulas that involve frequent repetitions, in an authoritative tone, by someone who is considered authoritative. And for many people this works—it just works."[2]

America in Peril

We can cite numerous initiatives by the Bush administration to control citizen activity here at home. Some, like the Patriot Act, were successfully passed by Congress and signed into law. Others introduced subsequently have not been immediately successful, but the basic principles are re-introduced again and again, under different names in different departments. Little by little they slip through and become law. This process continues and we should all be aware of it.

The USA Patriot Act

With the advent of mass production, mass transportation, mass marketing, mass communication and all the other good things that came into existence as America developed after the Civil War, the principal players became wealthier, more powerful, and very greedy. As the 20th century dawned, corruption became obscenely obvious so legislation was enacted to protect the working class and consumers. Monopolies were somewhat broken up during the pre-World War I period and social advances took place during the 1930s depression.

Big business made a comeback during World War II. From the late 1940s to the 1990s, legislation and public attitudes have decreased the power of labor while favoring business and investment. Large corporations previously broken up by anti-trust and anti-monopoly laws came together again to become even more powerful – conglomerating to reduce competition and minimize the payroll. Concern for the common person eroded and free enterprise became a buzz word as monopolies regained control of the economy. The neoconservative faction was still not satisfied. They wanted more control, not only domestically but globally. When the Bush administration captured the White House the neocons put their agenda on the table.

9/11 and the USA Patriot Act

Erosion of democracy was jump-started by 9/11. Just days later, then Att. Gen. John Ashcroft gave Congress a conveniently-available list of new government powers known as the "Uniting and Strengthening America by Providing Appropriate Tools Required to Intercept and Obstruct Terrorism Act." That mouthful simmers down to the acronym USA PATRIOT Act – or simply the Patriot Act.

The 342-page Patriot Act has ten titles containing more than 150 sections (see Appendix B for highlights). It was virtually impossible for the administration to have prepared that document in the few days following 9/11. Neither was it submitted according to protocol which would pass it through the White House Office of Management and Budget where comments would be invited from all agencies. It was simply delivered to Congress with the demand it be passed unchanged within a week. In spite of prevailing emotions, some lawmakers wanted a closer look. The judiciary committees in both houses began negotiations and some changes were achieved.

Ashcroft stepped up pressure, warning of imminent terrorist attacks and how Congress would be at fault if the US wasn't ready. Both House and Senate then burned midnight oil to craft nearly identical bills that rescinded most of the concessions previously negotiated. Before voting Congress recessed for the weekend and the dubious anthrax attacks created renewed panic and shut down the House for a week.

The Patriot Act finally became law October 26, 2001. Investigators can now conduct "sneak and peek" searches of suspects' homes, tap their landlines and cell phones, monitor their e-mail and internet activity – and more. Only too frequently have powers granted for one purpose been misused for another. Under the Patriot Act, Greenpeace could be investigated for terrorist activities and people protesting the wars on Afghanistan and Iraq could be investigated under the counterintelligence provisions. Had the Patriot Act been limited to terrorism it would have passed weeks earlier. Instead, a disproportionate amount of the Act can be applied to domestic criminal activities and even legitimate activities by citizens exercising freedoms of speech and expression.

Congress was concerned about certain portions that infringed on civil liberties, so it set expiration (sunset) dates for 16 sections of Title II and all of Title III which we will examine further, but first some background information.

The Foreign Intelligence Surveillance Act (FISA)

To grasp the full significance of the Patriot Act you must understand the difference between "intelligence gathering" and "law enforcement." J. Edgar Hoover's FBI started a series of counterintelligence programs (COINTELPRO) during the communist scare of the 1950s. They eventually extended to monitoring anti-war groups and anyone that spoke against US policy. Then the FBI was caught spying on a Vietnam war opposition group in Media, Pennsylvania. COINTELPRO was shut down in April 1971 and Senator Frank Church, chair of the Senate Select Committee to Study Government Operations, warned that FBI collection of domestic intelligence was a new form of unconstrained government operation that is always inclined to grow. Now with the FBI restricted to law enforcement and the CIA banned from operating in the US, it was not possible to conduct intelligence activities here at home.

Congress solved this dilemma with the 1978 Foreign Intelligence Surveillance Act (FISA) which set up special secret courts (FISA courts) from which the FBI had to obtain a warrant for foreign intelligence surveillance – electronic (phones and computers), physical searches, pen registers (recording the destination of outgoing communication), trap and trace devices (determining the source of incoming messages), and access to certain records. FISA warrants do not require the usual probable-cause justification as when a crime has been committed.

Foreign intelligence gathered by the FBI, as distinguished from the domestic intelligence used in law enforcement, cannot be used for evidence in criminal cases. It is secret. FBI agents cannot share FISA information with other FBI agents working on criminal cases, no matter how much it would help prosecution of a criminal case. In 1994 FISA was broadened to include some physical searches without warrant, without notice, or without letting the suspect know. But that information was still secret.

Melding Foreign Intelligence and Law Enforcement

All of this changed under the Patriot Act. Information sharing across the board was mandated. Standards for obtaining FISA warrants were lowered. Guaranteeing foreign intelligence as the "primary purpose" (i.e. only purpose) for a FISA warrant was changed to only requiring a "significant purpose" meaning the warrant was needed for foreign intelligence but could be used for criminal prosecution. Spying is allowed on people merely suspected of being foreign agents.

There was more. FISA search warrants can now be used repeatedly throughout the nation. These so-called roving warrants remain valid even when the investigation moves out of the issuing court's jurisdiction, thereby effectively taking judicial review out of the picture. There is no meaningful standard of "just cause" to obtain information such as consumer records, internet activity, educational records, library records, and more. And a permanent gag order prevents the institution providing the records from ever telling the subject of an investigation that their records were subpoenaed.

The CIA and FBI now work together and share information. Judicial review is unnecessary unless challenged, but challenges can be delayed at the government's request. The CIA still cannot operate within the United States or spy on US citizens anywhere, but they can accompany the FBI and benefit from the information obtained by them. The FBI can also share grand jury information with the CIA and national security agencies— even state and local police—as long as it pertains to foreign intelligence or international terrorism. Grand juries have nearly unlimited power to gather testimony, wiretap transcripts, phone records, business records and medical records in secret.

Section 802 of the Patriot Act creates the unprecedented new crime of "domestic terrorism." This criminalizes state crimes as domestic terrorism if any possible danger to human life is involved. A person cited for reckless driving could theoretically be tried in federal court as a domestic terrorist.

Immigrants and noncitizens fare worse. If they belong to or support an organization the Justice Department has designated a terrorist group, they are subject to detention even though the group may not threaten the US or even be a terrorist group at all. This is true even if the support given is humanitarian or intended to be humanitarian. Court cases have modified this activity somewhat but the threat of detention for noncitizens through misunderstood behavior is still severe.

The Treasury Department is charged with assembling a massive financial intelligence-gathering system that can be used by the CIA and they have subsequently issued extremely detailed regulations to carry out Title III of the Act (see Appendix B). It has made domestic banks virtual partners with the federal government in investigating terrorist funding and money laundering. A federal investigator can impose detailed and extreme "special measures," valid for 120 days, against domestic banks and other financial institutions once the Treasury Department makes the required "certifications." These previously unheard of special measures are not subject to court review.

Administrative Subpoenas—a.k.a. National Security Letters

Administrative subpoenas, or national security letters, can now replace a court order to obtain records. They allow investigators to trace private affairs over the internet, such as how people make and spend money, with whom they live, where they travel, what searches they make and what they read. National security letters cannot authorize eavesdropping on phone conversations or e-mail, but they are issued by the investigating agency and merely state the information needed for the case. They require no "just cause" or even a reasonable need for the information. The same gag order applies as to FISA warrants. Theoretically, they are to be judiciously used but in practice they became a convenience.

In late 2003 then Att. Gen. Ashcroft changed the 1995 policy of destroying records of innocent people when the investigation closed, to a new policy that keeps all information and distributes it freely among federal agencies. Information collected by national security letters is deposited in a new Investigative Data Warehouse using the same Oracle technology used by the CIA. In October 2004 Bush issued Executive Order 13388 making it easier to share this information with state, local, and tribal governments – in some cases with undisclosed entities of the private sector. Information in the database is now available for repeated use without justification. This database is also supplemented by consumer files obtained in the commercial sector.

National security letters are issued by more than 60 FBI field supervisors and deputies, amounting to about 30,000 a year – each applicable to numerous citizens. That's not counting national security letters issued by the Pentagon, Treasury Department and other US agencies. Although annual accountability reports to Congress are required, the executive branch keeps only bare-bones statistics and they are secret. Yet there have been no incidents reported where administrative subpoenas have helped to avert a terrorist attack.

Senator Pat Roberts, chair of the Senate Select Committee on Intelligence in 2005, said there is no proven abuse of these intelligence tools. That is not surprising, considering the secrecy and gag orders. Robert L. Barr Jr., former Georgia congressperson and CIA analyst, retorted that "the abuse is in the power itself," adding: "As a conservative, I really resent an administration that calls itself conservative taking the position that the burden is on the citizen to show the government has abused power, and otherwise shut up and comply."[3]

In March 2007 the Justice Department Insp. Gen. produced a 199-page report that stated "a significant number of [national security letter-related] violations are not being identified or reported by the FBI."[4] By 2005 the FBI had information from 143,000 requests on some 52,000 people in a database available to federal, state and local law enforcement agencies and some foreign governments. Agents were accused of ignoring instructions they didn't understand while using the letters as a matter of convenience. The report showed 22% (8,850) more national security letters were used than reported and few terrorism-related charges resulted—most were for fraud, money laundering and immigration violations.

The FBI also issued 739 emergency letters (not to be confused with national security letters) through a deal with three telephone companies which allowed the FBI, under "exigent circumstances," to obtain data with assurance that a court order was in process, although that was seldom the case. Since May 2006, emergency letters are still used, but with the promise of national security letter follow-up rather than a court order. Then in March 2007 the FBI issued an emergency letter template for use in exigent circumstances. Instructions for its use require an audit trail, but agents are told they needn't follow up with a national security letter. So now the FBI can obtain telephone records by just filling out a form.

A New Dawn for the Patriot Act Sunset Provisions

Section 303 of the Patriot Act provides that Title III in its entirety, which deals with terrorist financing, would expire on Oct. 1, 2005, unless Congress made it permanent. Congress repealed Section 303 so now the entire Title III is permanent. Section 224 provides that unless previously renewed by Congress, 16 sections of Title II would expire on the last day of 2005. They are:

Section 201—Authority to Accept Wire, Oral and Electronic Communication Relating to Terrorism.

Section 202—Authority to Accept Wire, Oral and Electronic Communication Relating to Computer Fraud and Abuse Offenses.

Section 203(b) – Authority to Share Electronic, Wire and Oral Interception Information.

Section 203(d) – Foreign Intelligence Information.

Section 204 – Clarification of Intelligence Exceptions from Limitations on Interception and Disclosure of Wire, Oral and Electronic Communication.

Section 206 – Roving Surveillance Authority under the Foreign Intelligence Surveillance Act of 1978.

Section 207 – Duration of FISA Surveillance of Non-United States Persons Who Are Agents of a Foreign Power.

Section 209 – Seizure of Voice-Mail Messages Regarding Warrants.

Section 212 – Emergency Disclosure of Electronic Communications to Protect Life and Limb.

Section 214 – Pen Register and Trap and Trace Authority Under FISA.

Section 215 – Access to Records and Other Items Under FISA.

Section 217 – Interception of Computer Trespasser Communications.

Section 218 – Foreign Intelligence Information.

Section 220 – Nationwide Service of Search Warrants for Electronic Evidence.

Section 223 – Civil Liability for Certain Unauthorized Disclosures.

Section 225 – Immunity for Compliance with FISA Wiretap.

When renewal of these 16 sections came up before Congress late in 2005, the deadline was extended twice. In early March 2006 a compromise agreement was reached. Section 224 (the sunset provision) was repealed and all sections were made permanent except Sections 206 and 215 which will sunset the last day of 2009 unless Congress makes them permanent.

In addition, in the "USA PATRIOT Improvement and Authorization Act of 2005," as it was called, Congress added several new provisions:

- Only libraries with internet access are subject to federal subpoenas for release of information on patrons.
- Recipients of federal subpoenas may contact a lawyer without providing that lawyer's name to a federal investigator.
- Recipients of federal subpoenas may challenge the gag order in court, but must wait a year to do so.
- People may sue the government if it leaks information obtained through new wiretapping and surveillance powers.

America in Peril

- The Justice Department must keep track of how often and under what circumstances the FBI secretly searches homes and seizes papers, and provide that information to Congress on certain prescribed dates.

This renewal legislation was signed into law March 9, 2006.

Court Decisions on the Patriot Act

National security letters ran into a snag on Sept. 6, 2007, when US District Judge Victor Marrero in New York ruled them unconstitutional for obtaining telephone and e-mail information from commercial companies. He said an indefinite gag order without judicial review violates the First Amendment and "offends the fundamental constitutional principles of checks and balances and separation of powers."[5] Marrero added that the "risk of investing the FBI with unchecked discretion to restrict such speech is that government agents, based on their own self-certification, may limit speech that does not pose a significant threat to national security or other compelling government interests."[6] Marrero's order affects only communications companies because that is the scope of the ACLU lawsuit which sparked it. He put a 90-day stay on his order to give the FBI a chance to appeal.

Three weeks later US District Judge Anne L. Aiken in Portland, Oregon ruled that wiretapping and secret searches authorized by FISA warrant or national security letter to gather criminal evidence, as opposed to foreign surveillance, violates the Fourth Amendment of the Constitution. The judge correctly identified the "seemingly minor change in wording" from *primary purpose* to *significant purpose* for obtaining FISA warrants as a maneuver to avoid need for probable cause, saying: "In place of the Fourth Amendment the people are expected to defer to the Executive Branch and its representation that it will authorize such surveillance only when appropriate," which is "asking this court to, in essence, amend the Bill of Rights, by giving it an interpretation that would deprive it of any real meaning."[7]

The status of court decisions cited here is where they stand at the time of this writing. Rulings by US District Courts are not necessarily binding nationwide until affirmed on appeal.

Bush's Signing Statements

President George W. Bush signed the legislation making most of the Patriot Act permanent amid much media fanfare in March 2006. The White House staff then brought out an addendum to the legislation just signed – called a "signing statement." This one indicated the President felt no obligation to inform Congress how the Patriot Act powers were used, saying: "The executive branch shall construe the provision...that calls for furnishing information to entities outside the executive branch ...in a manner consistent with the president's constitutional authority to supervise the unitary executive branch and to withhold information."[8] The unitary executive theory argues that Congress has limited power to control the executive branch.

Bush has taken this theory to extreme lengths, using it to bypass the law in several high-profile cases. When Congress passed legislation forbidding torture, Bush used a signing statement to say he would construe that provision "in a manner consistent with the constitutional authority of the president to supervise the unitary executive branch and as commander in chief... [in order to protect] the American people from further terrorist attacks."[9] Most of Bush's signing statements make general objections to what he sees as encroachment on his authority, infringement of his powers over foreign affairs, forcing him to submit information to or report to Congress, setting conditions for making executive appointments, or implying a legislative veto over his actions.

White House spokesperson Dana Perino defended Bush's actions, saying: "The signing statement makes clear that the president will faithfully execute the law in a manner that is consistent with the Constitution," at least according to the administration's ideas, "and there has not been one verified abuse of civil liberties using the Patriot Act." Right. That argument is used frequently to mollify criticism of secrecy. But if it's so clandestine we aren't supposed to know about it, how are we to get evidence to verify abuse? New York University law professor David Golove, who specializes in executive power issues, said, "On the one hand, they deny that Congress even has the authority to pass laws on these subjects like torture and eavesdropping, and in addition to that, they say that Congress is not even entitled to get information about anything to do with the war on terrorism."[10]

The Congressional Research Service (CSR) defines signing statements as "official pronouncements issued by the president contemporaneously to the signing of a bill into law that, in addition to commenting on the law generally, have been used to forward the president's interpretation of the statutory language; to assert constitutional objections to the provisions contained therein; and, concordantly, to announce that the provisions of the law will be administered in a manner that comports with the administration's conception of the president's constitutional prerogatives."[11]

Signing statements were used as far back as the early 19th century but have become more frequent and more controversial. They are neither provided for nor prohibited in the Constitution, but two significant reports on them were generated in 2006 – one by the American Bar Association (ABA) and the other by the Congressional Research Service.[12]

The ABA report says it voted to "oppose, as contrary to the rule of law and our constitutional separation of powers, a president's issuance of signing statements to claim the authority or state the intention to disregard or decline to enforce all or part of the law he has signed, or to interpret such a law in a manner inconsistent with the clear intent of Congress." This report focuses on the separation of powers and the constitutional requirement that a president either sign a bill or veto it. If vetoed, it goes back to Congress with reasons. Congress can then address those reasons or overrule the president with a super-majority vote. That cannot be done with a signing statement.

This report concluded that "the use, frequency, and nature of the president's signing statements demonstrates a 'radically expansive view' of executive power which 'amounts to a claim that he is impervious to the laws Congress enacts, and represents a serious assault on the constitutional system of checks and balances.'"

The CRS deplored signing statements as analogous to line-item vetoes which were ruled unconstitutional because they violate "the constitutional requirement of bicameralism and presentment by authorizing the president to essentially create a law which had not been voted upon by either house or presented to the president for signature." It called them "an expansive conception of presidential authority, coupled with a willingness to utilize fully mechanisms that will aid in furthering and buttressing that philosophy."

In a report issued the following year, the Government Accountability Office (GAO) determined that signing statements were issued for eleven of the twelve appropriations acts passed by Congress for fiscal year 2006.[13] Those eleven singled out 160 specific provisions to which the president took exception. The report identified twelve interconnected categories of concern or objection. The GAO then examined more closely 19 provisions from the 160, including at least one from each of the appropriations acts and each of the twelve categories of concern. They found ten of the selected provisions were implemented properly by the responsible agency, three required a special event to occur before being enacted and the events had not happened, but the remaining six provisions, a third of those examined, were not executed by the responsible agency as prescribed in the legislation.

Ambitions to Snitch, Snoop, and Data Mine

The Patriot Act did not end the neoconservative ambitions.

There followed a steady stream of actions designed to place more power in the president and the executive branch. Some of these did not reach fulfillment but were, nevertheless, building blocks of what was to come; including TIPS, TIA, and more.

Operation TIPS

With the Terrorism Information and Prevention System (TIPS), the Department of Justice planned to recruit at least 4% of the population as domestic spies – including workers who had access to people's homes, businesses, and transportation system operators – to report suspicious activity. The program started in May 2002 with police and law enforcement volunteers, then expanded to recruit long-haul truck drivers, delivery persons, letter carriers, utility employees, service providers, train conductors, longshoremen, dock workers, ship captains and more.

Opposition quickly rose from civil liberties and privacy groups – both liberal and conservative. John W. Whitehead of the conservative Rutherford Institute said: "What this means for the average citizen is that whatever you read, eat, or do – in the privacy of your home or out in public – will now be suspect in the eyes of your cable repairman, postal carrier, meter reader or others who, by way of the services they provide, will have access to your home."[14]

Majority Leader Dick Armey of the then Republican-controlled House insisted that Operation TIPS be banned in legislation creating the new Department of Homeland Security (discussed in the next chapter). Opposition was so strong by August that TIPS was scaled back to use only observers in public places. It didn't make any difference. When the Homeland Security Act became law in December 2002, Section 880 said that any and all activities to implement Operation TIPS was prohibited. Operation TIPS was dead before it got off the ground.

Or was it? Months before Congress blocked funding for TIPS, the Justice Department announced a closely related program under the same organization – called Citizen Corps. It would expand the number and mission of Neighborhood Watch Programs to make participants part of detecting terrorism. TIPS has been derailed but Neighborhood Watch thrives.

As this book goes to press, the media reports firefighters will be used to gather domestic intelligence because they enter hundreds of thousands of homes annually without a warrant. In several major cities they are being trained to recognize "suspicious" evidence and activity.

The TIA Program

In January 2002 the Pentagon established a program to "imagine, develop, apply, integrate, demonstrate, and transition all the information technologies, components and prototype, closed-loop information systems that will counter asymmetric threats by achieving total information awareness."[15] Thus several existing programs came together to create the Total Information Awareness (TIA) office.

Retired Adm. John M. Poindexter, former Reagan administration National Security advisor and a figure in the Iran-Contra scandal, was named TIA's first director.[16] He described TIA as a plan where "counterterrorism officials will use 'transformational' technology to sift through almost unimaginable large amounts of data...to find a discernable 'signal' indicating terrorist activity or planning." Many specialists questioned the technology but agreed that "if implemented as planned, it probably would be the largest data-surveillance system ever built."[17]

TIA became known through a Feb. 13, 2002, *New York Times* article by John Markoff. Liberals and conservatives alike became concerned. William Safire's Nov. 14, 2002, column in the same newspaper said TIA "has been given a $200 million budget to create computer dossiers on 300 million Americans."[18] From then on, opposition mounted.

In January 2003 Senator Russ Feingold introduced legislation to suspend work on TIA until Congress investigated the privacy issues. Senator Ron Wyden introduced legislation to prohibit TIA from operating in the US without specific Congressional permission. The next month legislation suspended TIA activities pending a Congressional report.

By May 2003 the program had been renamed *Terrorist* Information Awareness (rather than *Total*) which was more politically acceptable. It still didn't mollify the critics and the Defense Appropriations Act signed into law in October prohibited using funds for TIA and directed the office to close immediately.

Closing an office and terminating a program doesn't mean spying and data mining will cease. Two critical elements went to the Advanced Research and Development Activity (ARDA) which was then under the National Security Agency (NSA): The Information Awareness Prototype System which integrates the tools to extract, analyze and disseminate information was renamed "Basketball." The second was "Genoa II" which builds information technologies to anticipate and preëmpt attacks, renamed "Topsail" – Genoa being a headsail.

ARDA has now been taken away from the NSA, placed under the new US Director of Intelligence, and renamed the Disruptive Technology Office, which we will get to anon. Around October 2006 several universities – including Cornell, University of Pittsburgh and University of Utah – received a $2.4 million grant from the Department of Homeland Security to study what is called "sentiment analysis." They were charged with developing software to train computers to scan newspapers and track pertinent events and negative opinions worldwide.

As a database for the computer to work from they entered hundreds of articles on controversial subjects, such as Bush's term "axis of evil," words like "Guantanamo" and "global warming," and leaders such as "Hugo Chavez" of Venezuela and "Fidel Castro" of Cuba. The idea was to monitor global news faster and more comprehensively so DHS and the intelligence community could pinpoint potentially threatening patterns from massive amounts of information. Marc Rotenberg, executive director of Georgetown University Law Center, said "the effort recalled the aborted 2002 push...to develop a tracking system called Total Information Awareness."[19]

Again, it is naïve to think when a program is shut down, the forbidden technology will end. Like a shell game, it is shuffled to another department for continued development.

MATRIX

Shortly after 9/11, Florida law enforcement officials started using an intelligence gathering system called Multistate Anti-Terrorism Information Exchange (MATRIX) developed by Hank Asher, a pilot and alleged drug smuggler turned informant. Asher founded Seisint Inc. in Boca Raton, Florida, which owns MATRIX and houses its database.

MATRIX was a data-mining system like TIA. First it put government-created information into the database such as criminal history records, driver license data, vehicle registration data, incarceration/correction records, and more[20] — including digitized photographs and finger/thumb prints. Added to that were 20 billion records in databases held by private sources which a Seisint subsidiary had already collected to help creditors locate debtors. Using mathematical analysis it identifies anomalies that link people together and show suspicious behavior patterns. Analysts say MATRIX would do everything TIA was supposed to, except at the state level by a private company not subject to the same controls as a federal agency.

MATRIX soon spread to other states and the federal government to improve the exchange of information among law enforcement agencies. Even though California and Texas turned it down because of privacy and security concerns, 13 states were said to be initially interested. The Justice Department provided $4 million and the Department of Homeland Security (DHS) promised another $8 million along with a computer network.

According to a May 2004 *Washington Technology* article, MATRIX "ran into legal and political snags when many of the participating states became concerned that their state laws

America in Peril

would not allow them to transfer information about their citizens to the network's central repository. Some states also cited costs as a reason for leaving the project."[21] In early 2005, MATRIX was shut down, but only Connecticut, Florida, Ohio and Pennsylvania still remained in the network. That was not the end of the story. The shell game continued.

Patriot Act II

In February 2003—two months after TIPS had been scratched, while TIA was beginning to hit rocky seas in Congress, and as Cheney was being briefed on MATRIX—a Department of Justice secret draft of new legislation leaked to the public. The 120-page document dated Jan. 9, 2003, was called the "Domestic Security Enhancement Act of 2003." Quickly dubbed Patriot Act II and described as a frightening expansion of surveillance at the expense of privacy, it would:

- Apply an expansive definition of terrorism to some protest groups and end the need for a court order to spy on them.
- Make encrypting e-mail to hide plans for anything illegal, no matter how minor, a federal felony. (This was the first attempt, ever, to control domestic encryption.)
- Strip citizenship from any American who gives "material support" to any on the attorney general's terrorist organizations list.
- Legalize detaining people indefinitely without being charged or contacting a lawyer, and without releasing their names. Criminalize revealing a detained person's identity, no matter what their relationship to the detainee.
- Allow sharing of sensitive personal information among all law enforcement agencies. This would allow access to a consumer's credit report without a court order.
- Authorize secret arrests and detentions in immigration and other cases (such as material witness warrants) without filing criminal charges.
- Allow speedy deportation of legal immigrants based only on suspicions.
- Allow secret sampling and cataloguing and storing DNA, etc. of Americans merely suspected of being a terrorist without a court order, or the person's consent.
- Shelter federal agents engaged in illegal surveillance from crimi-

nal prosecution if they are following orders of high executive branch officials.

- Shield from civil liability any business or employee that reports "suspected terrorists" to the federal government, no matter how unfounded or malicious the tip may be.
- Allow the federal government to put gag orders on both state and federal grand juries, and take over their proceedings.

There is more in the details. These are not powers used in a democracy. They apply to protesters and any under the new "domestic terrorist" category established by the Patriot Act. Committing misdemeanors in a manner that can be construed as endangering human life can put the "domestic terrorist" label on you. Remember that "domestic terrorism" is a federal crime even though it may only have been caused by a speeding ticket.

The VICTORY Act

Reaction to the leaked Patriot Act II draft apparently discouraged Justice Department officials from introducing the bill. They still didn't give up. In June of 2003 Senator Orin Hatch of the Judiciary Committee circulated draft legislation that would expand wiretapping and investigative powers. It also linked terrorism with the drug war and banned a traditional form of paperless Middle East banking called Halawas.

Entitled the "Vital Interdiction of Criminal Terrorist Organizations Act of 2003," but dubbed the VICTORY Act (another sensation-stirring acronym), it created a new crime called "narco-terrorism," making it easier for the government to investigate the so-called narco-terrorist and prosecute fugitives and those accused of money laundering, and even nonviolent drug dealers. Some of the provisions seemed appealing, plus linking it to drugs and money laundering gave it respectability, but it also included significant portions of Patriot Act II.

The VICTORY Act apparently died in committee, or somewhere, but the concept flourished. Buried deep in the monstrous Intelligence Authorization Act for 2004 was a subtle redefinition of a "financial institution." Previously the term referred to banks, but it now includes stockbrokers, car dealerships, casinos, credit card companies, insurance agencies, jewelers, airlines, the post office and any other business where cash transactions would be useful in criminal, tax or regulatory matters. A gag order is also applicable, so the "financial institutions" cannot tell clients their records have been released. Congress passed this legislation in November 2003, but Bush didn't sign it into law until December 13. Why the unnecessary delay? He waited until the capture of Saddam Hussein dominated the media, distracting attention from his new executive power.

★ ★ ★ ★ ★

In this section I have reviewed several programs which were ostensibly cancelled. They are presented here for two reasons: to show the tenacity with which these ideas are pursued and to lay the groundwork for understanding later programs that were more successful. In the next chapter we will discuss the return of those two critical segments of the TIA program, noting how data bases are being compiled and how another program began which employs the key aspects of MATRIX. First, let's continue with more Bush administration initiatives.

National ID Cards and the Real-ID Act

The notion of a national ID card has surfaced repeatedly in past decades, but it was always dismissed due to police-state implications and privacy concerns. Amid the mass paranoia following 9/11, it again reappeared. Although the Bush administration appears to oppose a national ID card, the concept is gaining momentum.

The Common Access Card.

The Defense Department has for some time had plastic ID cards with embedded computer chips called Common Access Cards. Visible on the card are two photographs, two bar codes, a magnetic stripe and a gold computer chip. Described as looking like a driver's license on steroids, this smart card – which will encrypt e-mail, open doors to secure rooms, summon medical history, act as a debit card, and more – has been issued to thousands of military and civilian personnel. It will also allow Pentagon officials to track the bearer's actions, transactions and travel. All told, a good model for a national ID card.

Nationally-Standardized Driver's Licenses.

The federal government cannot issue a national ID card because the 2002 Homeland Security Act which cancelled TIPS also prohibited such a card, but that legislation didn't affect the states. The American Association of Motor Vehicle Administrators (AAMVA) devised a plan to include machine-readable biometric information on a nationally-standardized driver's license. The embedded identifiers would be linked to driver databases in all 50 states, Canada and the US State Department to check for outstanding tickets or other violations. The Justice Department and General Services Administration have worked with AAMVA on the project. International Biometric Group was awarded a contract in April 2003 to assist AAMVA in identifying one individual out of 200 million records. Although each state would have a separate database they would all interact. The federal government doesn't contribute towards the database but can access it. So much for prohibiting a federal ID card!

The AAMVA got a boost when the Real ID Act was signed by the president in May 2005, although it will not be effective until the end of 2009. This unfunded mandate requires all states to have uniform standards for driver's licenses plus "common machine-readable technology" for at least four pieces of biometric identification. This law was slipped through Congress without debate as an attachment to a spending measure for Afghanistan and Iraq. Some lawmakers are unhappy because privacy has not been adequately considered. Nothing in the Real ID Act requires encrypting biographical data, so high-tech ID cards loaded with information will up the ante for identity theft. Information will be collected by merchants and other entities and will be resold to companies who are in the business of compiling databases. It doesn't matter how well the states protect the data on driver's licenses because commercial companies will have the same information. Millions of driver's licenses are stolen or lost each year. The Real ID Act merely centralizes information so identity theft will be easier.

Radio-Frequency Identification Chips.

VeriChip Corp. of Florida has been aggressively trying to market its radio frequency identification (RFID) chip. Implanted chips have already been used to identify lost pets. In 2004 the Food and Drug Administration licensed VeriChip to sell implant chips for humans. As of September 2007 some 80 hospitals and 232 doctors have implanted 2,000 chips in people. CityWatcher.com, a video surveillance firm in Cincinnati, required workers in its secure areas to have chips implanted.

RFID chips are used by the Pentagon to track supplies and have even been attached to soldiers' dog tags. VeriChip wants to implant rice-grain-size chips under the skin of 1.4 million military personnel to replace dog tags. These would contain a digital photo, thumb print plus medical history. Some veterans and privacy organizations are balking, as are members of Congress. Senator Patrick Leahy questioned the safeguards on information, congressional oversight, endangerment to soldiers, and possible interception by the enemy.

In 2007 problems started surfacing. About 10% of the lab animals implanted with chips developed cancer. Serious injury can occur if an implanted chip is exposed to a strong electromagnetic field such as a MRI imager. Not only is the chip destroyed, but the person is seriously burned. Dr. Cheryl London plus preëminent cancer institutions recommend a 20-year trial period with animals before RFID chips are used in humans.

Secrets and Whistleblowers

The government is stepping up surveillance of the media

because of its part in publicizing information from whistleblowers. In May 2006 ABC News reported the FBI was monitoring reporters' phone calls in an effort to find whistleblowers and anonymous sources. The chief investigative reporter for ABC News, Brian Ross, acknowledged that this would discourage the reporting of fraud and waste, but said if that means using more shoe leather to make those contacts, that is what he would do.

Then in the May 2006 US Supreme Court ruling in *Garcetti v. Ceballos*, the court ruled: "When public employees make statements pursuant to their official duties, they are not speaking as citizens for First Amendment purposes, and the Constitution does not insulate their communication from employer discipline." This ruling meant that 20 million public employees cannot speak out against corruption or waste while on the job. It applies to government employees at all levels— including state agencies, public schools, colleges and hospitals.

The *Garcetti* decision undermines the 1989 Whistleblower Protection Act which gave federal employees First Amendment free speech protection if they reported government wrongdoing. Now the Supreme Court has gagged all public employees. In his dissenting opinion Justice David H. Souter said: "I would hold that private and public interest in addressing official wrongdoing and threats to health and safety can outweigh the government's stake in the efficient implementation of policy."[22]

Steven Shapiro, legal director for ACLU, added: "In an era of excessive government secrecy, the court has made it easier to engage in a government coverup by discouraging internal whistleblowing."[23] Stephen Kohn, chair of the National Whistleblower Center put it more bluntly: "The ruling is a victory for every crooked politician in the United States."[24]

It is true the Supreme Court's decision speaks only to an employee acting in an official capacity. There is still the possibility of a First Amendment shield if the employee acts outside the work environment as a private citizen. Los Angeles ACLU lawyer Peter Eliasberg said: "It basically says, if you go to the

LA Times you might get some protection. But if you report it in the office and up the chain of command, you don't have any protection."[25] It's still pretty dicey, particularly when the media's phones are being bugged. Many potential whistleblowers just won't risk their jobs.

Listen to what happened to a courageous whistleblower at DHS. In April 2007 the first cutter of the Coast Guard's $25 billion replacement program was delivered by Northrop Grumman—eight months late at double the cost. Even then the Lockheed Martin-furnished electronics could not process classified information but the Coast Guard was prepared to accept it anyway and fix it later at additional taxpayer expense. Systems engineer Anthony D'Armiento blew the whistle on this embarrassing activity and asked for an independent inspector general to investigate. He was placed on paid administrative leave and threatened with criminal investigation, then told he could return to his office to retrieve his computer. That was only a ploy so the DHS inspector general could question him without his attorney present. When D'Armiento refused to answer, he was escorted out at gunpoint, without his computer. The case is still pending at the time of this writing.

★ ★ ★ ★ ★

In this summary we addressed key programs aimed at giving the president unprecedented authority. Not all reached completion. Most have returned repeatedly under different sponsorship and departments. Others seemed to have disappeared in limbo. Or have they? We must constantly be on the alert. Next we will examine how government has been restructured to a more authoritarian state so it can administer these new rules.

Notes for Chapter 2

1. Graebner, William, *The Engineering of Consent: Democracy and Authority in Twentieth Century America*, (Madison: Univ. of Wisconsin Press, 1987), p. 38.
2. Goldstein, Ritt, "US: Patriotic Pride and Fear," *Asia Times*, 8 Jul 2004.
3. Gellman, Barton, "The FBI's Secret Scrutiny," *Washington Post*, 6 Nov 2005.
4. Smith, R. Jeffrey, "Report Details Missteps in Data Collection," *Washington Post*, 10 Mar 2007

5. CBS News/Associated Press, "Judge Strikes Down Parts of Patriot Act," 6 Sep 2006.

6. Eggen, Dan, "Judge Invalidates Patriot Act Provisions," *Washington Post*, 7 Sep 2007.

7. Keller, Susan Jo, "Judge Rules Provisions of the Patriot Act to be Illegal," *NY Times*, 27 Sep 2007.

8. Savage, Charlie, "Bush Shuns Patriot Act Requirement," *Boston Globe*, 24 Mar 2006.

9. CRS-RL33667 – "Presidential Signing Statements: Constitutional and Institutional Implications," a Congressional Research Service Report to Congress, prepared by Legislative Attorney T.J. Halstead of American Law Division, 20 Sep 2006, p. 9.

10. Savage, Charlie, op. cit.

11. CRS-RL33667, op. cit., p. 1.

12. See ABA Report – "Task Force on Presidential Signing Statements and the Separation of Powers Doctrine," Aug 2006; and CRS-RL33667 – *op. cit.*

13. B-308603 – "Presidential Signing Statements Accompanying the Fiscal Year 2006 Appropriations Acts," letter to Senator Robert C. Byrd and Congressman John Conyers, Jr. signed by GAO General Counsel Gary L. Kepplinger, 18 Jun 2007.

14. Branch-Brioso, Karen; "Federal Tipster Plan Gets Green Light Despite Opposition," *St. Louis Post-Dispatch*, 22 Jul 2002.

15. Information Awareness Office website – now defunct.

16. Retired Admiral John Poindexter was the highest ranking official in the Reagan administration criminally indicted for the Iran-Contra scandal. He was convicted in 1990 on five felony counts of lying to Congress, destroying official documents and obstructing congressional inquiries into the Iran-Contra affair, and sentenced to six months in jail. The conviction was overturned by a US Court of Appeals because Poindexter had been granted immunity to testify.

17. O'Harrow Jr., Robert, "US Hopes to Check Computers Globally," *Washington Post*, 12 Nov 2002.

18. *Wikipedia*, http://en.wikipedia.org/wiki/Information_Awareness_Office

19. Lipton, Eric; "Software Being Developed to Monitor Opinions of US," *NY Times*, 4 Oct 2006.

20. Other government-furnished data include pilot licenses, aircraft ownership, property ownership, Coast Guard registered vessels, state sexual offender lists, federal terrorist watch lists, corporation filings, Uniform Commercial Code filings, bankruptcy filings, civil court records, voter registration, address histories, and state-issued professional licenses.

21. Webb, Cynthia, "Total Information Dilemma," *Washington Post*, 27 May 2004.

22. *Garcetti v. Ceballos*, Supreme Court of the United States, No. 04-473, 3 May 2006.

23. Savage, David G., "Court Curbs the Speech of Public Employees," *Los Angeles Times*, 31 May 2006.

24. Holland, Gina (Associated Press), "High Court Trims Whistleblower Rights," Yahoo News, 30 May 2006.

25. Savage, David G. op. cit.

3

Big Brother Puts Down Roots

I do not believe that the kind of society I described [in my book, Nineteen Eighty-Four] *necessarily* WILL *arrive, but I believe ... that something resembling it* COULD *arrive. I believe also that totalitarian ideas have taken root in the minds of intellectuals everywhere.*
                                                                    —George Orwell, 1949

The phrase "Big Brother is watching" has become classic. In his novel. *Nineteen Eighty-Four*, George Orwell characterized Winston Smith as futilely standing alone against a post-World War III totalitarian state. Winston is systematically monitored by Thought Police who have telescreens, microphones and spies everywhere to discover and apprehend thought criminals who threaten the Party. Winston's job in the Ministry of Truth Records Department is to modify historical records to comply with the Party's version of history. Sometimes he constructs entire historical accounts from scratch. Then Winston falls into a forbidden love affair and is caught. He is sent to the Ministry of Love for reprogramming to understand the advantages of perpetual warfare. He is assured that the torture he undergoes is to alter his way of thinking, not to extract confessions. Winston succumbs to reprogramming but prides himself in maintaining a hatred of Big Brother. In the end, however, he finally comes to love Big Brother.

Nineteen Eighty-Four is scary. But we say it can't happen in our democracy. Are we sure? In this chapter I will discuss what seems to be ignored.

Department of Homeland Security

Shortly after 9/11, the Office of Homeland Security was set up with former Pennsylvania Gov. Tom Ridge as director. In May the next year the National Homeland Security Act of 2002 was introduced to establish a cabinet-level Department of Homeland Security (DHS). Congress passed the bill that November and sent it to the president. But there was serious debate over some last minute provisions: The president can change civil service workplace rules and pay scales. Dissatisfied workers can seek federal mediation but it is not binding. Liability exemptions for vaccine manufacturers are expanded. DHS can now contract with companies incorporated overseas to avoid taxes. Texas A&M gets an advantage in receiving grants for homeland security research, Homeland Security employees aren't guaranteed coverage under the Whistleblower Protection Act. All of these are in the final bill.

Bush signed the National Homeland Security Act the following week and the new department was officially opened on January 24, 2003, with Tom Ridge as the first Secretary.[1] Some 22 existing agencies and 170,000 personnel transferred to DHS, including the Federal Emergency Management Agency (FEMA), Secret Service, Coast Guard, Customs Service, Immigration and Naturalization Service, Border Patrol, Transportation and Safety Administration, and the FBI's National Infrastructure Protection Center. The transition was complete by the end of the fiscal year that September. The Act also moved the Bureau of Alcohol, Tobacco and Firearms from the Treasury Department to the Justice Department, alongside the FBI.

DHS analyzes information on terror threats collected by the

CIA, FBI, National Security Agency (NSA), and others; matches that intelligence against national vulnerabilities to detect terrorism and determine the type: cyber, nuclear, chemical, biological or whatever. DHS is responsible for border, coastline and travel security; protecting the nation's infrastructure and coördinating the national response to future emergencies.

With DHS's fiscal year 2007 spending bill, Bush issued a signing statement declaring his authority to edit DHS reports to Congress, saying he would interpret the Act "in a manner consistent with the president's constitutional authority to supervise the unitary executive branch."

It is beyond the scope of this chapter to delve into the entire operation of DHS. Here I will focus on what threatens our freedom, civil rights, and privacy.

ADVISE

It is encouraging to know that programs like TIPS, TIA, MATRIX, Patriot Act II, and VICTORY have fallen through the cracks. It's good they did, for it exemplifies how democracy should work, but we shouldn't become overconfident. That wasn't the end. DHS tried another program called "Analysis, Dissemination, Visualization, Insight, and Semantic Enhancement," a mouthful known by its acronym "ADVISE."

This is a computer system which collects massive amounts of data from blog sites and e-mail to government records and intelligence reports. It searches that data for patterns indicating terrorist activity. Data is then stored as links which show the relationships of people, behavioral patterns, places, organizations and events and this becomes available to federal intelligence and law enforcement agencies. State, local and private entities also are in the loop.

In February 2007 the Government Accountability Office (GAO) reported that ADVISE raised privacy concerns – the E-Government Act of 2002 calls for assessing those risks early on.[2] DHS officials claim assessment isn't required because the tool, itself, doesn't contain personal data but the GAO says its intended uses do involve personal data and could misidentify or mistakenly associate people with undesirable activity and crimes.

ADVISE has the same emphasis on broad collection and pattern analysis as TIA. DHS officials assure skeptics that privacy protection will be built in but Latanya Sweeney, founder of the Data Privacy Laboratory at Carnegie Mellon University said: "At this point, ADVISE has no funding for privacy technology."[3] She adds that there is no proposal for even state-of-the-art privacy technology.

Pilot tests scheduled for March 2007 were suspended after the GAO report. Then it was discovered that prior testing had been done using real people in the database without requisite privacy safeguards. Besides, the inspector general said ADVISE "was poorly planned, time consuming for analysts to use, and lacked adequate justifications."[4] With all that flak DHS declared the program terminated in early September 2007.

Did ADVISE join the fate of TIPS, TIA, MATRIX, Patriot Act II, and VICTORY? Maybe so, but it was only one of twelve data-mining projects DHS had going at the time and this one was getting too much bad press. Read on.

International TRAVEL – US-VISIT, ATS, and E-Passports

When the post-9/11 need for airport security sparked interest in "face recognition" to scan passing crowds for suspected terrorists, the National Security Entry-Exit Registration System was inaugurated. It required all males 18-45 years of age from 25 prescribed Muslim countries to register with the US government. Some 177,000 men did so and thousands were deported or detained.

After being forced to abandon the Entry-Exit Registration System because it was race biased, DHS pursued another means of controlling borders and ports of entry with a Computer-Assisted Passenger Prescreening System (CAPPS). In February 2003 DHS announced it would replace the older CAPPS with a newer CAPPS II. However, DHS's fiscal year 2004 appropriations bill banned using commercial databases for passenger risk assessments. CAPPS II was cancelled in July 2004 when legislation was proposed that would ban any computerized risk assessment of people not on the watch list. That still was not the end.

US-VISIT. Paralleling ADVISE and CAPPS II was still another program for international flights called United States Visitor and Immigrant Status Indicator Technology (US-VISIT) which went into use in January 2004. By the end of 2005 all US ports of entry were brought into the system. US-VISIT is not as discriminatory as the National Security Entry-Exit Registration System because all foreigners, not just certain races or ages, must be digitally photographed and fingerprint-scanned when entering the US. The original exit plan to use facial- and finger-print-recognition when visitors leave the US was canceled in late 2006 for lack of budget.

DHS claims US-VISIT has caught 372 people wanted for crimes or immigration violations, but it has never shown that it detected even one wanted terrorist. It would not have stopped Richard Reid—the "shoe bomber"—because he is a citizen of Britain which participates in a Visa Waiver Program. A July 2007 GAO report concluded: "Significant weaknesses in computer security controls threaten the confidentiality, integrity, and availability" of critical information and systems supporting the US-VISIT program, and "risk exists that unauthorized individuals could read, copy, delete, add and modify sensitive information"[5] So much for privacy.

Automated Targeting System (ATS). Another computerized system for assessing the terrorist risk of those entering the US, ATS has sized up millions of citizens and foreigners since its inception in 2002. Airlines and cruise ship lines must give DHS advanced information on passengers and crew that will be entering the US so it can be analyzed by the ATS computer system. This activity went unnoticed until a description of ATS was published in the November 2006 *Federal Register.* DHS planned to keep this data for 40 years and share it with local, state and foreign governments – even some courts and private contractors, but those on the list can't see it to challenge or correct it.

Information comes from travel and reservation agents when people make travel plans. This includes names, addresses, hotel and rental car records, where they are from, how they paid for the ticket, credit card information, contact information, next-of-kin, how often they buy one-way tickets, seating preferences, what they order to eat, and more. Border agents add license plate numbers and names of all people in the vehicle. Amtrak supplies passenger lists for trains going to and from Canada. According to Homeland Security, identifying high-risk individuals who aren't on any watch list is the aim of ATS.

Congressperson Marin Sabo said ATS is clearly illegal and the kind of computerized risk assessment we've been trying to avoid. Because computerized risk assessment of the general population is banned, ATS might also violate the Anti-Deficiency Act which makes it illegal to spend money not appropriated by Congress. Each year 87 million people enter the US by air, another 309 million arrive by land and sea. Every one of them is subject to ATS risk assessment. David Sobel, lawyer for Electronic Frontier Foundation, said: "It's probably the most invasive system the government has yet deployed in terms of the number of people affected."[6] Yet Homeland Security cannot claim ATS has apprehended even one terrorist.

DHS's Customs and Border Protection Agency (CBP) administers ATS. A May 2007 GAO report stated: "Federal privacy law requires agencies to inform the public about how the government uses their personal information.... [T]he current prescreening process allows passenger information to be used in multiple prescreening procedures and transferred among various CBP prescreening systems in ways that are not fully explained in CBP's privacy disclosures.... If CBP does not issue all appropriate disclosures, the traveling public will not be fully aware of how their personal information is being used during the passenger prescreening process."[7]

Europe's highest court struck down the ATS program in May 2007, giving the US and the European Union until July 31 to devise a new plan. By July they agreed to what looked reasonable, but was actually an expansion of the program—increasing the database to include racial and ethnic origin, political opinions, religious or philosophical beliefs, trade union membership, individual health information, traveling partners and sexual orientation. Although database fields were reduced from 34 to 19, data included in each field was significantly increased. Europe had to agree, however, because the US threatened to turn flights back.

The revised ATS program will be effective until July 2014. Records will be kept for 15 years but the US served notice that retention time is subject to further discussion. The DHS can also share data with other government agencies and other countries. ATS is back on track. Peter Hustinx, privacy supervisor for the European Union, has "serious doubts whether the outcome of these negotiations will be fully compatible with European fundamental rights."[8] Starting early in 2008 passengers on flights destined to the US must be checked against terrorist watch lists before the flight takes off, rather that after it is in the air. The final flight manifest must be transmitted to the DHS at least 30 minutes before takeoff.

E-Passports. In August 2006 the State Department began issuing new electronic passports (e-passports) which include remotely-readable biometric chips containing everything in the passport plus a digital photograph. Digital fingerprints and iris scans can be added later to facilitate US-VISIT. Port of entry officials can read passports with radio-frequency scanners from a distance and compare data with a database to verify identification. Privacy advocates object because anyone with a radio-frequency scanner can read the passport. Consequently, the covers and spine are now coated with a material that blocks radio-frequency waves unless the passport is open. Some still fear eavesdropping while the data is being scanned by an official. Of course the data is encrypted but encryption has never proved reliable in protecting sensitive information.

A 2004 law makes passports the only travel document accepted, with few exceptions. Since January 2007 all air travelers – citizens or foreigners – must show valid passports to enter the US. Starting in 2008, anyone entering the US by any means of transportation must show a passport.

Domestic Travel – Secure Flight

In August 2004, DHS's Transportation Security Administration (TSA) announced it would develop a "Secure Flight" system for domestic flights. According to the TSA website, "Secure Flight is to enhance the security of domestic commercial air travel within the United States through the use of improved watch list matching."[9] Currently, commercial aircraft operators check passenger lists against an extract from the federal terrorist watch list. Secure flight, when operational, will require aircraft operators to furnish TSA with passenger data for each flight starting 72 hours before scheduled takeoff. TSA will then check it against a more comprehensive expanded watch list, which is all TSA can legally do, since language in DHS's fiscal 2005 appropriations bill bans computerized risk assessment of people not on the watch list. Those on the flight manifest are not to be matched against any data base beyond the watch list without proper public notification early enough for comment.

But TSA did some cheating. In the concept-testing phase it used commercial data to try identifying people incorrectly placed on the watch list or those who have attempted to avoid detection by disguising their identities, to determine the accuracy of passenger-provided data. For this TSA used old passenger lists from June 2004. TSA issued privacy notices after-the-fact in the September/November 2004 *Federal Register*. Still they did not adequately explain procedures or admit a TSA contractor had amassed over 100 million individual data records containing extensive personal information without informing the public. The GAO reported the next year that "TSA did not fully disclose to the public its use of personal information in its fall 2004 privacy notices... [T]he public was not made fully aware of, nor had the opportunity to comment on TSA's use of personal information drawn from commercial sources... [T]he public did not receive the full protections of the Privacy Act."[10] The TSA published a revised privacy notice in the *Federal Register* on June 22 – retroactively and after the fact. In testimony before Congress on 21 March 2007, GAO expressed continued privacy concerns for Secure Flight.[11]

★ ★ ★ ★ ★

US-VISIT and ATS collect data on all international travelers arriving in the US. E-Passports collect more data on US citizens who plan to travel. Secure Flight for domestic travel also collects data. All of this information goes into various data banks, or so we are led to believe. Yet they are interacting entities. Together they equal the National Security Entry-Exit Registration System and CAPPS II, both of which were halted. Nevertheless, they live on in isolated segments to conjure up a false sense of privacy. Whatever the combination of all these programs is called, the reality is that no one – citizen or foreigner – can travel to, from, or within the United States without the government's approval. You cannot be issued a boarding pass until your name has been cleared by DHS. Freedom of movement has been restricted to that degree.

More exotic systems are being conjured up to monitor travelers. Face police will be at airports and other ports of entry. These so-called behavior-detection officers watch passengers for "micro-expressions" which supposedly reveal emotions and intentions. People's feelings are revealed in "facial flashes," or so the face police claim. They work in pairs to interact with passengers to create circumstances in which a passenger might feel uncomfortable. Behavioral-detection officers were posted at over a dozen US airports by August 2007. Plans are to have 500 on the job by the end of 2008. So, as one author warns, when you get to the airport you better be smiling.[12]

Joint Regional Information Exchange System

In May 2002, the Defense Intelligence Agency enlisted the California Justice Department and the New York City Police Department in a pilot program that developed into the Joint Regional Information Exchange System (JRIES) to share "sensitive but unclassified" knowledge about national security threats. This is "information that is not classified for national security reasons, but that warrants/requires administrative control and protection from public or other unauthorized disclosure for other reasons." It must meet one of nine criteria which include "Inter or intra-agency communications, including e-mails that form part of the internal deliberative processes of the US government, the disclosure of which could harm such a process."[13]

What started as a simple web portal where agencies could share intelligence now, according to a DHS press release, "allows multiple jurisdictions, disciplines, and emergency operation centers to receive and share the same intelligence information and tactical information – so that all users can have the same overall situation awareness."[14]

In February 2004 DHS expanded this network to all 50 states, 5 US territories, Washington DC, and 50 major cities to strengthen two-way flow of threat information. Although set up mainly to exchange "sensitive but unclassified" information, a platform has been provided to share SECRET intelligence with state offices and, some day, counties and elements of the private sector. The DHS press release states: "As a foundation of the Homeland Security Information Network initiative, the broadened JRIES community of users will include the state Homeland Security advisers, state adjutant generals (National Guard), state emergency operations centers, local emergency service providers including firefighters, law enforcement, and others."

The network is divided into workspaces. Largest is the National Situation Awareness workspace. Other permanent workspaces include Los Angeles International Airport and the Las Vegas Strip. Ed Manivian, chief of criminal intelligence for the California Justice Department, explains: "In Las Vegas, if they stopped a suspicious person on the strip, law enforcement could put that into the space, so everyone in the country would know about it. And if they threw a name out there, everyone could assist by checking their databases."[15]

Temporary workspaces come and go as needed, such as the Tournament of Roses Parade in Pasadena, California. In that workspace, for instance, pertinent maps and aerial photos are uploaded so Homeland Security teams nationwide know the parade route. It is easy to see that JRIES databases abound containing data on millions of citizens. These databases have been integrally linked with the FBI's 25-year-old Regional Information Sharing System that supports law enforcement and criminal justice agencies across the country. Here completes the tie between law enforcement and intelligence – both domestic and foreign. The military can also access JRIES databases to obtain domestic intelligence.

JRIES is nothing more than MATRIX all over again but using "distributed computing" to avoid MATRIX's mistakes. Instead of one massive database, geographically separated computer sites in different states are networked to be rapidly accessible with, usually, a single query. Yet those computers function essentially the same as MATRIX. One person said that if people knew what JRIES was looking at they would throw a fit.

Big Brother in the Sky and the National Applications Office

On 25 May 2007 the Director of National Intelligence made the nation's most powerful intelligence-gathering tools available to civilian security agencies – America's vast array of spy satellites. Then in October DHS Director Michael Chertoff set up the National Applications Office within the Department of Homeland Security to coördinate requests for spy satellite data. This data is much higher resolution than previous information from NASA and the US Geological Survey. It will likely come directly from the National Reconnaissance Office and include the full spectrum of data from MASINT (Measurement and Signature Intelligence), IMINT (Imagery Intelligence), and SIGINT (Signals Intelligence) satellites.

This new capability is said to enhance security at borders and seaports, protect critical infrastructure, assist security planning for large events and better manage natural disasters. Later it will be integrated into federal, state and local law enforcement work to watch ports of entry for smugglers, observe gang hideouts, monitor people by means of heat-detecting sensors, detect traces of chemicals and explosives and more. Only the intelligence community knows the full capabilities.

The *Wall Street Journal* described this spy satellite use as uncharted territory. New questions arise about privacy, warrant requirements for searches from space, and possible violations of the *Posse Comitatus Act* by using military intelligence for civil law enforcement. The article quotes from a 2005 study commissioned by the US intelligence community: "'There is little if any policy, guidance, or procedures regarding collecting, exploiting and dissemination of domestic MASINT,' ...[which] uses radar, lasers, infrared, electromagnetic data, and other technologies"[16]

The article doesn't mention IMINT or SIGINT satellites (later we will discuss NSA spying on phone calls, much of which is accomplished by the SIGINT satellites), but it did quote Gregory Nojeim of the Center for Democracy and Technology who warned: "You are talking about enormous power. Not only is the surveillance they are contemplating intrusive and omnipresent, it's also invisible. And that's what makes this so dangerous." Steven Aftergood of the Federation of American Scientists added: "It potentially marks a transformation of American political culture toward a surveillance state in which the entire public domain is subject to official monitoring."[17]

A National Police Force

When Congress renewed 16 sections of the Patriot Act due to expire 31 December 2005, it added a new Section 605, "Powers, Authorities, and Duties of United States Secret Service Uniformed Division" that is under DHS. The language reads:

> Subject to the supervision of the Secretary of Homeland Security, the United States Secret Service Uniformed Division shall perform such duties as the Director, United States Secret Service, may prescribe in connection with the protection of the following:[18]

The legislation then lists what shall be protected – mainly events attended by presidents, past presidents, their families, presidential candidates, other high government officials and foreign dignitaries. One significant sentence ends that list which covers a lot: "An event designated under Section 3056(e) of Title 18 US code as a *special event of national significance*" (emphasis added). The part which defines a special event of national significance says:

> When directed by the President, the United States Secret Service is authorized to participate, under the direction of the Secretary of Homeland Security, in planning, coördinating, and implementation of security at *special events of national significance, as determined by the President* (emphasis added).

That basically means anything the president desires. It could be as nondescript as a high school soccer game. The president can send the national police force to maintain order, selectively refuse admittance and make arrests. The national police are literally at the beck and call of the president for any task chosen. As Craig Roberts, senior research fellow at Stanford's Hoover Institution, states: "Like every law in the United States, this law will be extensively interpreted and abused. It has dire implications for free association and First Amendment rights. We can take it for granted that the new federal police will be used to suppress dissent and break up opposition."[19]

A National Intelligence Director

In December 2004 President Bush signed the "Intelligence Reform and Terrorism Prevention Act of 2004" establishing the office of the director of national intelligence which reports directly to the White House. Reporting to this new office are the 16 agencies in the country's intelligence community, including the FBI, CIA, NSA, Drug Enforcement Administration, National Geospatial-Intelligence Agency, Defense Intelligence Agency and the National Reconnaissance Office. The army, navy, air force, marines, and coast guard all have intelligence units, as do the departments of state, homeland security, energy and treasury.

This Directorship of National Intelligence was set up in partial compliance with 9/11 Commission recommendations. John D. Negroponte was sworn in as director of National Intelligence (DNI) and Air Force Gen. Michael Hayden as deputy director in May 2005.[20] Negroponte, a career US ambassador and foreign service officer, served in another shady segment of history. During his tenure as ambassador to Honduras (1981-1985), he allegedly helped make Honduras a staging area for Contra activity and death squads going into Nicaragua. He was also accused of using US aid to obtain compliance from Honduras. In later events, Organization of American States officials and other diplomats said the April 2002 coup to unseat Venezuelan President Hugo Chavez was supported by the US, and Negroponte was a key player. Many were surprised to see a career diplomat who seemed to disregard credible intelligence during Reagan's Central American cold-war policy, become the nation's intelligence czar.

National Counterterrorism Center

In August 2004 Bush signed an executive order establishing a National Counterterrorism Center (NCTC) which in December was codified under the director of national intelligence. Vice Adm. John Scott Redd was confirmed in July 2005 as the first director of NCTC. During his confirmation hearing, Redd said: "While there are many challenges ahead, bridging what has traditionally been referred to as foreign intelligence and domestic intelligence will be one of my top priorities."

Shocking! It was the express purpose of the Foreign Intelligence Surveillance Act and the FISA Courts to decisively separate foreign and domestic intelligence activities. Bridging them is a setback for civil liberties and privacy. Redd's later statement was no more assuring: "The NCTC will be the hub of an intelligence network that goes far beyond the traditional US intelligence community. The network will extend to all agencies of the federal government, to state and local governments and law enforcement agencies, to the private sector, and to liaison elements of foreign countries." That surely sounds like TIA.

Redd admitted the application of "information dominance" in fighting terrorism must be controlled because privacy and free expression "would be placed in jeopardy by unrestrained collection and exploitation of personal data," but then dismissed such concerns as impossible since new legislation has created "a Civil Liberties Board to oversee all US intelligence activities."[21]

Exactly what is this Privacy and Civil Liberties Board? Why do we never hear about it? Called the most invisible office in the White House, it was created the same time as NCTC but remained unstaffed during its first year. Five board members eventually were sworn in March 2006, but in Bush's budget released the previous month there was no money listed for the board. Asked why, Office of Management and Budget spokesperson Alex Conant denied the board was being suppressed by starving it of funds. He admitted it would have a full budget but explained officials decided not to itemize funding levels for certain White House offices. When it was "pointed out that funding for other White House offices such as the National Security Council was listed in the budget, Conant said: 'I have no explanation.'"[22] This board appears to be merely a façade to placate the public.

The Congressional Research Service (CRS) also foresaw problems with NCTC.[23] Its report referred to "potential civil liberties implications of collocating operational elements of the traditional foreign intelligence and domestic intelligence entities of the US Intelligence community…. [T]he possibility exists that unintentional mission creep and operational zeal could lead to situations in which rules designed to guide traditional foreign intelligence collection may be applied to US persons" and put their civil liberties at risk. CRS emphasized that the legislation creating NCTC specifically excluded "intelligence pertaining *exclusively* and *purely* to domestic terrorists and domestic counterterrorism" from NCTC's analytical responsibility (emphasis added), but the legislation does allow NCTC to receive, retain and disseminate domestic counterterrorism intelligence. More simply, NCTC can collect and share information on peaceful protest groups but they can't analyze it. Amazing! The FBI's Terrorist Screening Center of NCTC has compiled data from 26 terrorist-related databases to develop a master watch list. It will, of course, include the domestic intelligence that NCTC can't analyze. This list then forms the no-fly list for TSA, the visa watch for the State Department, the watch list for border guards and law enforcement. In February 2007 the media reported class action lawsuits against the government have been filed in California, Illinois and New York because some have waited over two years for citizenship papers. It's only supposed to take 120 days after the final interview, but because their names are similar to those on the FBI's watch list they are put on hold.

In September 2007 the Justice Department inspector general declared the NCTC master watch list full of errors and lacking key names. His report said the Terrorist Screening Center couldn't consistently get accurate and timely information to grass roots screening agents. The report noted some 700,000 names on the master watch list in the spring of 2007, four times the number three years earlier and about twice those from the previous year. GAO put the exact number at 755,000 records in

May 2007.[24] By late summer, Terrorist Screening Center Director Leonard C. Boyle claimed some 800,000 records with average growth of 20,000 names per month. This list screens 270 million people monthly–the approximate US population if they were all separate individuals.

The inspector general's team chose 105 records to examine. Of these 38% contained errors and inconsistencies, extrapolating to 380,000 erroneous records in the entire database. The report also identified 20 names of known or suspected terrorists not on the lists sent to front-line screening agents. In 2006 the watch list flagged almost 20,000 suspects but only a small fraction were denied entry or arrested. Officials won't talk about the database, discuss cases or confirm anyone's name. A spokesman for the Terrorist Screening Center said that to be in the database one must be a known or suspected terrorist or someone who supports and finances terrorists. Wow! This means over 800,000 such people are in the database! Only 20,000 were flagged–with very few resulting arrests? What is wrong with this picture?

Georgetown University law professor David D. Cole commented: "If being placed on a list means in practice that you will be denied a visa, barred entry, put on the no-fly list, targeted for pretextual prosecutions, etc., then the sweep of the list and the apparent absence of any way to clear oneself certainly raise problems." Marc Rotenberg, executive director of the Electronics Privacy Information Center, added "the size of the NCTC list and other terrorist-related databases underscores the severity of the 'false positive' problem, in which innocent people–including members of Congress–have been stopped for questioning or halted from flying because their names are wrongly included or are similar to suspects' names." Rotenberg added: "One of the seemingly insolvable problems is what do you do when someone is wrongly put on this list? If there are that many people on the list, a lot of them probably shouldn't be there. But how are they ever going to get off?"[25]

Perhaps the most visible misuse of this database is the "no-fly" list. In searching the internet for this term I found ten pages of those who have been barred from flying. A list compiled from ten hits on just the first page is displayed in Appendix-C. You only have to Google "no-fly list" to discover an avalanche of civil-rights abuses.

Privacy experts are warning America to prepare for a so-called "no-work" list. A provision in proposed immigration reform bills is for mandatory employee eligibility verification. Many think it would just affect immigrants. Not true. Every one of the 144 million people on the American workforce could eventually be in the database, 57 million of whom change jobs every year. Employers would have to check existing employees as well as prospective new-hires. Confirmation of Social Security status and legal immigration would be verified. Electronic Privacy Information Center's Mark Rotenberg says "people who aren't in the immigrant community assume it won't affect them. But for the system to work it has to encompass the entire American workforce." He added that proposed House and Senate bills "put the Social Security Administration and the Department of Homeland Security in the middle of every employment decision in the United States."[26]

This database for a no-work list already exists in Social Security Administration and US Citizenship and Immigration Service (USCIS) records that will be made available to employers. Currently there is a voluntary pilot program where 60,000 employers participate. This same article claims the program could rapidly be expanded and quotes Deborah Meyers, senior policy expert at the Migration Policy Institute, warning: "There are legitimate concerns in terms of privacy and the rights of individuals to access and correct their records." It also cites ACLU attorney Tim Sparapani who said people "are just beginning to understand the implications of it, and they're big. ...Pick your common surname. It's a nightmare for the system. And imagine not being able to work and provide for your family."

Another watch list, that either spun off of the National Counterterrorism Center's repository or contributed to it, is in the Treasury Department's Office of Foreign Assets Control (OFAC), is over 350 pages long with over 3,300 names of individuals and organizations. Most have never been in the US or suspected of being involved with financing terrorism, but many have common Muslim or Latin names. The list has been distributed to agencies and businesses such as financial institutions, credit bureaus, charities, landlords and even employers.

Bush's executive order issued after 9/11 expanded the OFAC list to unprecedented dimensions and puts common everyday business people under the pressure of looking for suspects. This has resulted in many false positives and lost opportunities. Yet they face stiff penalties – up to $10 million fine and/or 30 years in prison – if they inadvertently do business with any of the people or groups on the list. There is no minimum dollar amount. When in doubt, business personnel cancel the transaction rather than take a chance on penalties.

The Lawyers Committee for Civil Rights (San Francisco Bay area) has documented a list of OFAC incidents. A Roseville, California couple applied for credit to buy a treadmill. Wells Fargo told the seller to wait 72 hours because the husband's first name Hussein (a common Arab name) matched a name on the list and had to be investigated. He is a US citizen who has lived in Roseville over 30 years. Another Chicago resident named Muhammad underwent a credit search to buy a used car because his common Muslim name caused false matches that required checking. What would happen if he needed a job or housing?

People actually have been turned down for home loans. One northern California mental-health worker was denied a loan because he had an OFAC alert on his credit report. His middle name was Hassan which was an alias for Saddam Hussein's son. The discrepancy in birth dates would have indicated a false positive but the mortgage company didn't want to chance it. Another couple in Phoenix whose home was about to close escrow were told the sale could not proceed because the husband's name, a common Latino name, matched a name on the OFAC list.

The FBI's National Security Service

Bush consolidated intelligence gathering activities of the FBI in June 2005 by pulling together the Counterintelligence Division, the Counterterrorism Division, and the Directorate of Intelligence into a new National Security Service. Paradoxically, this split the FBI into two parts—law enforcement which remained under the FBI director with the new National Security Service essentially under the director of national intelligence. The head of this new service—the executive assistant FBI director of intelligence—is hired by the FBI director and the attorney general but the director of National Intelligence has veto power. This new executive assistant will "be subject to the coördination and budget authorities of the DNI as well as the same attorney general authorities that apply to other bureau divisions."[27] But in effect the director of National Intelligence controls the intelligence portion of the FBI budget and thereby the activities of all FBI agents and analysts working in the intelligence field.

A White House memorandum says the new National Security Service "will specialize in intelligence and other national security matters and respond to priorities set by the director of National Intelligence." That covers a wide field. Civil liberties advocates decry this new organization, likening it to a secret police force in America. Many FBI agents and Justice Department lawyers also oppose the new National Security Service.

The following October Negroponte released *The National Intelligence Strategy of the United States of America,* an apparently nondescript document with a collection of generalized statements which describe nothing. More enlightening is Negroponte's introduction which says, "The new concept of 'national intelligence' codified by the Intelligence Reform and Terrorist Prevention Act passed by Congress in 2004 has its origins in the tragedy of September 11, 2001 and President Bush's *National Security Strategy of the United States of America*." With that typical pointed reminder of 9/11 and reassertion of a terrorist threat while invoking Bush's strategy of preëmptive force, lessons from the past should warn us that this "new concept of national intelligence" is nothing more than turning preëmptive force inward. "In other words, the strategy is a strengthening and solidification of the existing Homeland/National Security apparatus into a more centralized structure (with more power and control in the hands of the Executive Branch)"[28]

The FBI's clandestine National Security Service fits snugly into that domestic policing scenario. While the CIA continues to control all overseas human intelligence operations, this new national service will be the agent for domestic surveillance.

The Disruptive Technology Office

We have seen how the Defense Appropriations Act for 2004 blocked funds for TIA and terminated the Pentagon's Information Awareness Office, followed by various elements of TIA being shuttled out of the DoD budget and continued under different names, sometimes with the same contractor. Two of the most important elements went to the Advanced Research and Development Activity (ARDA) which was under the National Security Agency (NSA).

One of these elements was "Genoa II," which was to build information-gathering technologies to anticipate and preëmpt attacks. It was then renamed "Topsail" under ARDA. A federal press release announcing a $3.7 million contract to SAIC for Topsail in October 2005 said: "The objective of Topsail is to develop decision-support aids for teams of intelligence analysts and policy personnel to assist in anticipating and preëmpting terrorist threats to US interests" – which is almost identical language to what was formerly used to describe Genoa II.

The other core element that went to ARDA – the most important and comprehensive element which ties together all the numerous information extraction, analysis and dissemination tools – was the Information Awareness Prototype System. This was renamed "Basketball" and was fully funded at least until September 2004. At that time Basketball was being tested at a research center run by ARDA and SAIC Corp. SAIC is a prominent Pentagon contractor for intelligence activities and the sole owner of Hicks & Associates, the company that had the TIA prototype contract. Basketball was described as a "closed-loop, end-to-end prototype system for early warning and decision-making." That's "exactly the same language used in contract documents for the TIA prototype system when it was awarded to Hicks in 2002."

It is unclear whether Basketball continues today under that name or a new one. Some sources interviewed for a February 2006 issue of *National Journal* wouldn't discuss classified projects and a spokesperson for SAIC declined to comment on the finished article. When NSA spokesperson Don Weber was asked about TIA programs that had been shifted to ARDA, he waffled out of an answer. This article reported that ARDA "is being taken out of NSA, placed under control of Negroponte's office, and given a new name. It will be called the 'Disruptive Technology Office,' a reference to a term of art describing any new invention that suddenly, and often dramatically, replaces established procedures."[29] TIA's new home is now with the Director of National Intelligence.

A Bizarre Transposition

There has been a drastic shuffling of chairs in high levels of government. It does indeed appear to be a game of musical chairs. It may be advantageous to make a few observations here.

CIA Director

Gen. Michael Hayden left his job as deputy director of National Intelligence to be confirmed as CIA director in May 2006. Hayden is still an active duty military officer with the

Pentagon and was once director of the National Security Agency (NSA). Although he promised at his confirmation hearings that his decisions as CIA director would not be influenced by the Defense Department, it is hard to imagine a career four-star general, still on active duty, not spicing his behavior with Pentagon thinking.

Secretary of Defense

After Rumsfeld's resignation, Robert Gates was confirmed as the secretary of defense in December 2006. When he was tapped for the job, he had been president of Texas A&M University since 2002. From 1999 to 2001 he was dean of the George Bush School of Government and Public Service which houses the former president's library. Most recently he was part of the Iraq Study Group cochaired by James A. Baker III and Lee Hamilton. Gates has over 25 years tenure in the CIA under six presidents. He joined in 1966 and was the first to rise from entry level to director. He retired as CIA director in 1993.

Gates' reputation was tarnished by the Iran-Contra scandal. In 1984 he wrote a memo to his boss, CIA Director William Casey, recommending bombing Nicaragua's military buildup and said the US should depart from its ineffective and halfhearted strategy to contain the Sandinista government, to make it clear that existence of a Central American regime closely aligned to Moscow and Havana was unacceptable. Later, by stonewalling and other evasive tactics, he escaped prosecution in the Iran-Contra scandal. Judge Lawrence Walsh, independent counsel investigating that affair, noted in his 1993 final report, "Owing to his senior status in the CIA, Gates was close to many figures who played significant roles in the Iran-Contra affair and was in a position to have known of their activities."[30]

Director of National Intelligence

Bush named retired Navy Vice Adm. John Michael McConnell to replace Negroponte as Director of National Intelligence (DNI) in January 2007. A 25-year veteran in the intelligence field and former director of the National Security Agency (1992-1996), McConnell was sworn in as DNI the next month.

Since his retirement in 1996, McConnell had been vice president of the security and intelligence consulting firm, Booz Allen Hamilton which contracts its services to the government. A former chair of Intelligence and National Security Alliance, the lobbying arm for the private intelligence industry, according to the *USA Today*, McConnell's appointment as director of national intelligence was part of "two current trends in intelligence gathering: the emphasis on technology, and the heightened role of private contractors in analyzing data and preparing reports that once might have been written by government intelligence officers."[31] R.J. Hillhouse reported that in 2007 the US was paying $42 billion a year[32] for private intelligence, up from $17.54 billion in 2000.[33] (In September 2006 the FBI started investigating the loss of CIA officers being lured to private companies for larger salaries.)

McConnell was the Booz Allen Hamilton vice president who signed a $63 million contract with the Pentagon in 2002 to help develop the TIA program—killed by Congress but according to *USA Today*, intelligence work "on that contract has continued, according to federal contracting records, which show the Pentagon paid Booz Allen about $2 million under that contract during 2006."

★ ★ ★ ★ ★

We now have the unique transposition of personnel in the turf war between the Pentagon and CIA. Star-rank military officers, albeit with extensive experience in the intelligence field, occupy the head positions of America's two most prominent civilian intelligence units. Meanwhile a career intelligence officer and past CIA director is in the top military seat. How this drama unfolds will be an interesting and suspenseful—possibly even democracy-threatening—chain of events to observe.

Notes for Chapter 3

1. Tom Ridge resigned Feb. 1, 2005, and was succeeded by Michael Chertoff.

2. GAO-07-293 – "Early Attention to Privacy in Developing a Key DHS Program Could Reduce Risks," report prepared by the GAO, Feb 2007.

3. Clayton, Mark, "US Plans Massive Data Sweep," *The Christian Science Monitor*, 9 Feb 2006.

4. Sniffen, Michael J. (AP), "DHS Ends Criticized Data-Mining," *San Francisco Chronicle*, 5 Sep 2007.

5. GAO-07-870 – "Information Security: Homeland Security Needs to Immediately Address Significant Weaknesses in Systems Supporting the US-VISIT Program," GAO report, Jul 2007.

6. Sniffen, Michael J. (AP), "U.S. Rates Travelers for Terror Risk," *Yahoo News*, 1 Dec 2006.

7. GAO-07-346 – "Aviation Security: Efforts to Strengthen International Passenger Pre-screening are Under Way, but Planning and Implementation Issues Remain," GAO report, 16 May 2007.

8. Lewis, Paul and Spencer S. Hsu, "Travelers Face Greater Use of Personal Data," *Washington Post*, 27 Jul 2007.

9. "Secure Flight Program," at http://www.tsa.gov/what_we_do/layers/scureflight/editorial_1716.shtm and links.

10. "Aviation Security: Transportation Security Administration Did Not Fully Disclose Uses of Personal Information During Secure Flight Program Testing in Initial Privacy Notices, but Has Recently Taken Steps to More Fully Inform the Public," letter from GAO to Congressional committees, 22 Jul 2005.

11. See GAO-07-630T – "Continuing Attention to Privacy Concerns Is Needed as Programs Are Developed," testimony of Linda D. Koontz of the GAO before the House Appropriations Committee's Subcommittee on Homeland Security, 21 Mar 2007.

12. See Davis, Patti, "At the Airport, You Better Smile," *Newsweek*, 16 Aug 2007.

13. "Scope of Sensitive but Unclassified Information," US Department of State Foreign Affairs Manual, Volume 12 – Diplomatic Security, Section 541, 4 Nov 2005.

14. DHS press release, "Homeland Security Information Network to Expand Collaboration, Connectivity for States and Major Cities," 24 Feb 2004.

15. Grimes, Brad, "Homeland Security Gets in the Groove," *Washington Technology*, 5 Apr 2004.

16. Block, Robert, "US to Expand Domestic Use of Spy Satellites," *Wall Street Journal*, 15 Aug 2007.

17. Schmitt, Eric, "Liberties Advocates Fear Abuse of Satellite Images," *NY Times*, 17 Aug 2007.

18. House Report 109-333 – USA PATRIOT Improvement and Reauthorization Act of 2005.

19. Roberts, Craig (Creators Syndicate), "Patriot Act Police Threaten Our Rights," Ocala.com, 31 Jan 2006.

20. General Hayden was formerly director of the NSA. He was later confirmed as CIA director in May 2006.

21. Redd quotations from National Counterterrorism Center home page; updated 23 Mar 2006 at http://www.nctc.gov (Redd's confirmation hearing link).

22. Isikoff, Michael, "Watchdog: What Ever Happened to the Civil Liberties Board?" *Newsweek*, 13 Mar 2006.

23. CRS Report, "The National Counterterrorism Center: Implementation Challenges and Issues for Congress," 24 Mar 2005.

24. GAO-08-110–"Terrorist Watch List Screening," a report by the GAO, 11 Oct 2007.

25. Pincus, Walter and Dan Eggen, "325,000 Names on Terror List," *Washington Post*, 15 Feb 2006.

26. Friedman, Lisa; "Employee Verification System Would Affect All Workers, Privacy Experts Say," *Inland Valley Daily Bulletin* (Ontario, CA), 12 Jun 2006.

27. White House Memorandum; "Strengthening the Ability of the Department of Justice to Meet Challenges to the Security of the Nation," 29 Jun 2005.

28. Chin, Larry, "The New National Security Strategy of the United States: Towards an Even More Dangerous International Security Apparatus," *Online Journal*, 29 Oct 2005.

29. Quotations here from Shane Harris, "TIA Lives On," *National Journal*, 23 Feb 2006.

30. Wayne Madsen Report, 9 November 2006

31. Kelley, Matt and Richard Willing, "Nominee Played Big Role in Outsourcing Intelligence," *USA Today*, 5 Jan 2007.

32. The $42 billion for intelligence contracting must have been from both the Director of National Intelligence budget and the Pentagon's. DNI Mike McConnell announced in October 2007 that his office spent $43.5 billion in fiscal year 2007 – about 70% of which is believed to have gone to contractors. The Pentagon is thought to have spent another $10 billion in private intelligence contracts.

33. Scahill, Jeremy, "The Mercenary Revolution: Flush with Profits from Iraq War, Military Contractors See a World of Business Opportunities," *Independent*, 15 Jan 2007.

4

Big Brother's Martial Arm

*To increase the efficiency of the Department of Defense, you first
have to abolish it. It's far too large.*
                                    —Admiral Hyman Rickover, 1982

Admiral Rickover, known as the father of the nuclear navy,
had second thoughts about his profession toward the end of his
career and told Congress in 1982, "We'll probably destroy ourselves," adding, "I'm not proud of the part I played."[1] That was
back when the Pentagon wasn't active in domestic activities.
The situation has expanded considerably since then.

Pentagon Intelligence Ambitions

Pentagon officials did not want to be shunted aside by the
intelligence shakeups following 9/11 and the invasion of Iraq.
Traditionally Pentagon intelligence agencies have engaged in
"technical means" of intelligence gathering—using electronics,
satellites and such technologies intended to provide tactical and
strategic support for military commanders. But the Pentagon's
"human intelligence" activities—spies, covert operations, interro-
gating prisoners, counterterrorism, and counterproliferation—
increased after 9/11. Epitomizing this expansion was the estab-

lishment in 2003 of an undersecretary of defense for intelligence — the first in history — with purview over the Defense Intelligence Agency (DIA) and subservient intelligence agencies of the various military services. Stephen Cambone, appointed as the new undersecretary, said in May of that year that existing agencies will continue as they have been. His job was to keep them on the right track following Pentagon policy. In other words, what the defense secretary wants, not the CIA nor the DIA.

Also controlled by this new undersecretary were the National Security Agency (NSA), the National Reconnaissance Office (NRO), and the National Geospatial Intelligence Agency (NGA) — at that time called the National Imagery and Mapping Agency. Those three agencies had been under the Department of Defense but they reported to both Defense Secretary Rumsfeld and CIA Director George Tenet. In the bureaucratic turf war this new undersecretary post gave Rumsfeld an edge in authority.

Cambone was quickly confirmed by the Senate, but the Office of the Director of National Intelligence (DNI) wasn't established until the end of 2004. On paper, the DNI oversees all intelligence activities, but budgetwise it doesn't work that way, for the DNI controls only the CIA budget — only 12% of the total intelligence budget. The Pentagon maintains 85% of that budget, so defense officials have a competitive edge over the DNI.

By 2005 some lawmakers became concerned the Pentagon was engaged in intelligence activities that circumvented congressional and DNI oversight because they involve "possible propaganda efforts and highly technological initiatives [that] might be masked as so-called special access programs, the details of which are highly classified." They feared the Pentagon was creating "parallel functions to what is going on in intelligence, but is calling it something else."[2]

Just what were these new intelligence activities that created so much concern? To cast light on that question, we must remember what information broke into the news in late 2004.

Strategic Support Branch

The story goes that the Strategic Support Branch was started in April 2002 under the Defense Intelligence Agency because Rumsfeld wanted to end the Pentagon's dependence on the CIA for human intelligence. It was first known by the code word Project Icon but has had several names since then. It operated for at least two years in Iraq and Afghanistan. Teams worked with "newly empowered" special operations forces. According to then chair of the Joint Chiefs of Staff, General Richard B. Myers, focus of the Strategic Support Branch is on possible future areas of US involvement such as the Philippines, Somalia, Yemen, Indonesia and Georgia. This shift to allowing special forces supported by "special missions units" to operate furtively in friendly as well as unfriendly countries during peacetime is a significant jump.

A future aspiration, possibly already implemented, is a Pentagon-controlled espionage school and intelligence operation commands in every overseas region. I suspect the new African Command (AFRICOM) announced in February 2007 is an intelligence operation command. It includes all of Africa except Egypt and is to be fully operational by October 2008. AFRICOM is not a typical war-fighting geographic command but is set up specifically to enhance counterterrorism. Rather than have a main headquarters in one country it will have five "nodes" in west, south, east, north and central Africa where area-specific "regional integration teams" will relate to their location.

Just days after Bush signed the law creating a Director of National Intelligence in December 2004, information started filtering into the media about a secret Pentagon plan allowing for a major expansion in gathering human intelligence (normally CIA turf). According to Pentagon officials this secret new Strategic Support Branch was established with "reprogrammed" funds, not congressionally approved funds.

Although Pentagon officials say they will remain accountable to Congress, "they also assert that defense intelligence missions are subject to fewer legal restraints than Rumsfeld's predecessors believed." For instance, Title 10 of the US Code requires the Pentagon to report all deployment orders or other types of formal direction to position US forces for combat. Cambone issued guidelines in January 2005 that special operations forces may "conduct clandestine HUMINT operations ...before publication" of deployment orders.[3] This is in consonance with the War on Terrorism being a "different kind of war" that requires more secrecy and fewer restraints.

Title 50 of the US Code requires the administration to keep Congress "fully and currently informed of all intelligence activities," but "traditional...military activities" and "routine support" are exempted. The Pentagon interprets "traditional" and "routine" more expansively when applied to the War on Terrorism.

Operations already started overseas skirt the technical distinction between clandestine and covert. Clandestine operations are those conducted secretly. Covert operations are those the US denies any connection with. The latter have stricter legal requirements which require the consent of the president and prompt notification of both parties and in both houses of the legislature.

Mission Creep into Domestic Spying

It is unclear how much this elbowing for position by the Pentagon affects domestic intelligence and spying on US citizens, but the concept of "mission creep" already accounts for some aspects of domestic spying by the Pentagon. For instance, the National Geophysical-Intelligence Agency (NGA), according to DOD Directive 5105.60, is a Combat Support Agency of the Department of Defense.[4] It supports policy makers and military forces by providing timely, relevant and accurate geospatial intelligence – which involves using satellite information to show activities and conditions on earth. Thus geospatial intelligence can be used to determine if the soil is too wet to support heavy armored vehicles or detect covert weapons proliferation.

Before the 9/11 attacks NGA only spied on the US to assist in natural disasters such as providing images of forest fires or floods. Now the agency has opened an Americas Office to support compiling images of more than 130 urban areas. It also gets other assignments like mapping the Washington DC mall and America's power transmission-line grid, along with disaster exercises. About twice a month NGA is called upon to support homeland security events. It routinely provides aerial photos and 3-D images of large events or potential terrorist targets, such as political conventions and nuclear power plants.

All this cannot be done without obtaining data on US citizens or private companies. Although NGA claims it is not interested in such data, domestic spying is possible and there is no oversight. "In most cases it is not intrusive," says the NGA's associate general council, Laura Jennings. Steven Aftergood, government secrecy project director of the Federation of American Scientists, objects: "What it boils down to is 'Trust us. Our intentions are good.'...If they deviate from their own rules, how would it be discovered? I am not satisfied that they have an answer to that question."[5] In May 2007, as noted above, data from America's vast array of spy satellites became available to DHS's National Applications Office.

The Counterintelligence Field Activity

An even more poignant example of "mission creep" is the Pentagon's Counterintelligence Field Activity (CIFA). After 9/11 the Bush administration declared the entire continental US a theater of military operations for the first time since the Civil War. CIFA was created by DOD Directive 5105.67 in February 2002. Counterintelligence, also called counterespionage, is the function of finding and identifying espionage activities.

CIFA's mission is to "develop and manage DOD counterintelligence programs and functions that support the protection of the department...as well as to detect and neutralize espionage against the department."[6] That mission statement mandates two general functions for CIFA: First to be a central point for collection, evaluation, and analysis of all DOD counterintelligence information. CIFA does not, itself, gather information; it is to develop and manage an integrated DOD counterintelligence program and to oversee DOD-wide counterintelligence investigations, operations and functional services. Its second function to identify and neutralize espionage activities which target the DOD – involves functioning as a law enforcement activity with regard to countering *espionage* activities. However, "CIFA shall not engage in the investigation, apprehension or detention of individuals suspected or convicted of *criminal* offenses" (emphasis added). Thus CIFA's functions are strictly limited to counterintelligence/counterespionage activities.

At least that was the mission of CIFA articulated in 2002 and 2003. Then the mission began to creep. *The Wall Street Journal* reported that "CIFA was originally charged with protecting the military and critical infrastructure from spying by terrorists and foreign intelligence services. But in August [2003] Paul Wolfowitz, the deputy defense secretary, issued a directive ordering the unit to maintain a 'domestic law-enforcement database that includes information related to potential terrorist threats directed against the Department of Defense.'"[7]

Complementing that, Wolfowitz also initiated a new reporting procedure known as Threat and Local Observation Notice (TALON)[8] whose reports contain anything that might remotely be considered a threat. Information is neither checked nor validated before it feeds into the database CIFA was directed to maintain. Contrary to law and custom, the Pentagon is collecting raw and unverified information on US citizens exercising their right to free speech, such as attendees at Mothers' Day rallies, the Raging Grannies and Code Pink (discussed below). Furthermore, this questionable information can be used by the FBI and local law enforcement agencies.

TALON has been described by Pentagon officials as the place where all the "dots" are stored. Connecting those dots is done by data mining—extracting patterns from large volumes of raw information. Senator Richard Shelby of the Senate Intelligence Committee reported in December 2002 that CIFA and the Justice Department are developing data mining techniques to discover possible terrorist threats which means a lot of snooping and a lot of citizen records being assimilated—even misunderstood—in the process.

Not much was heard about CIFA after that until late 2005 when the *Washington Post* reported: "The White House is considering expanding the power of a little-known Pentagon agency called the Counterintelligence Field Activity...from an office that coördinates Pentagon security efforts...to one that also has authority to investigate crimes within the United States such as treason, foreign or terrorist sabotage, or even economic espionage."[9] That is a big creep from a mission that originally forbade any law enforcement except in regard to military espionage. (Sabotage is deliberately destroying or obstructing to acquire political or military gain. Espionage refers to spying or using spies.) A four-page Pentagon memo, "Review of the TALON Reporting System," acquired in February 2006 by the ACLU under a Freedom of Information Act request, indicated TALON had 13,000 entries including 2,821 reports on America citizens. The memo said "an examination of the system led to deletion of 1,131 reports involving Americans, 186 of which dealt with 'anti-military protests or demonstrations in the US'."[10]

That April the Pentagon announced 260 entries should not have been there. Spokesman Whitman claimed less than two percent of the 13,000 database entries provided through the TALON system shouldn't have been there. So the remaining 12,740-plus "suspicious incidents" are legitimate, according to the Pentagon. If there is that much actual evidence of terrorism in America we are in big trouble. Our jails should be bulging. Nevertheless, CBS News noted in late 2005 that the TALON database "includes the monitoring of peaceful anti-war and counter-military recruitment groups.... The Pentagon now collects domestic intelligence that goes beyond legitimate concerns about terrorism and protecting US military installations."[11]

About this time the Pentagon petitioned Congress to amend the Privacy Act so the FBI could share information on US citizens with the Pentagon, CIA and others should that information pertain to foreign intelligence matters. This sparked a critical backlash. Senator Ron Wyden of the Senate Select Committee on Intelligence warned we "are deputizing the military to spy on law-abiding Americans in America. This is a huge leap without even a [congressional] hearing." Kate Martin, director of the Center for National Securities Studies, claimed the data-sharing amendment "removes one of the few existing privacy protections against creation of secret dossiers on Americans by government intelligence agencies," noting the Pentagon's "intelligence agencies are quietly expanding their domestic presence without public debate."[12]

Other claims were made about CIFA's dipping into domestic spying. *The Wall Street Journal* said it was working with the FBI and other civilian agencies doing tasks such as background checks on foreign workers and government employees. A secret briefing paper obtained by NBC showed the military was collecting information like people's names and vehicle license numbers and concluded that "we have noted increased communication and encouragement between protest groups using the internet," but no "significant connection" between incidents, such as "recurring instigators at protests" or "vehicle descriptions."[13] So the Pentagon definitely was monitoring who attends protests, the vehicles they drive and what they do on the internet.

This same article noted that contracts amounting to at least $33 million since March 2004 have been awarded to four giant corporations—Lockheed Martin, Northrop Grumman, Unisys Corporation and Computer Sciences Corporation—to compile databases from government data, commercial information and internet communications—all justified as a means to finding terrorists, spies and saboteurs. One contract to Northrop Grumman called "Person Search" is designed "to provide comprehensive information about people of interest." A similar contract with Computer Sciences Corporation dubbed "The Insider Threat Initiative," intends to "develop systems able to detect, mitigate, and investigate insider threats" as well as the ability to "identify and document *normal* and abnormal activities and behaviors" (emphasis added).

In December 2005 the Pentagon gave CIFA authority to assign domestic cases to the counterintelligence units of the military services that have over 4,000 trained investigators at home and abroad. This is one more step beyond CIFA's previous mission to only *collect and process* information *from* those units. This new tasking authority meant CIFA can now *make* domestic assignments *to* the army, navy, and air force to gather information.

By January 2007 a new aspect of this aggressive expansion into domestic spying came to public attention. The Pentagon has been using national security letters, also known as administrative subpoenas, to obtain banking and credit records on people suspected of terrorism or espionage, including hundreds of Americans. The CIA, also severely restricted in domestic intelligence gathering and prohibited from domestic law enforcement, has used a handful of national security letters since 9/11, but the Pentagon is believed to have issued thousands by this date.

Unlike those issued by the FBI, Pentagon (and CIA) national security letters are not compulsory because Congress has repeatedly rejected post-9/11 requests by both agencies to issue mandatory letters. Nevertheless, the non-compulsory letters are very intimidating and most recipients are motivated to comply. Besides being illegal, they also interfere with investigations by the FBI or state and local law enforcement officials.

Even more troubling, military officials indicated in early 2007 they planned to incorporate the records obtained into CIFA's database. Vice President Dick Cheney told *Fox News*:

"This is an authority that goes back three or four decades. It was reaffirmed in the Patriot Act.... It's a perfectly legitimate activity. There's nothing wrong with it or illegal. It doesn't violate people's civil rights. And if an institution that receives one of these national security letters disagrees with it, they're free to go to court to try to stop its execution."[14]

It is true that in the 1970s the US Supreme Court ruled a person's bank records and a listing of what numbers a person calls are not private and can be obtained with good reason. However, the US Congress then passed legislation making them private except for very serious reasons such as national security investigations. In such cases the FBI is the legal authority for obtaining the required records. Technically, of course, the Pentagon is merely asking to see these records, but they put up a pretty intimidating bluff.

Newsweek revealed in April 2006 Pentagon officials have had ongoing meetings discussing a possible merger of CIFA with the Defense Security Service (DSS) which is an older agency that investigates the security arrangements of defense contractors, and has millions of classified files generated from security background checks on defense-contractor employees. Following a hiatus because of the controversy over CIFA's data bank on war resisters, a committee led by Robert Rogalski, deputy undersecretary of defense for intelligence, started meeting regularly during March and April of 2006 to discuss consolidation.

"Both Pentagon insiders and privacy experts fear that if CIFA merges with, or, in effect, takes over DSS, there would be a weakening of the safeguards that are supposed to regulate the release of the estimated 4.5 million security files on defense-contractor employees currently controlled by DSS."[15] These secret files are stored in an abandoned mineshaft in Virginia and CIFA has already requested access several times. DSS rejected the requests because CIFA would not provide adequate reason. A merger would weaken that control. But it would also give CIFA control over the DSS inspectors which could lead to inspectors having to perform the additional task of seeing that contractors are adequately protecting "sensitive but unclassified" information. Control of those inspectors is something CIFA wants but doesn't have. There was much media coverage of this proposed merger in April 2006 but since then the issue seems to have disappeared from scrutiny.

> CIFA is becoming the superpower of data mining within the US national security community. Its "operational and analytical records" include "reports of investigation, collection reports, statements of individuals, affidavits, correspondence, and other documentation pertaining to investigative or analytical efforts" by the DOD and other US government agencies to identify terrorist and other threats.[16]

This is all happening with no Congressional oversight.

The Army's 902nd Military Intelligence Group

When the Total Information Awareness (TIA) program was killed by Congress, there was an exception created for tools and techniques that would benefit "counterterrorism foreign intelligence." Described above is how the prototype system and Genoa II went to the NSA and then was assimilated by the Director of National Intelligence. Three of TIA's data mining and artificial intelligence programs went to the 902nd Military Intelligence Group – which was set up during World War II as part of the army's command structure. It is separate from CIFA but is the Pentagon's largest counterintelligence unit with hundreds of personnel spread across the country.

Besides having access to TALON, the 902nd makes extensive use of the Joint Regional Information Exchange System (JRIES) which has been expanded to all 50 states by DHS. This plus other military units can also access the JRIES which has been set up to provide the military with terrorist-related information on US citizens without violating prohibitions on the military "collecting" domestic intelligence. JRIES is one of the systems that still provides this information. Another is the internet.

★ ★ ★ ★ ★

Besides all this expansion of domestic powers within the Pentagon, a new regional command will further buttress the Pentagon's reach into citizen control – the Northern Command.

Northern Command

A month after the 9/11 attack the Pentagon reshuffled existing commands to improve homeland defense. (The term "homeland security" is used to refer to civilian activity and "homeland defense" to the military.) The North American Aerospace Command (NORAD) and the US Space Command, both based in Colorado and under Air Force General Ralph E. Eberhart in 2002, had the responsibility for protecting US skies as well as overseeing the military satellites and computer networks. The Joint Forces Command headquartered in Virginia guards the ocean approaches. In January 2002 the Pentagon decided to combine these three commands under a new Northern Command (NORTHCOM) – a regional command,[17] with Eberhart in charge.[18] It was publicly announced in April but NORAD still retained its identity because it is a joint command with Canada.

NORTHCOM is charged with the defense of North America, including Canada and Mexico with responsibilities for military aircraft guarding America's airspace, Navy ships patrolling coastal waters out to 500 miles, command over federal troops based in the US, and even many National Guard Activities. It is authorized to respond to any of a dozen scenarios including terrorist attacks, insurrections or domestic violence including conspiracies, natural disasters and epidemics. It will also oversee the new Joint Task Force Civil Support trained for response to chemical, biological or nuclear attacks. Which means NORTHCOM provides military support for civil authorities and has to maintain good working relations with state and local law enforcement agencies in fighting terrorism and training first responders to emergencies. It also helps the National Guard in

3,200 communities build 22-person response teams to support "civil authorities in minimizing the damage and recovering from domestic chemical, biological, radiological, nuclear or high-yield explosive mass-casualty attack."[19]

There are now 55 of these teams – one for each state and territory. The Muscatatuck Urban Training Center in southern Indiana has been used by NORTHCOM for simulated anti-terrorist exercises such as nuclear detonations by terrorists in the United States. The Army in 2007 allocated $100 million to develop this sprawling complex for urban warfare training all year round.

This newborn active role of the military in civil activities on US territory bothered many citizens and members of Congress. Conflict with the ancient but revered *Posse Comitatus Act* was suspected.

Posse Comitatus Act of 1878

Following the Civil War, Union troops were sent into the South during the reconstruction era to provide law enforcement. The resulting oppression by the Union Army caused Congress to end the occupation in 1878 with the *Posse Comitatus Act* which literally means "power of the country" or "force of the country." The "posse" often assembled by frontier sheriffs to chase outlaws was a shortened form of the phrase. In short, the act disallows using the military as a domestic police force on US soil "except in cases and under circumstances expressly authorized by the Constitution or Act of Congress." It has since evolved to symbolize the isolation of civilian affairs from military influence. It reads in full:

> Whoever, except in cases and under circumstances expressly authorized by the Constitution or Act of Congress, willfully uses any part of the Army or Air Force as a *posse comitatus* or otherwise to execute the laws shall be fined under this title or imprisoned not more than two years, or both.[20]

The wording of the act has hardly changed since 1878. The

courts have interpreted the act to distinguish between actually enforcing the law – searches & seizures, making arrests and other police-type activity – and helping law enforcement officials by furnishing equipment, facilities and training. Only direct or active participation is forbidden – acting "as a *posse comitatus* or otherwise to execute the laws" is illegal. While under the control of state governors the national guard is excluded from the Act. When the national guard was called up for airport security following 9/11, Bush let the governors do the calling up so *Posse Comitatus* would not be violated.

Congress can legislate exceptions as it desires and the president can issue a National Security Decision Directive when necessary. Some recent exceptions to the *Posse Comitatus Act* were:

- Authorizing federal soldiers to patrol the border for drugs in 1986.
- Sending US Army and Marine troops to assist the national guard during Los Angeles riots following acquittal of police officers accused of beating Rodney King in 1992.
- A 1997 law authorizes coöperation of the military with the Justice Department if there has been a chemical or biological attack.
- Another allows the president to call in the military if it is needed to protect life and property.
- Still another allows military coöperation with the Justice Department in obtaining intelligence or in performing searches and seizures if human life is in immediate danger.
- Section 104 of the Patriot Act provides that the military may be called in if there has been an attack on the US with weapons of mass destruction.

"Taken together, all these measures give the President authority to use the military in most conceivable emergency situations."[21] Retired Army Colonel Dennis Corrigan who taught law at the Judge Advocate General's school advises caution because soldiers are more adept at facing an enemy on the battlefield than for confronting civilians or protecting Constitutional rights. He says there "should be a partnership between the military and civilian sectors—the civilian doing the confrontation and the military providing support. I'm not sure, even with what's going on today, that Congress wants the military arresting people."[22]

How about spying on the American people? That leads into another story.

The Errant National Guard Unit

The first key objective for the June 2005 Strategy for Homeland Defense and Civil Support is to: "Achieve maximum awareness of potential threats." It goes on to elaborate: "Together with the Intelligence Community and civil authorities, DOD works to obtain and promptly exploit all actionable information needed to protect the United States. Timely and actionable intelligence, together with early warning, is the most critical enabler to protecting the United States at a safe distance."[23]

That sounds pretty efficient on paper. But how will it affect democracy's privacy and our Constitutionally-protected rights against unreasonable searches and seizures? One event gives us a clue—what I call the errant California National Guard unit. Perhaps it was just a rogue unit, or maybe it was influenced by the new Strategy for Homeland Defense and Civil Support. At any rate it gives us a "heads up." The *San Jose Mercury News* (California) has been instrumental in bringing this heretofore clandestine intelligence unit to public attention.

On 26 June 2005, the same month the new homeland defense strategy was released, this newspaper made public that a special Domestic Watch Unit had been quietly set up within the California National Guard. Known officially as the Information Synchronization, Knowledge Management and Intelligence Fusion program, it had "'broad authority' to monitor, analyze and distribute information on potential terrorist threats" which is "part of an expanding nationwide effort to better integrate military intelligence into global anti-terrorism initiatives."[24] The two-person unit was set up in 2004 by then guard commander Maj. Gen. Thomas Eres.[25] The job description for his job said the director of this new unit was to have broad authority but was expected to use first-rate judgment and show meticulous discretion. This same article said top national guard officials tried to play down public concerns, quoting guard spokesperson Lt. Col. Stan Zezotarski, "We do not do any type of surveillance or human intelligence or mixing with crowds," claiming "the National Guard does not operate in that way. We have always had a policy where we respect the rights of citizens."

Colonel Robert J. O'Neill, director of a Domestic Watch unit and a veteran intelligence officer, said they access sensitive national security information and share it with local and state law enforcement officials by integrating into the local system to give them information they lack. He said his unit doesn't violate laws which forbid spying on Americans.

E-mails obtained by the *San Jose Mercury News* reveal a more sinister story about this "expanding *nationwide* effort" established without approval from the governor or the state legislature (emphasis added). People objecting to the war in Iraq planned a Mothers' Day rally at the Vietnam Veteran's Memorial near the state capitol building in Sacramento to demand return of California National Guard troops by the following Labor Day. In what has been described as a courtesy to the military, an aide to Governor Schwarzenegger alerted the National Guard of the event. Word went up the line to Maj. Gen. Eres. E-mails cited by this newspaper show the information was forwarded "to our Intel. folks who continue to monitor."

The day of the rally turned out to be rainy so only a few dozen people showed up. Among them were the Raging Grannies (a women's singing group with a median age of 72), Gold Star Families for Peace (an organization of families that have lost loved ones in war), and Code Pink (women working against war).

When Domestic Watch activities became public, spokesperson Zezotarski claimed only media reports and websites were monitored and that no one went to the rally. "It's nothing subversive," he said, but "who knows who could infiltrate that type of group and stir something up? After all, we live in the age of terrorism, so who knows?" But Christopher Pyle, the former Army intelligence officer who exposed domestic spying by the military in 1970, scoffed at such a defense. He said the guard's job "is not to investigate individuals, but to clear streets, protect facilities, and help first responders."[26] Pyle warned against dangerous "mission creep" from Domestic Watch, which in the 1970s led to the army collecting files on over 100,000 people and using aggressive practices to undermine anti-war groups during the Vietnam War.

State Senator Joe Dunn called a hearing on the guard's Domestic Watch activities, asking the guard to preserve all relative documents and information. That same day, June 27, claiming it was before seeing Dunn's letter, the guard erased the computer of a retired colonel who had overseen the special intelligence unit. Dunn then requested the computer's hard drive so technicians could recover whatever possible. But acting guard commander, General Alexander, said he could not comply because federal officials were conducting their own investigation. Dunn said the Pentagon had no say over this state matter and accused the guard of stonewalling his investigation. Then the guard said the erased hard drive was government property and not subject to subpoena.[27]

Hearings were convened in July 2005. Internal Guard e-mails presented as evidence indicated its high-level interest in the Mothers' Day rally. When George O'Connell, counsel for the guard, was asked if the guard kept files on US citizens, he replied: "Senator I don't know what you mean by files." Dunn then asked Guard Lt. Col. Joseph Righello the same question and was told: "I don't know." Lawyer O'Connell said the subpoenaed documents represented "the bulk" of the information desired. But Righello later admitted there was still a "large amount of material" that was classified or marked "official use only." In addition, at least 18 guard officials refused to testify and Gov. Schwarzenegger would not order them to do so.[28]

A shake-up started in late July 2005. Schwarzenegger removed one lieut. col. from his job as spokesperson and another, Lieut. Col. Zezotarski, was told not to speak to the media anymore. The big shuffle came on November 16. Domestic Watch was quietly disbanded with no formal announcement. Colonel O'Neill was terminated December 31. Another member of Domestic Watch was transferred. It "was the right thing to do," said Col. David Baldwin, director of Plans and Operations for the California National Guard. "The Civil Support Division was not formed in accordance with military doctrine and it was an organization that did not have the approval of the legislature in the governor's budget."[29] Investigators from the US Army's Inspector General's Office said they found no evidence the guard collected information on US citizens, but refused to release their report.

Still, Dunn expressed concerns that what happened in California was actually part of larger and more sinister activity throughout the US. Through contacts with guard officials in other states he heard reports of similar units established elsewhere. Dunn said: "The question is, was there a federally inspired program, post 9/11, to get around a law that prevents domestic spying?... It appears that could be a possibility here."[30]

Dunn's concern has real validity in light of official statements by General Eberhart, commander-in-chief of NORTHCOM who told the national guard in 2004 that "we can't let culture and the way we've always done it stand in the way" of gathering intelligence.[31]

Federal Control of the National Guard

According to our constitution, the governor is commander-in-chief of the national guard in that state in time of peace. The president can take command of the national guard for federal duty during wartime but, during peacetime, the governor must give permission for the national guard to be nationalized – even in time of emergency, major disaster or the like.

All of that changed in October 2006. Included in the 2007 Defense Authorization Bill was language giving the president power to call up the 440,000-strong national guard under disaster and emergency conditions without the governor's consent, even over the governor's objections. The governors of all 50 states opposed that measure.

The *Posse Comitatus Act of 1878* bars federal troops – including a federalized national guard – from exercising law enforcement on US soil. Any exception must be authorized by the constitution or by congress. Congress made one exception 200 years ago with the *Insurrection Act of 1807* (10 U.S.C. 331-334). Article 333 of that act reads:

> The President, by using the militia or the armed forces, or both, or by any other means, shall take such measures as he considers necessary to suppress, in a State, any insurrection, domestic violence, unlawful combination, or conspiracy, if it:(1) so hinders the execution of the laws of that State, and of the United States within the State, that any part or class of its people is deprived of a right, privilege, immunity, or protection named in the Constitution and secured by law, and the constituted authorities of that State are unable, fail, or refuse to protect that right, privilege, or immunity, or to give that protection; or (2) opposes or obstructs the execution of the laws of the United States or impedes the course of justice under those laws. In any situation covered by clause (1), the State shall be considered to have denied the equal protection of the laws secured by the Constitution.

The October 2006 appropriations bill adds "natural disaster, epidemic or serious public health emergency, terrorist attack or incident" to the conditions under which the national guard can be federalized if the president determines that "authorities of the state or possession are incapable of maintaining public order." The National Governors Association wrote congress that this change is "a dramatic expansion of federal authority during natural disasters that could cause confusion in the command-and-control of the national guard and interfere with states' ability to respond to natural disasters within their borders."[32] It does, indeed, vastly expand executive branch power and judging from previous examples, the language of that expansion will be interpreted liberally. This is an important expansion should the administration ever decide to impose martial law.

Military Influence on Civilian Law Enforcement

Local law enforcement agencies have for decades been drifting toward a paramilitary flavor. Perhaps most noticeable for military type violence are the Special Weapons And Tactics (SWAT) teams. Formation of the first SWAT team is credited to the Los Angeles Police Department and organized as D Platoon of the Metro Branch in 1967.

Since then SWAT teams have spread to every local law enforcement force of any significant size as well as state and local levels. They come under numerous names including Special Response Team, Special Response Force, Hostage Rescue Team, Special Reaction Team, Special Operations Group and Special Operations and Response Team.

Team members are usually dressed military style in battle fatigues and combat boots with Kevlar helmets and vests, face shields, ballistic shields and sometimes night vision goggles. Trained in crowd control techniques and hostage rescue, they use special weapons such as tasers, flashbang grenades, smoke grenades and bean bags. Other equipment often used are communications devices, submachine guns, shotguns, carbines, high-powered rifles for markspersons (snipers), pepper spray, tear gas, and even boot knives. Many units have armored personnel carriers and grenade launchers; some have helicopters.

In addition to crowd control and hostage rescue, SWAT teams are used to deliver dangerous papers as during drug raids which usually take place late at night or before dawn when the targeted individuals can be caught off guard. Because these raids normally involve unannounced, forced entry, SWAT teams are also equipped with battering rams and other forced-entry devices. Some 44,000 such raids a year result in numerous wrong addresses, subjecting minor offenders and bystanders to unnecessary violence. Deaths have resulted, even to innocent people.

To supply these civilian paramilitary units with equipment the Department of Defense has a Technology Transfer Program. Legislation passed in 1990 and 1996 allows transfer of excess personal property to federal and state agencies. Under the Bush administration the transfer became more than just personal items and went to more than just federal and state agencies. A law signed by Bush in December 2002 (Section 1401 of Public Law 107-314) instructs the Secretary of Defense to "designate a senior official of the Department of Defense to coördinate all Department of Defense efforts to identify, evaluate, deploy and transfer to federal, state, and local first-responders technology items and equipment in support of homeland security."

The purported DOD vision for this Technology Transfer program is even more explicit, stating: "In order to fulfill the strategic objective of the DOD's Strategy for Homeland Defense and Civil Support to 'improve national and international capabilities for homeland defense and homeland security,' the DOD will promote the integration and sharing of applicable DOD technology, items, and equipment with federal, state, local, and tribal authorities and the private sector. Sharing technologies, capabilities, and expertise strengthens the nation's ability to respond to hostile threats and domestic emergencies."[33] Note that it emphasizes homeland defense over homeland security – that is, NORTHCOM over the Department of Homeland Security. Also, the sharing now extends to tribal authorities and the private sector, the latter presumably the private contractors or mercenaries. Having mercenaries available to meet "domestic emergencies" is scary. We'll look at those potential "domestic emergencies" in more detail in Chapter 10.

So now the sharing is almost unlimited and can include sophisticated equipment normally unavailable to local police such as grenade-launchers, armored-personnel carriers, even tanks. Thus when 26 armored personnel carriers were returned from loan in South America they were sold to police departments for their SWAT teams.

Another example of technology sharing is with the Pinellas County Sheriff's office of Florida. Through a program funded by the Department of Justice through a company called Visage, the Pinellas County Sheriff's Department has developed one of the most advanced biometric technology face-recognition systems in the country. Since 2002 it has established a database of over 4.5 million faces and that database is expanding. Now the DOD is working with Pinellas County to acquire that capability and share it with other civilian law enforcement agencies.

Observers are concerned over the military meddling in civilian law enforcement. Marina Lowe, staff attorney for ACLU of Utah warns those "two roles are diametrically opposed. Law enforcement has the goal of using minimum force and trying to protect people's constitutional rights. Whereas the military tends to use a lot more force, has different objectives and often relaxes civil liberties to achieve security in times of war." Civil Libertarian Diane Cecilia Weber wrote in a CATO Institute paper: "The sharing of training and technology by military and law enforcement agencies has produced a shared mindset, and the mindset of the warrior is simply not appropriate for the civilian police officer charged with enforcing the law."[34]

★ ★ ★ ★ ★

Air Force General Victor E. Renuart Jr. assumed command of both NORAD and NORTHCOM in March 2007 and is helping NORTHCOM assume the geographic dimensions envisioned by the neoconservatives and the Pentagon.

Initiatives to Conquer North America

President Dwight D. Eisenhower, in his farewell address to

the nation, issued a solemn warning: "In the councils of government, we must guard against the acquisition of unwarranted influence, whether sought or unsought, by the military-industrial complex. The potential for the disastrous rise of misplaced power exists and will persist."[35] The conquest of North America is being accomplished by the confluence of those two streams—the flow of economic ambitions of America's huge corporate empire and the Pentagon's unsatiated thirst for power. This is nothing more than the military-industrial complex emerging from its adolescent years—pushed along, of course, by the neoconservative agenda.

Let me first address the economic stream.

NAFTA and the SPP

The North American Free Trade Agreement (NAFTA)—an economic treaty among the US, Mexico and Canada—went into effect in January 1994. It was drafted in secret during the George H.W. Bush administration by over 1,000 advisors from the corporate community; a minuscule five from environmental groups; and none from consumer, labor or health groups. Not by chance did the Chiapas rebellion in Mexico start the same day. The peasants correctly foresaw the deplorable labor conditions and slave wages that eventually occurred—a condition leading to Mexico's $20 billion indebtedness to the US with billions of dollars in Mexican oil sales held as collateral.

The imbalance of trade caused by devaluation of the peso and the resulting drop in US exports garnered a net gain of only 11,000 US jobs—a far cry from the 190,000 predicted and an insignificant percentage of America's 125 million jobs. Exacerbating the US unemployment figure, more illegal but cheap Mexican labor started migrating to the US to obtain better-paying employment, or just to get a job—which led to our current immigration dilemma.

Canada also suffered. Many jobs and companies moved to the US, Canadian companies were taken over by American corporations, and unemployment rose. A year after NAFTA went into effect, even advocates of the pact admitted it was oversold regarding the jobs and wealth it would bring in all three countries. The true benefiters from NAFTA were the large American corporations. Terry Karl, director of the Center for Latin American Studies at Stanford University, said the people were defrauded by NAFTA "because to sell the pact politically its benefits had to be exaggerated, its promise had to be exaggerated, and its potential problems had to be downplayed."[36]

NAFTA expires after 15 years—at the end of 2008. The "Three Amigos" summit at Waco, Texas in March 2005 launched a sequel to NAFTA called the Security and Prosperity Partnership of North America (SPP). Leaders of Mexico, Canada and the US met for the first of what was to become annual summit meetings to review planning for the free movement of people, goods and services throughout the continent. Subsequent meetings were held in Cancun, Mexico in March 2006 and Montebello, Canada in August 2007. Only 30 top business executives from the three countries were invited to the last encounter.

Before exploring the Montebello summit, let us look at the flow of Pentagon activity.

NORTHCOM, NORAD and the BPG

During his April 2002 announcement on the creation of NORTHCOM, Rumsfeld said that the new command would "be responsible for land, aerospace and sea defenses of the United States" and would "operate within the US in support of civil authorities."[37] General Richard Myers, then chair of the Joint Chiefs of Staff, elaborated that NORTHCOM's geographic responsibility included "the continental United States, Alaska,[38] Canada and Mexico, portions of the Caribbean and the contiguous waters out—in the Atlantic and Pacific oceans, out to a minimum of 500 miles," and that NORTHCOM would also be "responsible to civil authorities for chemical, biological, radiological, nuclear, major conventional explosive events" and for potential "support for natural disasters – hurricanes, floods, and fires."[39]

The US wants Canada to join NORTHCOM and Canada already is a token member of the North American Defense Command (NORAD) with a general as deputy commander, but NORAD is a functional command rather than a regional command. For all practical purposes NORTHCOM and NORAD are the same – occupying the same headquarters at Peterson Air Force Base at Colorado Springs; the same US general commands both and they have the same chief of staff. The only difference is the Canadian general who is deputy commander of NORAD but not connected with NORTHCOM. In December 2002, then Canadian Prime Minister Jean Chrétien refused to extend Canada's participation in joining NORTHCOM.

Nevertheless, that same month it was announced that an interim Binational Planning Group (BPG) headquartered at Peterson Air Force base was being set up to explore the expansion of NORAD's function to defend against maritime threats and land attacks (air threats being the prime mission of NORAD), and to provide civil support. More specifically, the BPG was tasked to prepare response plans for terrorist attacks, natural disasters and other emergencies; to improve coördination of military support to civilian agencies; and to find better ways to coördinate maritime surveillance, sharing intelligence and evaluating threats.

The BPG mandate was to expire in two years, when it was unofficially expected that NORAD would merge with NORTHCOM. Later the BPG was extended to May 2006 with the unofficial expectation that Canada would then join NORTHCOM. Two months before that expiration date the BPG recommended a maritime mission and warning system for NORAD. The US and Canada followed that recommendation when they secretly signed a renewed NORAD agreement in April 2006. Now the missions of NORAD and NORTHCOM perfectly coincide.

The renewal of NORAD gave control of Canada's territorial waters to the US. At the outset, four years prior when formation of NORTHCOM was first announced, Canada agreed that "US troops could be deployed to Canada and Canadian troops could cross the border into the United States if the continent was attacked by terrorists who do not respect borders, according to an agreement announced by US and Canadian officials."[40]

North American Union (NAU)

It is easy to see that Security and Prosperity Partnership (SSP) and the Binational Planning Group (BPG) coincide geographically for it is logical to the military-industrial as well as the neocons viewpoint that these two initiatives should be combined—which is what the advocates of these agreements had in mind. They envision a North American Union (NAU) and hold up the European Union (EU) as a model. There is a world of difference in the process, however. The EU was crafted over some four decades with much public and parliamentary debate. The planned NAU timetable is a mere five years—to be completed in 2010—with negotiations wrapped in secrecy from the public and Congress. Even the SSP is a unilateral agreement among the "three amigos" that has never been presented to legislators or taxpayers for approval prior to the August 2007 summit at Montebello. The secrecy, of course, is necessary if the corporate giants and their 30 representatives at Montebello are to get the conditions they desire.

For this reason the third SSP summit at Montebello, Canada was shrouded in security. Conference planners admitted US troops arranged that security. A $1 million, 10-foot-high fence was designed to keep the 10,000 expected protesters miles away from the hotel where the meeting took place. The completion of a "North American Plan for Avian and Pandemic Influenza" was announced to the media—which was a secondary focus of the summit, for it certainly couldn't have been the sole accomplishment of a meeting advised by 30 corporate representatives.

There is much guessing and speculation on what else transpired at Montebello but no firm information seems to be forthcoming. The secrecy of SSP and BPG is holding fast, and carrying over to a military-industrial vision of a North American Union. The neoconservative agenda progresses virtually unnoticed.

Notes for Chapter 4

1. UPI dispatch "Retiring Admiral Rickover Predicts World Will 'Probably Destroy' Itself," *Santa Barbara News Press*, 29 Jan 1982, page A-12.

2. Jehl, Douglas and Eric Schmitt, "Pentagon Seeks to Expand in Intelligence-collecting," *NY Times*, 19 Dec 2004.

3. Gellman, Barton; "Secret Unit Expands Rumsfeld's Domain," *Washington Post*, 23 Jan 2005.

4. NGA was established 1 Oct 1996 as the National Imagery and Mapping Agency (NIMA), but its name was changed in 2003 when it was put under the DOD.

5. AP, "US Makes Spy Images Inside US," posted on *Wired News*, 26 Sep 2004 at http://www.wired.com/news/technology/0,1282,65091,00.html?tw=wn_tophead_6

6. DOD Directive 5105.67; "Department of Defense Counterintelligence Field Activity (DOD CIFA)," 19 Feb 2002, Section 3.

7. Block, Robert and Gary Fields, "Is Military Creeping into Domestic Law Enforcement?" *Wall Street Journal*, 9 Mar 2004.

8. Wolfowitz resigned as deputy secretary of defense in March 2005 to become World Bank president. He was succeeded by Gordon England, former secretary of the navy and the first deputy secretary of DHS.

9. Pincus, Walter, "Pentagon Expanding its Domestic Surveillance Activity," *Washington Post*, 27 Nov 2005.

10. Pincus, Walter; "Protesters Found in Database," *Washington Post*, 17 Jan 2007.

11. Myers, Lisa, Douglas Pasternak and Rich Gardella, "Is the Pentagon Spying on Americans?" NBC News, 13 Dec 2005.

12. Pincus; 27 Nov 2005, op. cit.

13. Myers, Pasternak and Gardella, op. cit.

14. Savage, David G., "Cheney Defends Pentagon," *Los Angeles Times*, 15 Jan 2007.

15. Hosenball, Mark, "America's Secret Police?" *Newsweek*, 13 Apr 2006.

16. Meyers, Pasternak and Gardella, op. cit.

17. Four other regional commands at the time were Central Command (Middle East, Central Asia and Eastern Africa), European Command (Europe and the remainder of Africa), Pacific Command (Pacific and Indian Oceans and East/Southeast Asia), and Southern Command (Central and South America). A new Africa Command was announced in February 2007 to cover all of Africa except Egypt (which will remain under the Central Command). There are also functional commands not geographically constrained, such as Military Airlift Command and Special Forces Command.

18. Eberhart was replaced on 6 Nov 2004 by Adm Timothy J. Keating who was replaced by AF Gen Victor E. Renuart Jr. on 19 Mar 2007.

19. *Strategy for Homeland Defense and Civil Support*, US DOD, Jun 2005.

20. 18 U.S.C. 1385; *Posse Comitatus Act of 1878* (Revised 6 Jan 2003).

21. Isenberg, David, "The US Military: A Creeping Civilian Mission," *Asia Times*, 5 Dec 2003.

22. Badger, T.A., "1878 Military Law Gets New Attention," AP, 24 Nov 2001.

23. *Strategy for Homeland Defense and Civil Support*, op. cit.

24. Nissenbaum, Dion, "Program Raises Spying Concern," *San Jose Mercury News*, 26 Jun 2005.

25. Eres was forced to retire in Jun 2005 because he allegedly failed to prove his shooting, misused military flights and misused anti-drug and anti-terrorist funds.

26. Nissenbaum, op. cit.

27. This is a Catch-22 situation. The *Posse Comitatus Act* allows the US to supply training and equipment to state and local authorities, but when used illegally that equipment becomes government property unavailable to state investigators.

28. Davis, Aaron C., "Legislator Confronts Guard over Documents," *San Jose Mercury News*, 20 Jul 2005.

29. Garcia, Edwin, "Under Pressure, Guard Dismantles Spy Unit," *San Jose Mercury News*, 2 Dec 2005.

30. Davis, op. cit.

31. Nissenbaum, op. cit.

32. Peterson, Kavan, "Governors Lose in Power Struggle over National Guard," Stateline.org, 12 Jan 2007. Available at http://www.stateline.org/live/printable/story?contentId=170453

33. "1401 Technology Transfer Program Overview," published by the Office of the Assistant Secretary of Defense for Homeland Defense and America's Security Affairs, 2006. Available at http://www.defenselink.mil/policy/sections/policy_offices/hd/offices/techTrans/techTrans_process/index.html

34. Lamb, Jonah Owen; "Unholy Alliance: Military and Police Technologies Sharing Sends Shivers up Civil Libertarians' Spines," *Salt Lake City Weekly*, 5 Jul 2007.

35. *Public Papers of the Presidents, Dwight D. Eisenhower,* 1960, pp. 1035-1040.

36. *San Jose Mercury News*, 4 Feb 1995.

37. Rumsfeld, Donald H.; "Special Briefing on the Unified Command Plan," News transcript of the US DOD, 17 Apr 2002.

38. NORTHCOM geographically covers Alaska but the troops based there are under the Pacific Command.

39. Myers, General Richard; "Special Briefing on the Unified Command Plan," News Transcript of the US DOD, 17 April 2002.

40. *Edmonton Sun*, 11 Sep 2002. Cited in Michel Chossudovsky, "Canada's Sovereignty in Jeopardy: The Militarization of North America," *Global Research*, 17 Aug 2007, at http://www.globalresearch.ca/PrintArticle.php?articleId=6572

5

Invading Privacy

> *The accumulation of all powers; legislative, executive, and judiciary; in the same hands; whether of one, a few, or many; and whether hereditary, self-appointed, or elective; may justly be pronounced the definition of tyranny.*
> —James Madison

I have so far outlined programs, legislated or otherwise, that became known to the public. During 2006 other programs started surfacing which had been kept secret from Congress and the citizens—which Bush had authorized shortly after the 9/11 attacks. Here we will look at some just recently discovered.

NSA's Terrorist Surveillance Program

In December 2005 *The New York Times* exposed a secret operation by the National Security Agency (NSA) called the "Terrorist Surveillance Program." In a clandestine October 2001 presidential order, the NSA was directed to eavesdrop on all international telephone calls and e-mail communication originating in the US without obtaining the court-issued warrants required for domestic surveillance. We are told it watches for key words that might indicate terrorist activity. Messages containing those key words would be investigated further. Air Force Gen.

Michael V. Hayden was the director of NSA at the time this program started (later to become assistant director of National Intelligence and the CIA director) and is credited with being the mastermind of the plan.

Overseas Calls from the US

A few select congressional leaders were reportedly briefed when the Terrorist Surveillance Program began but it is not clear how much they were told. Apparently none of the minority Democrats were fully informed. Congresswoman Nancy Pelosi, now speaker of the House, said she was told several times that Bush had something going with NSA. She expressed concerns on those occasions but said Bush's statement Saturday "raises serious questions as to what the activities were and whether the activities were lawful."[1]

That Saturday statement was Bush's December 17 radio address when he admitted authorizing the spying program. Then, and in a press conference two days later, Bush contended Congress authorized him to use force against Al Qaeda, and that authorized him to intercept telephone calls and e-mails without a warrant. Plus, Article II of the Constitution, he claimed, made him commander-in-chief of the armed forces. The Congressional Research Service (CRS) doubted such expansive interpretations and said the legal rationale "does not seem to be well grounded."[2] CRS was particularly critical of the claim that Congress had included eavesdropping when it legislated "all necessary and appropriate force" against terrorists and said provisions of federal wiretap laws render such justification meaningless.

Bush insisted the Terrorist Surveillance Program is "a highly classified program that is crucial to our national security," and "is a vital tool in our war against the terrorists." He claimed the "American people expect me to do everything in my power, under our laws and constitution, to protect them and their civil liberties and that is exactly what I will continue to do as long as I am president."[3] Incongruously, this flagrant violation of law and Constitution threatens the very civil liberties Bush claims to be protecting.

Whistleblowers Alert the Media.

NSA is America's largest and most secretive spy agency with a mission to monitor communications abroad and break any codes used. Obtaining information from radio, telephone and other types of electronic signals is called signals intelligence and it is lawful for the agency to monitor such signals originating in a foreign country even if it is communication with someone in the US. But for signals originating in the US, the Foreign Intelligence Surveillance Act (FISA) requires a warrant.

A dozen current and former NSA officials anonymously discussed the Terrorist Surveillance Program with reporters for *The New York Times* because they were concerned about the program's legality and oversight. At the White House's request, the *Times* delayed publication for a year and then omitted portions officials claimed could help terrorists. The whistleblowers were concerned about unlawful searches and seizures forbidden by the Fourth Amendment and said many inside the NSA disapprove of the program and want nothing to do with it. Others point out the program is unnecessary because all that is required is to follow FISA procedure.

In late January 2006, Gen. Hayden, then deputy director of National Intelligence, said if the spying program had been in place before 9/11 many of the hijackers would have been apprehended. Hayden failed to mention that the NSA, CIA and FBI knew about two of the hijackers in January 2000 but didn't follow up. He also conveniently forgot to mention the NSA interception of attack warnings the day before which were not translated until the day after. He further claimed warrantless spying allowed NSA to act more rapidly with less information than using FISA courts, suggesting that a warrant would require too much evidence.

FISA courts do require some evidence to show the target has

a connection to terrorism, but the law makes FISA courts the "exclusive means" for intelligence agents to eavesdrop on Americans. It is not difficult to get a warrant. Only one in 400 are rejected. It is also permissible to eavesdrop for 72 hours before obtaining a warrant. Yet Atty. Gen. Alberto Gonzales labeled FISA too cumbersome for a program of "a military nature" that required "maximum speed and agility to achieve early warning."[4] He also called FISA irrelevant because of the president's powers. James Bamford denounced the administration's position, saying: "In essence, NSA seemed to be on a classic fishing expedition, precisely the type of abuse the FISA court was put in place to stop."[5]

The next month Gonzales told the Senate Judiciary Committee there "has not been any serious disagreement about the program the president has confirmed. There have been disagreements about other matters regarding operations, which I cannot get into."[6] Gonzales confined his testimony to the announced program, saying it is legal. Senator Diane Feinstein complained that Gonzales "provided none of the documents the committee required for proper oversight, and his assurances alone did not allay my concerns. Instead he propounded a radical legal theory of presidential power largely unconstrained by either Congress or the courts."[7]

In 1975 when Senator Frank Church chaired a select committee on intelligence, he visited NSA and was appalled, saying: "That capability at any time could be turned around on the American people and no American would have any privacy left, such is the capability to monitor everything: telephone conversations, telegrams, it doesn't matter. There would be no place to hide." He added that if a dictator ever took over America, NSA "could enable it to impose total tyranny, and there would be no way to fight back." Church worried: "I know the capacity that is there to make tyranny total in America, and we must see to it that this agency and all agencies ...operate within the law and under proper supervision, so that we never cross over

...the abyss from which there is no return."[8]

That was in 1975 when NSA spying only extended to telephone calls and telegrams. Today we have e-mail, cell phones and the internet carrying personal correspondence and information. Russell D. Tice, an 18-year veteran at NSA who worked on some of the most secret programs, was one of the whistleblowers. When he questioned the spying program, NSA authorities had him examined by a psychologist who diagnosed him paranoid. Tice consulted an independent psychologist who could find no problems. Nevertheless, NSA revoked his security clearance and fired him, so he went to the media and told the *Times* NSA could monitor every domestic and international phone call as they pass through switching centers to sort out words and phrases terrorists use. Although Bush says he gave orders to listen to only a small number of Americans, Tice says the number being monitored could potentially be in the millions.

Atty. Gen. Gonzales wrote in *The Wall Street Journal*: "The NSA's Terrorist Surveillance Program is narrowly focused on the international communications of persons believed to be members or agents of Al Qaeda or attributed terrorist organizations."[9] The devil is in the details. Perhaps the truth comes from examining the words and program-names used. Maybe the Terrorist Surveillance Program Gonzales refers to does just what he describes, but there could be another program beyond that. Suspicion of such was heightened during House judiciary committee hearings when a Justice Department official waffled in answering the question on whether the administration thought it legal to monitor purely domestic phone calls without a warrant if terrorism was suspected. He couldn't positively say it hadn't been done. I'll get to that, but first let's see how the administration avoids legal action in the courts.

Terrorist Surveillance Program Ruled Unconstitutional.

US District Judge Anna Diggs Taylor in Detroit shocked the government in August 2006 by ruling the Terrorist Surveillance

Program unconstitutional because it violated free speech, privacy and separation of powers (First & Fourth Amendments) as well as the FISA statute. She ordered surveillance stopped. In her 43-page opinion she stated: "Plaintiffs have prevailed, and the public interest is clear, in this matter. It is the upholding of our Constitution."[10] She added: "There are no hereditary kings in America and no powers not created by the Constitution."

The government's response was that the president has authority to order this surveillance but to prove it would reveal secret information. Taylor said she'd reviewed the secret information and found it irrelevant. She called the secrecy argument "disingenuous and without merit." An editorial on her ruling concluded that "one judge in Michigan has done what 535 members of Congress have so abysmally failed to do."[11]

The government appealed to the Sixth US Circuit Court of Appeals, which allowed the surveillance to continue until the appeal is decided. Justice Department spokesperson Charles Miller said the government's argument on appeal is that the president has Constitutional authority to eavesdrop because it protects civil liberties. The ACLU asked the Sixth Circuit to uphold Taylor's decision because: "The government's sweeping theory of executive power would allow the president to violate any law passed by Congress. This theory presents a profound threat to our democratic system."[12]

The oral arguments before a three-judge panel in January 2007 worried the administration enough that two weeks before Gonzales announced an abrupt reversal of the administration's stance. In a two-page letter to Senators Patrick Leahy and Arlen Specter of the Judiciary Committee, Gonzales said the FISA court had just issued orders allowing NSA to eavesdrop on international communications regardless of whether they originate in the US or abroad when probable cause exists that one of the parties is a terrorist or associated with a terrorist group. Gonzales added that surveillance under the Terrorist Surveillance Program would now be conducted with a FISA warrant.

That sounds fine but the entire agreement is secret—"an unnamed judge on the secret court in a nonadversarial proceeding that apparently cannot be appealed, had issued orders that apparently both granted surveillance requests and set out some ground rules for how such requests would be handled."[13] The judge is unidentified. It appears a separate warrant will not be issued for every instance; instead a blanket warrant covering a large segment of monitoring over a prescribed time seems to have been issued. Anonymous statements from those supposedly familiar with the program say the warrant is "programmatic," meaning one warrant covers an entire program. That being the case, this entire exercise is contrary to the stated purpose of the Foreign Intelligence Surveillance Act.

Why did it take over four years to come up with a satisfactory plan that would involve the FISA court? ACLU Executive Director Anthony D. Romero said, "It's clearly a flip-flop because they saw the writing on the wall. But it still does not address questions about whether the president broke the law. Complying with FISA now does not make his actions over the last 4½ years legal."[14]

Unabashed, the administration says although eavesdropping is currently carried out under court order, that arrangement is voluntary and the president still has authority to order warrantless wiretapping if necessary. During May 2007 hearings Senator Russ Feingold asked National Intelligence Director Michael McConnell if he could promise Bush would no longer sidestep the FISA court process. McConnell replied: "Sir, the president's authority under Article II is in the Constitution. So if the president chooses to exercise Article II authority, that would be the president's call." Later he said there were no current plans to resume warrantless wiretapping, but added, "I'd just like to highlight, Article II is Article II, so in a different circumstance, I can't speak for the president what he might decide."[15]

The Sixth Circuit's panel evaded the issue in its July 6 ruling. Its two-to-one decision merely said plaintiffs couldn't prove personal harm and dismissed the case. It also recognized the state secrets privilege. The dissenting judge said at least the plaintiffs who are lawyers suffered harm because they now have to use extraordinary measures and suffer extra expense to communicate with their clients overseas. He agreed with the district court's decision that warrantless wiretapping violates FISA and the First and Fourth Amendments. The two majority-opinion judges were appointed by the Bush family. The dissenting judge was a Clinton appointee. The ACLU is considering taking this case to the Supreme Court.

Does the President Have a Preëminent Role in Foreign Affairs?

In a speech at Georgetown University Law Center in September 2006, Atty. Gen. Gonzales criticized judges who ruled against the administration's programs. After saying federal judges shouldn't put their personal views above the president's decisions in wartime, he stressed the Constitution makes the president commander-in-chief and alleged the US Supreme Court has consistently acknowledged the president's preëminent role in foreign affairs, adding, "The Constitution, by contrast, provides the courts with relatively few tools to superintend military and foreign policy decisions, especially during wartime. Judges must resist the temptation to supplement those tools based on their own personal views about the wisdom of the policies under review." He cautioned federal judges against feeling immune to criticism because of their lifetime appointment, advising, "A proper sense of judicial humility requires judges to keep in mind the institutional limitations of the judiciary and the duties expressly assigned by the Constitution to the more politically accountable branches."[16]

Louis Fisher, a specialist in Constitutional law at the Law Library of the Library of Congress, refuted the false notion that the executive branch has exclusive authority pertaining to foreign affairs. Those who champion unlimited presidential power rely heavily on the Supreme Court case *United States v. Curtiss-*

Wright Export Corp (1936). In a separate opinion which is extraneous to the court's decision and not binding, Justice George Sutherland cited a statement made in 1800 by John Marshall which said the president "is the sole organ of the nation in its external relations."[17] That statement is the main source of Bush's assertion today that he is the only one to make decisions regarding foreign affairs.

But if you go back to 1800 and to Marshall, you discover at that time he was a representative in Congress, not chief justice of the Supreme Court. Marshall was not speaking for the judicial branch and just because he later became chief justice, it does not give that statement any weight as a judicial precedent. In addition, Marshall's statement is cited out of context because it was made regarding implementation of the *Jay Treaty* and he was defending President John Adams' authority to extradite a British citizen charged with a murder on a British ship. In the same article Fisher explained: "Marshall meant merely that when the United States enters into a treaty with an extradition provision, it is the president's duty under the constitution to see that the treaty is faithfully carried out. He meant that, and nothing more." In this case the president, under the constitution, was the sole organ for implementing the treaty – Article II charges the president with faithfully executing the law and Article VI makes treaties part of the supreme law of the land. There are constitutional checks and balances on formulating treaties and foreign policy. A statement made with reference to executing a treaty has no bearing on formulating a treaty.

Fisher then deplores this "sole organ" doctrine which has been employed in three recent legal arguments:

1) US Department of Justice. Its 42-page white paper from January 2006 attempted to justify NSA eavesdropping by referring to the "President's well-recognized inherent constitutional authority as Commander-in-Chief and sole organ for the nation in foreign affairs." Later in the California lawsuit the DOJ argued that the state secrets privilege "embodies central aspects of the Executive's re-

sponsibilities under Article II of the Constitution as Commander-in-Chief and as the nation's organ for foreign affairs."

2) Judge Richard Posner, a Reagan appointee to the US 7th Circuit Court of Appeals. In his book *Not a Suicide Pact* he erroneously writes: "In *United States v. Curtiss-Wright Export Corp* (1936), the Supreme Court held that the United States acquired the powers of a sovereign nation by its successful revolution against Great Britain rather than by a grant in the Constitution; the nation is prior to the Constitution."[18] That wasn't a "holding" of the court, it was just supplemental editorializing by Justice Sutherland. Fisher points out that any hereditary sovereign powers perceived to have been acquired from British monarchy would have gone to the Continental Congress because there was no presidency at that time.

3) John Yoo, Professor of Law at University of California, Berkeley. In his book *War by Other Means* he writes that "the Constitution grants the President the leading role in foreign affairs. The statement that the President is the 'sole organ for the nation in foreign affairs' was not manufactured by the Bush administration, but in fact comes from a 1936 Supreme Court case that recognized the President's control over diplomacy and the setting of foreign policy."[19] The holding in that case recognized no such thing but was only the extraneous opinion of Justice Sutherland.

Nowhere in his career as congressman, secretary of state or chief justice did John Marshall ever imply that the president had the predominant say in foreign policy. In fact, "in *Little v. Barreme* (1804) he stated that when a presidential proclamation in time of war conflicts with a statute enacted by Congress, the statute prevails."[20] Furthermore, the *Curtiss-Wright* case was not about presidential power and the decision in that case did not address presidential powers. It was about Congress delegating legislative power.

To finally put the 1936 case to rest, along with Sutherland's editorializing, in *Youngston Co. v. Sawyer* (1952) Justice Robert Jackson said "the president might act in external affairs without congressional authority, but not that he might act contrary to an act of Congress." More recently, the D.C. US Circuit Court of Appeals opined: "To the extent that denominating the President as the 'sole organ' of the United States in international affairs constitutes a blanket endorsement of plenary Presidential power over any matter extending beyond the borders of this country, we reject that characterization."[21]

What Do We Not Know?

Now back to the eavesdropping. "According to John E. McLaughlin, who was deputy director of the Central Intelligence Agency in the fall of 2001 and was among the first briefed on NSA spying, this eavesdropping was the most secret operation in the entire intelligence network, complete with its own code word—*which itself is secret*"[22] (emphasis added). If even the code word for the program was so secret it can't be divulged, then it is not wise to believe they received a complete briefing. It looks like there is more to this very secret program than what Gonzales was talking about in his *Wall Street Journal* article. We must look deeper.

Russell Tice told the House Government Reform Subcommittee he was concerned about another, much broader "special access" electronic surveillance program which is wider in scope than what has been exposed by *The New York Times*. He thought it violated the Constitution but it was too secret to talk about. Tice said further he couldn't even brief the NSA inspector general because that office was not cleared to hear the information.

Gonzales also implied there was more to NSA's activities. In testimony before the House Judiciary Committee in April 2006, he said he wouldn't rule out the president's legal authority to authorize spying on Americans exclusively in the US without a warrant: "The administration, assuming the conversation related to Al Qaeda, would have to determine if the surveillance were crucial to the nation's fight against terrorism." Gonzales added the clincher when he again admitted to disagreement within the administration on the monitoring program but said it "did not relate to the program the president disclosed. [It] related to something else and I can't get into that."[23] These are almost the same words he used two months before with the Senate Judiciary Committee. What the president disclosed was surveillance in which one end of the communication is outside the United States; what Gonzales could not get into is, in his own words, "something else."

Congress did learn more about that "something else" in May 2007 when former Deputy Atty Gen. James B. Comey testified. Comey related how he, Atty. Gen. John Ashcroft, FBI Director Robert S. Mueller III and chief counsel Jack L. Goldsmith almost resigned in March 2004 when the terrorist surveillance program had to be re-authorized. Comey was the No. 2 in the Justice Department until he resigned in August 2006, but in March 2004 he was acting attorney general while Ashcroft was hospitalized for surgery. Here's how the story went.

The crisis started when Comey refused to renew a presidential order on spying. The Justice Department's Office of Legal Counsel, under Goldsmith, had reviewed the program and said it was illegal. In an effort to bypass Comey, Andrew Card (then White House chief of staff) and Alberto Gonzales (then White House counsel) went to Ashcroft's hospital bed to get his approval. Comey, Mueller and Goldsmith beat them there and Ashcroft refused to override Comey. At a White House meeting a few days later, Bush called Comey aside and they reached an agreement on how to proceed. Details on Comey's refusal and the agreement reached were not disclosed. Ashcroft refused to answer questions but Mueller confirmed Comey's account, saying: "The discussion was on a national, a NSA program that has been much discussed, yes."[24] Goldsmith also confirmed Comey's testimony.

Gonzales was again called to testify before the Senate on July 24 and asked why he hadn't previously disclosed the 2004 standoff. Gonzales merely repeated that the disagreement was not about the Terrorist Surveillance Program but about something else. The reader should look closely at the phrasing. Gonzales says the discussion was not about the Terrorist Surveillance Program. Mueller says it was about a program that has been very much discussed. Considering the Terrorist Surveillance Program as pertaining only to overseas phone calls, the only other NSA program that has been very much discussed is NSA data mining at the phone companies, which will be discussed below. Then enters Mike McConnell.

On July 31, Director of National Intelligence McConnell stepped in to get Gonzales off the hook. He wrote to Senator Arlen Specter of the judiciary committee that shortly after 9/11 Bush signed one single executive order to authorize numerous intelligence activities of which the Terrorist Surveillance Program was only one. But McConnell added that it is the only one that can be discussed publicly because it's the only one the President has announced.

If the statements of all these men – Gonzales, Mueller and McConnell – are considered together, the logical conclusion is that it was the NSA data mining at phone companies that was the controversy in Ashcroft's hospital room, for this program has been much discussed, but has not been officially acknowledged. How it was altered to satisfy Comey during his White House meeting remains a mystery. Or was some other means used to get Comey's compliance? Nevertheless, McConnell's statement was the first instance someone in the administration publicly admitted undisclosed spying activities, and that the eavesdropping on overseas phone calls which Bush confirmed in December 2005 was only one part of a much broader program.

Now to that "something else" Gonzales referred to.

Data Mining by NSA

In December 2005 domestic spying by NSA became publicly known at last. Mark Klein who had worked at AT&T for 22 years revealed a bizarre story. In 2002 a NSA agent talked with management at the San Francisco switching center where he worked. Construction of a secret room next door began the following year. Although NSA hired its own people, Klein was assigned to connect internet fiber optic circuits to a splitting cabinet, with the split-off portion going to that secret room. All the customer's internet traffic passing through the switching station had a copy shunted to the secret room.

The AT&T Lawsuit.

Electronic Frontier Foundation (EFF), a San Francisco-based public interest group for digital rights, sued AT&T in 2006 for helping NSA scoop up domestic and international phone/internet records on its customers. Millions of records were datamined without a warrant. Klein's affidavit said: "I learned that fiber optic[25] cables from the secret room were tapping into the WorldNet [AT&T's internet service] circuits by splitting off a portion of the light signal." It was not exclusively WorldNet traffic being diverted, but also that going to and from other domestic and international internet providers. Klein's affidavit also said the secret room contained Narus STA 6400 data-mining equipment "known to be used particularly by government intelligence agencies because of its ability to sift through large amounts of data looking for programmed targets." Through conversations with other employees he learned that secret rooms were likewise being built in other cities including Seattle, San Jose, Los Angeles and San Diego. Klein's affidavit continued that "unlike the controversy over targeted wiretaps of individuals' phone calls, this potential spying appears to be applied wholesale to all sorts of internet communications and countless citizens."[26] The ACLU in Michigan and the Center for Constitutional Rights in New York filed lawsuits against the federal government regarding NSA spying on US citizens.

The Plot Thickens—More Companies Involved

Another bombshell surfaced on May 11. USA Today revealed that besides AT&T, Verizon and BellSouth had also been allowing NSA to gather calling records from tens of millions of customers. White House spokesperson Dana Perino issued a disclaimer of sorts, saying: "There is no domestic surveillance without court approval."[27] Referring to "surveillance" was misleading because it refers to eavesdropping, not data mining.

NSA doesn't listen to conversations. They collect phone numbers and e-mail addresses of both caller and called, how the call was routed, day and time—what law enforcement officials call pen registers and trace and trap devices. Telephone companies routinely collect this information for business and billing purposes. AT&T has two large databases in a system called *Daytona*. One called *Hawkeye* contains nearly every domestic phone call made over the last five years; the other, *Aurora*, does the same for e-mail.

The government insists that FISA court approval is not required when only phone numbers and routing are collected. Others disagree. The information collected, when matched with other data bases, easily reveal identity, Social Security numbers, street addresses and much more personal information about the callers. Furthermore, the Communications Act prohibits telecom companies from releasing customer proprietary information except under specific stringent conditions.[28] Section 2702 of the Electronic Communications Privacy Act of 1986 did essentially the same for cell phones and the internet, saying "a provider of remote computer service or electronic communication service to the public shall not knowingly divulge a record or other information pertaining to a subscriber or customer...to any government entity."[29] Companies that violate this law are subject to damages of at least $1,000 per violation per customer.

USA Today gave further credence to the EFF lawsuit against AT&T, the largest American telecommunications company, by bringing Verizon and BellSouth into the picture—the second and third largest companies respectively. Number four in America's telecommunications hierarchy, Quest, says it was approached by NSA officials but turned them down.

Nobody—the government, AT&T, Verizon, BellSouth, or Quest—denies that NSA has access to telecommunications data.

AT&T said they "do not comment on matters of national security, except to say that we only assist law enforcement and government agencies charged with protecting national security in strict accordance with the law." Verizon similarly said they "do not comment on national security matters, we act in full compliance with the law and we are committed to safeguarding our customers' privacy." BellSouth "does not provide any confidential customer information to the NSA or any government agency without proper legal authority." Quest, which claimed it refused NSA's request, wouldn't "talk about this. It's a classified situation."[30]

Brian Ross of ABC News commented: "I don't know how it is they feel that they have some sort of classified information about national security. But it well might be that there's some sort of sweeping national security letter that is involved here.... A 2006 version of the Church Committee is needed to investigate the anti-terror programs created in the scary aftermath of 9/11."[31] Section 2709 of the Electronic Communications Privacy Act of 1986 once gave the FBI director authority to demand phone billing records, but that was ruled unconstitutional under the First, and possibly the Fourth, Amendment in the case of *ACLU v. Ashcroft* (2004).

On the evening of May 11, Bush said on TV that "the government does not listen to domestic phone calls without court approval." Watch the wording! It is true the government isn't listening to conversations, as far as we know anyway; it is analyzing calling patterns. Senator Wayne Allen said the White House assured him that "telephone customers' names, addresses and other personal information has not been handed over to the NSA as part of this program."[32] That's also probably true but, as mentioned, that information can easily be acquired from phone numbers and e-mail addresses. For instance, I entered my phone number in a Google search and four pages of hits came up giving my name and address and listing every research paper I have posted on the internet. There was a link to click for more information (at a price). Something as simple as Google tells a lot about a person.

On May 15 BellSouth denied *USA Today's* allegation and a day later Verizon followed suit. On June 30, *USA Today* published a "note to our readers" to correct a reporting flaw: "At the heart of our report is the fact that NSA is collecting phone call records of millions of Americans.... [W]e originally reported that the telephone companies were *working under contract* with the NSA. We've concluded that we cannot establish that Bell-South or Verizon *entered into a contract* with the NSA to provide the bulk calling records"[33] (emphasis added). It was undoubtedly a national security letter, not a contract.

AT&T also issued a misleading statement saying it "does not allow wiretapping without a court order nor has it otherwise given customer information to law enforcement authorities or government agencies without legal authorization."[34] Wiretapping is listening in on phone conversations, not gathering call records. Interpretations of what is legally authorized can also become skewed. For example: In May 2006 Atty. Gen. Gonzales said the records allegedly monitored by NSA were only business records. He explained that the 1979 Supreme Court decision in *Smith v. Maryland* ruled that "those kinds of records do not enjoy Fourth Amendment protection. There is no reasonable expectation of privacy in those kinds of records."[35] What Gonzales didn't explain is that the Electronics Communication Privacy Act of 1986 was passed in reaction to the *Smith v. Maryland* decision. Gathering business records doesn't violate the Fourth Amendment but it is breaking the 1986 privacy law.

On May 17, in order to clear the atmosphere for Gen. Hayden's confirmation as CIA director, the White House relented and provided a briefing on the NSA program for members of the House and Senate Intelligence Committees. The briefing was classified and the legislators cannot comment on it.

Domestic spying continued to draw flak. Adm. Bobby Ray Inman, director of NSA from 1977 to 1981, told *Democracy*

Now: "My own view, this activity was not authorized by a [Congressional] resolution to use whatever force you need to do. There clearly was a line in the FISA statutes which says you couldn't do this."[36]

Anticipating the use of state secrecy privilege to stop federal lawsuits, the ACLU filed complaints in over 20 states demanding utilities commissions and state attorneys general investigate the telecommunications companies involved with NSA spying.[37] It also launched a nationwide campaign for citizens to make their local utility commissions aware of their privacy concerns. Before I get to these lawsuits in state courts, let me explain the state secrets privilege.

State Secrets and Catch-22

Merely stamping a document SECRET doesn't automatically make revealing its contents a crime. The Espionage Act of 1917 made revealing information detrimental to the security of the United States a criminal act. It makes no mention of whether it is stamped SECRET or not and that Act has been virtually unchanged since it was passed. There has been no legislation signed into law, yet, that criminalizes the disclosure of information just because it is stamped SECRET. Such a law would criminalize whistleblowing and prevent Congress from getting information necessary to perform its oversight function. There would be no check or balance over the executive branch.

However, just because America hasn't passed an Official Secrets Act doesn't mean it hasn't been tried. In 1957, Senator Norris Cotton proposed making the disclosure of any classified information a crime but Congress wouldn't buy it. A bill to criminalize the revealing of anything stamped SECRET was introduced in 2000 by Senator Richard Shelby. It actually got through Congress, but President Bill Clinton vetoed it. Whew, that was close!

Shelby tried again right after 9/11, but Atty. Gen. Ashcroft told him it wasn't necessary. That still wasn't the end. In August 2006 Senator Christopher Bond introduced "A Bill to Prohibit the Unauthorized Disclosure of Classified Information" (S. 3774). It was identical to Shelby's and would have eliminated a need to prove that disclosure damaged national security. The bill was read twice and referred to the Committee on the Judiciary where it died with the 109th Congress.

Nick Schwellenbach, a reporter-researcher and blog editor at the Project on Government Oversight in Washington D.C., pointed out that had Bond's legislation been in effect we would never have learned about such things as the My Lai Massacre, the Pentagon Papers, Pentagon coverups of multi-billion dollar weapons systems overruns and test failures, the Abu Ghraib torture outrage or the Iran-Contra Scandal. He added that "some lawmakers are seeking to sharply reduce their own ability to defend democracy and the public interest, and leave out in the cold those conscientious government employees who want to expose government malfeasance."[38]

Although not specified in the US Constitution or laws, the state secrets privilege was upheld in a 1953 Supreme Court decision (*United States v. Reynolds*) regarding the 1948 crash of a B-29 bomber on a secret mission. This extraordinary executive privilege "allows the government to tell a judge that a civil case may expose information detrimental to national security, and ask that testimony or documents be hidden or a lawsuit dismissed."[39] In the past, judges have always granted this request. The ultimate decision lies with the judge. But in 1953 the state secrecy privilege was actually used to shield sensitive documents. Today it is being used to snuff out lawsuits before they begin. It was used to block lawsuits by Sibel Edmonds (a translator for the FBI), Jeffrey Sterling (a linguist for the CIA), Maher Arar (flown on a secret CIA rendition flight to Syria for torture), Khaled el-Masri (flown on a CIA flight to Afghanistan for torture), and a patent claim for a fiber-optic cable coupler used in eavesdropping,

Likewise, attempts to squelch NSA spying activities have

been made in every branch of the federal government and at state level. State secrecy obstacles were encountered in all attempts. I will list a few:

Judicial Branch

Although the government is not involved in the AT&T lawsuit, the Justice Department filed a motion for dismissal, invoking a "state secrets privilege" because matters expected to be presented in the case involve secret information that can't be discussed. The motion claimed the lawsuit would gravely harm national security if it were allowed to proceed. Later the government turned to the state secrets tactic in an attempt to sidetrack lawsuits in Oregon, Michigan and New York.

Law Professor William Weaver, senior advisor to the National Security Whistleblowers Coalition, said: "The privilege is being used to hide criminal activity – embarrassing activity – and protect the president from adverse publicity and close off the investigation." EFF attorney Lee Tien said: "Everything that might actually give somebody an opportunity to respond to what they're saying is hidden in the secret parts." Another EFF lawyer, Kevin Bankston added that the government is "basically saying that no one could ever go to court to stop illegal surveillance so long as they claim it's for national security. It leaves them completely unaccountable and leaves the communications companies that are colluding with them unaccountable."[40]

This same article said that when classified declarations were given by the CIA and NSA to presiding US District Judge Vaughn R. Walker in the San Francisco AT&T case, the judge asked how the plaintiffs would be able to respond to the declarations. Dep. Asst. Atty. Gen. Carl J. Nichols answered: "They won't be, frankly, your honor. They won't be in the sense that they will not be able to see nor rebut our showing.... Unfortunately, or fortunately, that is the way it is done, and that is the way it has to be done. Because to do otherwise would be to disclose facts to a number of people, the result of which would harm

America in Peril

national security."

Judge Walker didn't agree. On 20 July 2006, for the first time in US history, a court rejected the state secrets argument because the details of the case were so widely known that there were no secrets to reveal. Walker said: "The compromise between liberty and security remains a difficult one. But dismissing this case at the outset would sacrifice liberty for no apparent enhancement of security." He also indicated the case had some merit because "AT&T cannot seriously contend that a reasonable entity in its position could have believed that the alleged domestic dragnet was legal."[41]

DOJ attorneys appealed Walker's decision to the US 9th Circuit Court of Appeals in San Francisco. Meanwhile, another unexpected event occurred. A federal multi-district litigation panel in Washington DC consolidated 17 class-action lawsuits against telecommunication companies from 13 federal court districts into one case to be heard in San Francisco – in the courtroom of Chief Judge Vaughn Walker. Lawsuits against the government were not included. By November the number of consolidated lawsuits against BellSouth, Cingular Wireless, Sprint, MCI, Verizon, AT&T, and cable provider Comcast reached 48. Also, in December 2006, AT&T completed an $86 billion buyout of BellSouth – they are now one company.

On November 17th the government requested that work on all 48 cases be frozen until the 9th Circuit ruled on Walker's failure to dismiss. The 9th Circuit hadn't scheduled a hearing and all briefs on appeal had until April 2007 to be submitted. Walker refused to freeze the cases.

The government then asked that all 48 cases be combined into one jumbo lawsuit because that would make them easier to dismiss on the state secrets privilege. Electronic Frontier Director Cindy Cohen rebutted that each company should be sued individually. Walker agreed and reduced the 48 cases to just five, one against each company, all to be tried in San Francisco. Despite the pending appeal, and over the protests of government attorneys, Walker ruled on 20 February 2007 that the cases could proceed in the discovery phase to gather evidence.

Administrative Branch

Shortly after NSA spying became publicly known, the Justice Department started an investigation into its legality. It seemed unlikely that one branch of the administration would find fault with another branch. It didn't. On 10 May 2006 the Justice Department's Office of Professional Responsibility (OPR) told Congress the investigation couldn't continue because NSA "refused to grant Justice Department lawyers the necessary security clearance to probe the matter."[42]

Congressman Maurice Hinchey pressed NSA on who denied the clearances. It turned out that Bush, himself, personally blocked the investigation. Gonzales told the Senate in July the president withheld permission for the security clearance because he wanted to limit the number of people who had access to the program. A *Boston Globe* editorial noted that the OPR has conducted highly classified investigations for 31 years and, until now, it has never been prevented from pursuing an inquiry.

Similarly, Representative Edward Markey asked the Federal Communications Commission (FCC) which oversees and regulates telecommunications, to investigate newspaper reports about telecom companies giving NSA access to call records. FCC Chair Kevin Martin, a Republican, said such a probe would require access to "highly sensitive classified information" and the "commission has no power to order the production of classified information." His May 22 reply to Markey said: "The classified nature of the NSA's activities makes us unable to investigate the alleged violations."

Markey retorted: "We can't have a situation where the FCC, charged with enforcing the law, won't even begin an investigation of apparent violations of the law because it predicts the administration will roadblock any investigation citing national security." Unfortunately: "On May 5, President George W.

Bush delegated to the [director of National Intelligence] the authority to waive liability for national security matters if they are done in coöperation with the head of an agency or department, according to a notice in the *Federal Register*."[43]

Legislative Branch

Even Congress has been declawed. After the USA *Today* article, Senator Arlen Specter, then chair of the Senate Judiciary Committee, said he would call the phone companies involved to testify. That changed on June 6 when he deferred "earlier plans to subpoena telephone executives after Vice President Dick Cheney said they would be precluded on national security grounds from answering questions about reported disclosure of phone records."[44] Cheney had maneuvered behind Specter's back to block telephone companies from testifying. In a three-page letter dated June 7, Specter fumed: "I was surprised, to say the least, that you sought to influence, really determine, the action of the committee without calling me first."[45] Specter has been criticized for backing down, but if he hadn't it would have been the same story—state secrets and national security.

State Level Subpoenas and Lawsuits

A group of citizens and the ACLU filed a complaint with Maine's Public Utilities Commission (PUC) in May 2006 alleging that Verizon was passing information to the NSA. Verizon was uncoöperative, claiming the PUC lacked authority to investigate involvement with NSA because that information is protected by the state secrets privilege. Shenna Bellows, executive director of the Maine ACLU said: "We were surprised to see Verizon make the state secrets argument because only the government, not private entities, can assert that privilege. Use of the state secrets argument indicates that Verizon lawyers may have worked closely with federal government lawyers in drafting a response to the commission."[46]

Doug Cowie, a retiree from the Maine PUC, also filed a complaint saying the "PUC is supposed to determine whether the complaint has merit or not." Two months later the PUC did ask Verizon "to swear under oath to the veracity of a May press release the company issued in response to the *USA Today* allegations."[47] This was asking Verizon to clarify that it was not supplying records to the government because the ambiguity of its press release left some doubt. About an hour after the PUC-set deadline for an answer, the US Justice Department announced it was suing the state of Maine.

The Justice Department invoked the state secrets privilege and said an answer from Verizon would endanger the country. Cowie said if "Verison's public statements had classified information in them, they would have gone to jail." Minutes later Verizon answered the PUC saying that due to the pending lawsuit it could not verify its May press release. The ACLU then got involved because no legal basis exists for the government to sue the state for enforcing state laws. Shenna Bellows stated that claiming Verizon's answer would endanger national security "doesn't pass the straight-face test."

Missouri's Public Service Commissioner was sued by the DOJ in US District Court in July 2006 to stop him from seeking information about AT&T giving phone records to NSA in violation of Missouri's privacy laws. The DOJ lawsuit said an AT&T answer could harm national security and that the federal government preëmpts state law regarding foreign-intelligence gathering and national security. Therefore, the DOJ claimed, Missouri lacked authority to subpoena such highly classified and sensitive information. Missouri's Public Service Commissioner noted that the government cited no legal justification for AT&T to violate Missouri law.

A New Jersey case had a different twist. In May Atty. Gen. Zulima Farber subpoenaed five telecommunications carriers to produce any documents indicating information had been given to NSA, suspecting that state consumer-protection laws may have been violated. The feds stepped in warning that New Jersey was treading on federal turf. Asst. US Atty. Gen. Peter Keisler informed telecommunications companies that if they complied with the subpoena they would violate federal laws and executive orders. In June 2006 the federal government sued New Jersey's attorney general in US District Court to stop Farber's quest for information about telephone companies giving call records to NSA.

Revising FISA to Fit the Bush Agenda

In April 2007 National Intelligence Director McConnell proposed legislation to revise the Foreign Intelligence Surveillance Act to address new technologies such as cell phones, e-mail and the internet. It would allow the NSA to eavesdrop on foreigners without a FISA warrant, extend duration of warrants to one year, strip the power to hear spying claims from all but secret FISA courts, and retroactively grant civil immunity to telecom companies and internet providers that coöperated with NSA. The latter would moot the 48 lawsuits pending in Judge Walker's courtroom. The new bill would also give legal protection to government workers involved with the domestic spying program. Kate Martin, director of the Center for National Security Studies, said the proposed legislation would allow so much uninhibited spying that the protections of FISA would be nullified. When legislators asked McConnell what was wrong with the present FISA process, he said it was too secret for all Americans to know. Oh!

In the new Democrat-controlled Congress the proposed bill was making zero headway. The administration then conveniently wrapped up years of work on the National Intelligence Estimate that hyped Al Qaeda's growing threat. The national terrorist threat level was upped. Republican Representative John Boehner leaked secret information that an unnamed FISA judge blocked warrantless NSA wiretapping of communications that pass through switching stations in the US. Modern fiber-optic technology routes most global messages through US routing stations, even when both sender and receiver are overseas. NSA's foreign spying was curtailed at a time, according to the administration, when the US was vulnerable to high threat.

This put lots of pressure on the legislators at a time when Congress was about to adjourn for its August recess. The Bush administration upped the rhetoric about Democrats being at fault if a terrorist attack occurred while they were out. National Intelligence Director McConnell met with legislators in a secret session to cobble together a slimmed down emergency bill. In panic Congress patched together the Protect America Act of 2007 – a bill most of the legislators did not fully understand and which legitimized more than eavesdropping on foreign messages. By cleverly changing a few words, and through McConnell's stubborn insistence, the new legislation also allowed collecting business records, physical searches and trap-and-trace devices. The final act was almost what McConnell had originally asked for. Bush signed it into law in August.

The Protect America Act of 2007 was temporary and expires in six months, but any spying authorization under it could stay in place for a year beyond the act's expiration date. Nevertheless, when the bill expired, so would any immunity for telecommunications companies which the bill might have provided. Pressure continues from the administration to make the act permanent.

Litigation and Legislation Continues

Three days after the Protect America Act of 2007 was signed, the ACLU petitioned the FISA court to release information on rulings regarding NSA eavesdropping, the January 2007 FISA warrant allowing the Terrorist Surveillance Program to continue, the May 2007 rulings that a court order is needed for foreign communications passing through a US router and that any surveillance involving a wire or fiber optics in the US requires court approval. The ACLU claimed these unusual disclosures are justified because the administration has been using these secret rulings for political purposes.

Some FISA court officials were vexed that court decisions were used to advance the administration's agenda. Chief Judge Colleen Kollar-Kotelly said the court would consider the request and released an order in August saying the ACLU's request warrants further briefing and gave the government two weeks to respond. Then the ACLU had a further two weeks to file a rebuttal. At the time of this writing no decision has been made.

When the Bush administration appealed US District Judge Vaughn R. Walker's refusal to grant "state secrets" privilege in the cases against telecommunication companies, the case was heard on August 15, 2007, before a skeptical and sometimes hostile three-judge panel of the 9th Circuit Court. All three of the judges had been appointed by a Democratic president. Before the 9th Circuit announced its decision, and possibly in an attempt to preëmpt the court's unsympathetic attitude, Intelligence Director McConnell confirmed publicly for the first time that telecommunication companies assisted with the administration's warrantless data mining program.

It was apparent McConnell's admission would help plaintiffs in the lawsuits pending in Judge Walker's courtroom, but he may have had other motives. He took a gamble between helping the plaintiffs and making the lawsuits moot. His strategy was aimed at frightening a skittish Congress into granting AT&T, Verizon and the others immunity. He pointed out that a civil settlement requiring a $1,000 payment to each customer would bankrupt the companies. He also played the acting-in-good faith card, making it clear this immunity was a key element in updating the Foreign Intelligence Surveillance Act.

Bush entered the fray at the end of August. Wanting authority to grant immunity to companies that coöperated with NSA's data mining program and to avoid confirming any particular company was involved, he asked the attorney general to intervene on behalf of anyone charged with privacy violations for coöperating in spying activities, whether or not they actually did—the "neither confirm nor deny" mindset.

Treasury's *Swift* Monitoring System

In June 2006 *The New York Times* revealed another secret spying program—the Terrorist Finance Tracking Program. The *Los Angeles Times* and the *Wall Street Journal* also picked up on the stories. A few weeks after 9/11, Bush issued a presidential order directing the Treasury Department to lead an effort to disrupt terrorist financing. Administration officials put a lot of pressure on the newspapers not to print the story, but the editors thought differently. Bill Keller, executive editor of *The New York Times*, said: "We have listened closely to the administration's arguments for withholding this information, and given them the most serious and respectful consideration. We remain convinced that the administration's extraordinary access to this vast repository of international financial data, however carefully targeted use of it may be, is a matter of public interests."[48] Keller stated in an open letter that he and other editors concluded that national security isn't at risk because the administration is continually touting its terrorist- finance-tracking activities.

The *Los Angeles Times* article said "Bush administration officials asked the [LA] *Times* not to publish information about the program, contending that disclosure could damage its effectiveness and that sufficient safeguards are in place to protect the public." Editor Dean Baquet explained: "We weighed the government's arguments carefully, but in the end we determined that it was in the public interest to publish information about the extraordinary reach of this program. It is part of the continuing national debate over the aggressive measures employed by the government."[49]

Although government officials say the program is limited to tracing suspicious transactions that might lead to a terrorist, *The New York Times* found that "counterterrorism officials have gained access to financial records from a vast international database and examined banking transactions involving thousands of Americans and others in the United States." One former senior counterterrorism official, even though he approves of the program, said: "The capability here is awesome or, depending on where you're sitting, troubling." He observed that tight controls are in place but, nevertheless: "The potential for abuse is enormous."[50]

So what is this spying program, touted by the Bush administration as a vital tool in terrorist tracking that has played behind the scenes since 2001? When Bush issued his executive order, the Treasury Department went right to the nerve center for global banking—the Belgium-based Society for Worldwide Interbank Financial Telecommunication (SWIFT). This consortium of some 7,900 institutions in over 200 countries involves virtually every commercial bank and other financial institution. SWIFT moves some 11 million transactions involving about $6 trillion daily. It does not monitor routine banking as done by individuals such as credit card purchases and ATM transactions, but rather most of its transactions are across national borders and by-wire transfers.

The Treasury Department saw SWIFT as the key to discovering terrorist money transfers into the US and elsewhere without having to go through the painstaking process of getting approval from the vast number of financial institutions involved. The CIA wanted to obtain the data covertly but Treasury officials chose to be up front because they were sure SWIFT would coöperate. However, since SWIFT did not have the capability to search its own records, the US—presumably the CIA—provided that technology.

It turned out the consortium was coöperative but not without a written subpoena, so the Treasury Department writes a national security letter every month. These are issued in secret and not reviewed by any judge or grand jury. The data received is neither all-inclusive nor time sensitive. Apparently a block of data is obtained every month for transactions involving specific countries, institutions, organizations or individuals. Recently the Treasury Department has had to pacify SWIFT by allowing every search to be audited, so the government contracted Booz

Allen Hamilton of McLean, Virginia to do this. Data is stored by the CIA in Virginia but can be accessed by other agencies.

Justification for the national security letters relies on the 1977 International Emergency Economic Powers Act. Because this use of emergency powers has extended over decades, SWIFT and others involved began to worry. L. Richard Fischer, a lawyer and expert in the field of banking privacy, told *The New York Times* he was troubled that broad and nonspecific national security letters were used to collect and analyze such a massive volume of financial data. He said it bypasses bank privacy laws which require some sort of justification and due process for access. At a minimum, he felt the activity was inappropriate.

The SWIFT monitoring program, run by the CIA and overseen by the Treasury Department, is considered the largest and most extensive of several secret programs to track terrorist financing. Key segments of the banking industry have been kept in the dark but administration officials say classified briefings were given to some members of Congress and the 9/11 Commission. Those briefings were reported to have been stepped up when it became clear *The New York Times* was going to publish information about the program. However, Representative Sue Kelly, then chair of the Oversight and Investigations Subcommittee of the House Committee on Financial Services, said "No one on the full committee had been informed about the program in its nearly five years of existence, even though it is squarely within the committee's jurisdiction." She added that many "people in Congress who should have been briefed by the administration were not. What else is it that we don't know?"[51]

Some Republicans on the subcommittee fulminated over the newspaper articles, but not all. Representative Ron Paul said: "Quite frankly, I don't think the terrorists were tipped off to anything. We have been monitoring financial activities for 30 years. They know what's going on." Democrat Representative Barney Frank said he was offered a briefing just before the newspaper stories broke, but he declined because it would be in secret and he couldn't discuss it. Frank said: "To be honest, I have come to believe that people in this administration have a different view of democracy than I have."[52]

Rounding out the Spying Spectrum

So not only is the government invading citizen privacy by gaining access to telephone and e-mail communication, banking records, library activity and an assortment of other records and activity, they have also encroached on our postal system and our internet activity. Some events that have come to public attention indicate how they are going about this.

Is the Government Opening Our Domestic Mail?

Bush signed the Postal Accountability and Enhancement Act in December 2006 – ostensibly as a statute directing some reform measures for the US Postal Service and prohibiting government agents from opening first-class mail without a warrant. Bush then issued one of his famous signing statements saying he would construe the language "which provides for opening an item of a class of mail otherwise sealed against inspection in a manner consistent, to the maximum extent possible, with the need to conduct searches in exigent circumstances."[53]

The postal reform bill was guided through Congress by Senator Susan Collins who asked Bush to clarify his intent. She said the legislation "does nothing to alter the protections of privacy and civil liberties provided by the Constitution and other federal laws. The Foreign Intelligence Surveillance Act of 1978 and other federal criminal rules require prior judicial approval before domestic sealed mail can be searched."[54] Representative Henry Waxman added that "despite the president's statement that he may be able to circumvent a basic privacy protection, the new postal law continues to prohibit the government from snooping in people's mail without a warrant." Kate Martin, director of the Center for National Securities Studies in Washington added: "The signing statement claims authority to open domestic mail without a warrant, and that would be new and quite alarming."[55]

American Civil Liberties Union attorney Ann Beeson said the ACLU will request clarification on how the exception Bush claims will be used, and if mail has already been opened. She stated: "The signing statement raises serious questions whether he is authorizing opening of mail contrary to the Constitution and to laws enacted by Congress. What is the purpose of the signing statement if it isn't that?"[56]

White House spokeswoman Emily Lawrinmore denied the signing statement was a claim to some new authority. She said: "In certain circumstances – such as the proverbial 'ticking bomb' –the Constitution does not require warrants for reasonable searches. Bush, himself, had cited the need to "protect human life and safety against hazardous materials and the need for physical searches specifically authorized by the law for foreign intelligence collection."[57]

ACLU's Beeson allowed it was constitutionally permissible to open packages suspected of containing a bomb, but Bush's "signing statement uses language that's broader than that exception," pointing out Bush used the phrase "exigent circumstances"–which ranges from an imminent danger to a prolonged emergency such as the war on terror, adding, "The question is: What does that mean and why has he suddenly put this in writing if it isn't a changed policy?"[58] A very important question.

The FBI Wants to Monitor Our Internet Activity

In January 2007, news reports reminded us that for over a year the FBI has been trying to get a better handle on what Americans do on-line. Under the guise of fighting child pornography, the government had been trying to have internet providers keep each individual's records for a longer period of time to make it easier to find out what websites are visited and what is purchased on-line. Most companies already keep them for one to three months, which privacy advocates maintain is adequate for investigating crimes. It is already easy to get what is needed for that purpose. Laws passed since 9/11 allow the FBI to merely send a letter ordering certain specific records be kept longer.

But keeping *all* records for lengthy periods can be interpreted as another move toward total surveillance of all Americans. Leslie Harris, executive director for the Center for Democracy and Technology says she doesn't believe "it's realistic to think we would create this enormous honeypot of information and then say to the FBI, 'You can only use it for this narrow purpose.'" Electronic Frontier Foundation attorney Kevin Bankston added, "There's been no showing that mass surveillance of internet users, mandated by the government, is necessary for law enforcement. If this passes, there would be a chilling effect on free speech if everyone knew that everything they did on the internet could be traced back to them."

When pinned down, the government seems to offer a variety of justifications for retaining internet records. As Harris points out: "I've been in discussions at the Department of Justice where someone would say, 'We want this for child protection.' And someone else would say 'National security,' and someone else would say, 'Computer crimes.' We're operating in the wild, wild West here." Harris sums it up this way: "We have an environment in which we're collecting more and more information on the personal lives of Americans, and our laws are completely inadequate to protect us."[59]

The FBI's Point-and-Click Surveillance System

Back in the old days of Gangbusters and Hoover's FBI, after the G-man got a wiretap warrant he had to ask the telephone company to hard-wire a connection to the circuit. No more. Nowadays we have "back doors" to communications equipment. The Communications Assistance for Law Enforcement Act of 1994 requires these devices instantly to switch on a wiretap for the FBI or other law enforcement agency. A court order is still required—theoretically—and the phone company or internet provider must open the circuit, but these are just incidental to the way things are being run today. It effectively gives the FBI push-button control to eavesdrop.

This back-door availability is complemented by the FBI's so-called point-and-click surveillance system which is touted as an instant wiretap on almost any kind of communications devices —land lines, cellular phones, internet telephony, text messages, the whole gamut. Officially this capability is called the Digital Collections Systems Network, but more commonly referred to as DCSNet. It includes at least three collection components. First of the known components is DCS-3000, called Red Hook which performs pen-registers and trap-and-trace surveillance. DCS-5000 uses wiretaps focused on spies or terrorists. DCS-6000 listens in on the content of digital messages. Seeing those designations makes you wonder if there are DCS-1000, -2000, and -4000 components—and what they do.

DCSNet all together provides a surveillance system allowing "FBI agents to play back recordings even as they are being captured (like TiVo), create master wiretap files, send digital recordings to translators, track the rough location of targets in real-time using cell-tower information, and even stream intercepts outward to mobile surveillance vans."[60] All of this is handled in a network of FBI wiretap rooms interconnected by a network run by Sprint. It is not hard to speculate on secret activity involving DCSNet having been authorized by Bush's post 9/11 presidential order which covered many areas including the Terrorist Surveillance Program and NSA data mining.

The Privacy and Civil Liberties Board

Then there is the Privacy and Civil Liberties Board, commonly called the White House privacy board. Ever heard of it? It is a five-member panel, with one Democrat on board, created in 2004 whose report to Congress in March 2007 put a stamp of approval on NSA's warrantless eavesdropping program and the Treasury Department's international banking tracking, saying they don't violate anyone's civil liberties. But given some of the board members' ties with the Bush administration, the Democrat-controlled Congress was skeptical. Representative Bernie Thompson, chair of the House Homeland Security Committee, dismissed any perceived credibility in the report: "Their current findings and any additional conclusions they reach will be taken with a grain of salt until they become fully independent."[61]

Meanwhile, Congress has not adequately investigated the legality of any spying programs. Neither have they produced legislation to protect whistleblowers. Oversight programs discussed between White House officials and some senators would do no more than legitimize warrantless spying while not even penetrating the surface of what that spying amounts to. Congress does have recourse in situations when the administration won't provide answers. But instead, the legislative branch seems to go through meaningless motions while tacitly yielding to the White House's contention that the executive branch has constitutional authority never before realized or practiced. We should seriously heed Benjamin Franklin's advice: "Those who would sacrifice a little freedom for a little security deserve neither."

Notes for Chapter 5

1. Kuhnhenn, James (Knight Ridder); "Bush Defends Spying in US," *San Jose Mercury News*, 18 Dec 2005.
2. Lichtblau, Eric and Scott Shane, "Basis for Spying in US is Doubted," *NY Times*, 7 Jan 2006.
3. AP, "Bush Vows to Continue Spying on Americans," *NY Times*, 17 Dec 2005.
4. Ragavan, Chitra, "The Letter of the Law," *US News & World Report*, 27 Mar 2006.
5. Bamford, James, "The Agency That Could Be Big Brother," *NY Times*, 25 Dec 2005.
6. Shane, Scott and David Johnston, "Mining of Data Prompted Fight over Spying," *NY Times*, 29 Jul 2007.
7. Feinstein, Diane; "US Senator Diane Feinstein Responding to Your Message," e-mail from Senator Feinstein to Jan Aldridge, 8 Apr 2006.
8. Bamford, op. cit.
9. Gonzales, Alberto R., "America Expects Surveillance," *WSJ*, 6 Feb 2006.
10. Karush, Sarah (AP), "Judge Nixes Warrantless Surveillance," *Yahoo! News*, 17 Aug 2006.
11. Taylor quotations in editorial; "Ruling of Law," *NY Times*, 18 Aug 2006.
12. AP, "ACLU Seeks Again to Block Wiretaps," *NY Times*, 14 Nov 2006.
13. Liptak, Adam, "White House Shifting Tactics in Spy Cases," *NY Times*, 19 Jan 2007

14. Eggen, Dan, "Court Will Oversee Wiretap Program," *Washington Post*, 18 Jan 2007.

15. Risen, James, "Administration Pulls Back on Surveillance Agreement," *NY Times*, 2 May 2007.

16. Sniffen, Michael (AP), "Gonzales Cautions Judges on Interfering," *LA Times*, 29 Sep 2006.

17. Fisher, Louis, "President's Game? History Refutes Claims to Unlimited Power over Foreign Affairs," *Legal Times Online.* 4 Dec 2006.

18. Posner, Richard A., *Not a Suicide Pact: The Constitution in a Time of National Emergency* (NY: Oxford Univ Press, 2006) p. 4.

19. Yoo, John, *War by Other Means: An Insider's Account of the War On Terror* (NY; Atlantic Monthly Press, 2006), p. 102.

20. Fisher, op. cit.

21. Fisher, op. cit.

22. Bamford, op. cit.

23. AP; "Gonzales Draws Criticism from Panel Chief," *NY Times*, 6 Apr 2006.

24. Grier, Peter, "Support for Attorney General Gonzales Slips Further," *Christian Science Monitor*, 2 Aug 2007.

25. Fiber optics use light to transmit data, as opposed to electricity in wires.

26. Klein, Mark, affidavit to support Electronic Frontier Foundation's lawsuit against AT&T, 6 Apr 2006, at http://www.wired.com/news/technology/1,70621-0.html.

27. Cauley, Leslie; "NSA Has Massive Database of Americans' Phone Calls," *USA Today*, 11 May 2006.

28. 47 U.S.C. 222(c)(1); Communication Act of 1934 as modified by the Telecom Act of 1996.

29. 18 U.S.C. 2402(a)(3); Electronic Communication Act of 1986.

30. Cauley, op. cit.

31. Democracy Now, 16 May 2006. At http://www.democracynow.org/print.pl?sid=06/05/16/145201

32. Squeo, Anne Marie, "Bush Seeks to Quell Storm over Telecom Monitoring," *Wall Street Journal*, 12 May 2006.

33. AP, "*USA Today* Admits NSA Report Flaws," *San Jose Mercury News*, 1 Jul 2006.

34. Searcey, Dionne and Anne Marie Squeo, "More Phone Firms Fight Claims They Supplied Call Data to NSA," *Wall Street Journal*, 17 May 2006.

35. Pincus, Walter, "Gonzales Rationale on Phone Data Disputed," *Washington Post*, 25 May 2006.

36. Goodman, Amy, *Democracy Now*, 17 May 2006, http://www.democracynow.org/article.pl?sid=06/05/17/159213

37. As of mid-2006 ACLU had filed complaints in Arizona, Colorado, Connecticut, Delaware, Florida, Iowa, Kansas, Massachusetts, Missouri, Nebraska, Nevada, New Jersey, New York, Oregon, Pennsylvania, Rhode Island, Tennessee, Texas, Vermont, Virginia and Washington.

38. Schwellenbach, Nick, "An Official Secrets Act Might Keep Congress in the Dark," *Nieman Watchdog*, 25 Aug 2006, at http://www.niemanwatchdog.org

39. Singel, Ryan, "Feds Go All out to Kill Spy Suit," *Wired News*, 2 May 2006, at http://www.wired.com/news/technology/security/1,70785-0.html

40. Carey, Pete, "US: Lawsuit a Risk to Secrecy," *San Jose Mercury News*, 14 May 2006.

41. AP, "Judge Rules Against Bush in Spying Lawsuit," *MSNBC.com*, 20 Jul 2006.

42. AP, "NSA Stymies Justice Dept. Spying Probe," *NY Times*, 11 May 2006.

43. FCC and Markey quotes in Reuters; "FCC Chief Says Won't Probe NSA Call Program," *NY Times*, 23 May 2006.

44. Reuters; "Senate Panel Backs off Telecoms in Spying Probe," *NY Times*, 6 Jun 2006.

45. Kuhnhenn, James (Knight Ridder); "Senator: Cheney Blocking NSA Probe," *San Jose Mercury News*, 8 Jun 2006.

46. "Verizon Refuses to Come Clean about Wire-tapping," *New Standard* (Syracuse, NY). 23 May 2006, at http://newstandardnews.net/content/index.cfm/items/

47. Roychoudhuri, Onnesha, "DOJ Quashes Wiretapping Inquiries," *In These Times*, 20 Nov 2006.

48. Lichtblau, Eric and James Risen, "Bank Data Secretly Reviewed by US to Fight Terror," *NY Times*, 22 June 2006.

49. "Newspapers Reject Government Request to Kill Story," *Editor & Publisher*, 22 Jun 2006.

50. Lechtblau and Risen, op. cit.

51. Andrews, Edmund L., "Republicans Criticize Lack of Briefings on Bank Data," *NY Times*, 12 Jul 2006.

52. Kelly, Paul and Frank quotations in Andrews, op. cit.

53. Meek, James Gordon, "W Pushes Envelope on US Spying," *NY Daily News*, 4 Jan 2007.

54. Schmid, Randolph E. (AP), "Privacy Questioned under New Law," *San Jose Mercury News*, 5 Jan 2007.

55. Waxman and Martin quotations in Meek, op. cit.

56. Schmid, op. cit.

57. Meek, op. cit.

58. Schmid, op. cit.

59. Harris and Bankston quotes in Reinan, John, "Feds Pushing for Internet Records," *Grand Haven Tribune* (MI), 6 Jan 2007.

60. Singel, Ryan, "Point, Click...Eavesdrop: How the FBI Wiretap Net Operates," *Wired*, 29 Aug 2007.

61. Yen, Hope (AP), "White House Panel OKs Surveillance Plans," *San Jose Mercury News*, 6 Mar 2007.

6

A Nation of Secrets

Without some form of censorship, propaganda in the strict sense of the word is impossible. In order to conduct a propaganda there must be some barrier between the public and the event. Access to the real environment must be limited, before anyone can create a pseudo-environment that he thinks is wise or desirable.
— *Walter Lippmann*[1]

Walter Lippmann played a dramatic role on the American scene during the 20th century as an influential author, journalist and political commentator. In his Harvard days he cofounded the Harvard Socialist Club and edited the *Harvard Daily*. Early in the 20th century he supported Theodore Roosevelt's Progressive party and cofounded the *New Republic* magazine. Then he went from Socialist to Democrat and became an adviser to President Woodrow Wilson, was a member of the American delegation to the Paris Peace Conference in 1919 and helped draft the covenant of the League of Nations. During those years he had a rosy view of democracy, believing that if Americans were given the facts they would participate fully in politics and world affairs, and become an educated electorate.

After World War I, Lippmann changed this viewpoint. Seeing how the masses were manipulated through effective pro-

America in Peril

paganda techniques, he adopted the belief that the populace was more like a herd of beasts which had to be guided by an intellectual elite. He maintained it could not be left to the press to form public opinion – modern leadership required experts to formulate what the press will present, what he called "preëmptive management." Regarding the public, Lippmann coined the word "manufacturing consent."[2]

His quote posits that a barrier must be placed between the public and the real environment – between America's citizens and the activities of government. This barrier has manifested itself as a wall of secrecy which threatens the very democracy we Americans are so proud of. In 2004 the minority staff of the US House of Representative Committee on Oversight and Government Reform prepared an 81-page report entitled *Secrecy and the Bush Administration*. After detailing how the Bush administration has narrowed the scope and application of laws promoting open government, analyzing how the administration has expanded laws that restrict public access to government information and examining how the administration has limited congressional access to federal records, the report concludes:

> This review of the nation's open government laws reveals that the Bush Administration has systematically sought to limit disclosure of government records while expanding its authority to operate in secret. Through legislative changes, implementing regulations, and administrative practices, the Administration has undermined the laws that make the federal government more transparent to its citizens, including the Freedom of Information Act, the Presidential Records Act, and the Federal Advisory Committee Act. At the same time, the Administration has expanded the reach of the laws authorizing the Administration to classify documents and to act without public or congressional oversight. Individually, some of the changes implemented by the Bush Administration may have limited impact. Taken together, however, the Administration's actions represent an unparalleled assault on the principle of open and accountable government.[3]

In the following pages I will examine that unparalleled assault on the principle of open and accountable government.

Hiding the Workings of Government

Within the greater social sphere of America and the world, the Bush administration has employed various devices. Topmost of these is control of information released by government departments and agencies. Much has been written on the secrecy used to muzzle the Joint Congressional Investigation of 9/11 and the 9/11 Commission itself. Likewise for Bush's justification for invading Iraq. Without repeating that information here, we will look at some prime examples of secrecy here at home.

Cheney's Secret Energy Task Force

Within days of the 2001 inauguration, as one of its first actions, the new administration created a cabinet-level task force chaired by Vice President Cheney to prepare the National Energy Policy of the United States. In less than four months, this task force submitted its final report to the president with over 100 recommendations for executive action or legislation including increased oil and gas drilling on public land and a new look at nuclear power. Controversy rose before that, however.

By April 2001, various members of the media had reported that this task force met privately with representatives from energy companies who were major contributors to the administration's election campaign. This prompted ranking members of the Democrat party on the House Energy and Commerce Committees to request a Government Accountability Office (GAO) investigation of the process used to develop the National Energy Policy—asking who had been consulted and what topics were discussed at the meetings. The GAO reported:

> [W]e initiated contact with the Office of the Vice President (OVP).... From the outset OVP did not respond to our request for information, including descriptive information on the process by which the National Energy Policy report was devel-

oped, asserting that we lacked statutory authority to examine [task force] activities. We were also denied the opportunity to interview staff assisting the Vice President on the [task force] effort.... The Vice President denied us access to virtually all requested information.[4]

Having met with almost total noncoöperation from the vice president and the White House, the comptroller general, head of the GAO, in February 2002 filed suit in the US District Court for the District of Columbia. Seven government agencies (Departments of Energy, Interior, Transportation, Commerce, and Agriculture, Environmental Protection Agency and Office of Management and Budget) were ordered to turn over documents, but about a third of the pages were censored out. Nothing came from the White House that would answer the primary questions on the process and who acted as advisors—just 77 pages of trivial information from Cheney's office. Then in December 2002, the district court threw out the GAO's case, saying the comptroller general lacked authority to sue because only six individual members of Congress requested the investigation and lawsuit, not a committee.

While the GAO lawsuit was going on, other organizations took Cheney to court. On 17 July 2001, the public interest law firm Judicial Watch announced it was suing Cheney under the Federal Advisory Commission Act and the Freedom of Information Act. Judicial Watch expressed concern "that energy policy is being made in secret by individuals and interests with a financial and political stake in particular policies."[5] Meanwhile, White House Press Secretary Ari Fleischer and others on 22 January 2002 insinuated that the Sierra Club had been consulted. A week later the Sierra Club issued a press release saying its members were only allowed to meet with Cheney's task force after the energy plan was drawn up and released and then they joined Judicial Watch in the suit against Cheney and his task force. The litigation demanded a full accounting of which private industrialists helped craft the National Energy Policy.

Two months later, a federal judge ordered the seven energy companies involved to release thousands of documents concerning Cheney's energy policy and in May Federal Judge Emmet Sullivan, over White House objections, ruled the lawsuit could continue. He said Cheney and the White House were seeking a ruling from him that "would eviscerate the understanding of checks and balances between the three branches of the government on which constitutional order depends."

Later that year Judge Sullivan ordered Cheney either to turn over the requested documents or provide a list justifying why each one was being withheld. The White House appealed the case, claiming the Constitution granted executive immunity from having to divulge that information. The US Court of Appeals rejected the Bush administration's appeal, saying that Cheney had no legal grounds for refusing the judge's order. Then the White House appealed to the Supreme Court—the same court that appointed George W. Bush to the White House two years earlier. The high court granted *certiorari*—hearings were set for spring of 2004 with a decision in June.

Before that happened Cheney and Supreme Court Justice Antonin Scalia went on a January hunting trip in Louisiana. Scalia rejected conflict of interest accusations, saying: "I do not think my impartiality could reasonably be questioned," adding, "Social contact with high-level executive officials have never been thought improper for judges who may have before them cases in which those people are involved in their official capacity, as opposed to their personal capacity."[6] Then it came out the two didn't just happen to meet at the hunting resort. Scalia was an invited guest of Cheney on Air Force 2. Law professor Stephen Gillers says this "means Scalia is accepting a gift of some value from a litigant in a case before him."[7]

Two ranking members of the Senate's Judiciary and the Governmental Affairs Committees did not buy Scalia's reasoning. On January 22 they requested Chief Justice William Rehnquist to provide "canons, procedures, and rules" on the recusal of justices from cases in which "their impartiality might reasonably be questioned, " adding: "When a sitting judge, poised to hear a case involving a particular litigant, goes on vacation with that litigant, reasonable people will question whether that judge can be a fair and impartial adjudicator of that man's case or his opponent's claims."[8]

Rehnquist replied, "The high court does not have a formal policy or rules for reviewing decisions by justices on whether to withdraw from a case." However, federal law states that "any justice or judge shall disqualify himself in any proceeding in which his impartiality might be questioned."[9] Meanwhile, Cheney still claimed immunity from a subpoena. Justice Department lawyers representing Cheney and the White House argued that "judicial power cannot extend to ordering the vice president to disclose details about the way the president gets advice." Judicial Watch filed briefs countering that "Cheney's claims to immunity were laughable after a 1997 Supreme Court decision that discovery could proceed against then-President Bill Clinton in a case brought by sexual-harassment accuser Paula Jones."[10]

On 24 June 2004 the Supreme Court ruled 7 to 2 the vice president enjoyed executive privilege so does not have to reveal secret details of his energy task force. Years later, in July 2007, an unidentified former White House official leaked a list of almost 300 individuals and groups connected with the energy industry who had visited Cheney's office during the time of the task force. That list was only partial. By contrast, only 13 environmental groups were invited late in the process, and then only to a single session.

Dodging the Seven-Member Rule

Congress passed a law in 1928 that became known as the Seven-Member Rule which provided:

An Executive agency, on request of the Committee on Government Operations of the House of Representatives, or of any seven members thereof, or on request of the Committee on Government Affairs of the Senate, or any five members thereof, shall submit any information to it relating to any matter within the jurisdiction of the committee.[11]

Executive agencies have traditionally provided information requested under the Seven-Member Rule even though the Committee on Government Operations was renamed.[12] Not the Bush administration. Ashcroft's Justice Department interpreted the statute's reference to the Committee on Government Operations as not applicable to the Committee on Government Reform and refused to provide the requested material. Two cases were involved.

A request from 18 members of the House Committee on Government Reform came in April 2001 for unadjusted 2000 census data from the Department of Commerce. It was refused. In May, 16 members took the Bush administration to court. A Los Angeles Federal District Court ruled against the administration in January 2002, so the administration appealed to the 9th Circuit in San Francisco. There the case was combined with another by two state legislators requesting the same data. On 8 October 2002 the Court ruled in favor of the legislators but didn't mention the House committee's case. When the Commerce Department released the data to the legislators it also gave it to the 16 House committee members. The House appeal was rendered moot and no legal precedent on the Seven-Member Rule was established.

In February 2004 media reports indicated the Bush administration had withheld the true cost of its Medicare Drug Program and furnished to Congress numbers $100 billion less than calculated. Requests for the withheld documents by ranking members of three House committees were refused. In March 19 members of the Government Reform Committee invoked the Seven-Member Rule to obtain that information from the Department of Health and Human Services (HHS). They were given four documents already in the public domain, so the 19 members made a second request in April and were refused.

Other Instances of Hiding Government Activities

White House Visitor Logs. While investigating lobbyists access to the White House, the *Washington Post* sued the US Secret Service in 2006 for copies of the visitor logs for the vice president's office, his legal counsel, his chief spokesperson and other top aides and advisors. US District Judge Ricardo M. Urbina rejected the executive secrecy argument and ordered the Secret Service to release the records. In December the Bush administration asked the US Court of Appeals for Washington D.C. to reverse Urbina's order. In their 57-page brief government lawyers claimed the Secret Service only has temporary custody of the records which are ultimately controlled by the vice president and that Congress has excluded presidential and vice-presidential records from public access. The appeal is still pending. In September 2006, records revealed in a similar lawsuit that key figures in the Jack Abramoff lobbying scandal made over a hundred visits to the White House.

Requests from Ranking Minority Members of Congress. During the first four years of the George W. Bush administration, Representative Henry A. Waxman, the ranking minority member of the House Committee on Government Reform, made over 100 requests for information under the committee's jurisdiction. In every instance the request was ignored, refused or answered late and inadequately. Five of the no-response instances are:

- On 13 June 2004, Waxman requested information from Cheney to clarify why his chief of staff was briefed beforehand on a $7 billion, sole-source contract to Halliburton for work on Iraqi oil infrastructure.
- The same month, ranking members of eight House committees requested documents from Bush regarding torture at Abu Ghraib prison and elsewhere.
- In October 2003, Waxman requested that HHS provide copies of correspondence with the True Values Coalition. Waxman was investigating that Coalition's "hit list" of over 150 scientists researching HIV/AIDS with National Institute of Health funding. He was concerned that science was being politicized.
- Between March and July 2003, Waxman made several requests

of Bush and National Security Adviser Condoleezza Rice for documents explaining why the president falsely reported in his State of the Union address that Iraq was seeking uranium from Africa.

• In June and July 2003, Waxman requested information from White House Senior Adviser Karl Rove and then White House Counsel Alberto Gonzales about meetings and phone conversations Rove had with companies in which he owned stock.

Ranking members of other committees had similar problems. In November 2003, the White House Office of Administration informed the appropriations committees of both houses the White House would only respond to requests signed by committee chairs.

EPA Library Closings. The Environmental Protection Agency (EPA) discovered in February 2006 its EPA Library budget for fiscal year 2007 had been drastically cut – from $2.5 million in 2006 to half a million. By March its Chicago library had been shut down. In October two more were closed. Those three serviced the entire middle United States in their essential function of helping to safeguard America's health and environment. Five were reported closed in February 2007.

The EPA Library network of 27 facilities were begun in 1971 to support ten regional offices, two research centers and twelve laboratories – to say nothing of serving thousands of citizens with information ranging from basic sciences to records on local hazards from waste, pollution and toxic substances. In 2005, according to Public Employees for Environmental Research, this network handled over 134,000 EPA-generated research requests and housed 50,000 documents which are only available at the EPA libraries

At first the closings were excused as simple budgetary moves. As criticism mounted, the excuse moved to a technological advance when EPA spokesperson Jessica Emond said, "EPA's library modernization is providing better access to a broader audience. When libraries go digital, everyone benefits." When confronted with the loss of information, she responded, "EPA has implemented a stringent agenda to ensure that no essential material gets lost and has followed the American Library Association (ALA) guidance by developing criteria for reviewing its library collection." Unconvinced, ALA president Leslie Burger retorted: "The [ALA's] loose collection of resources is a good starting point for thinking about collection development policies but does not constitute ALA guidance and criteria."[13]

Another question is the ability to digitize the entire collection when some documents are hundreds of pages long with complicated graphics and maps. The same article quoted Michael Halpern of the Union of Concerned Scientists who doubted the digitalization story. If that were true, he claimed the "EPA's plan is backwards. A thoughtful and deliberate digitalization of all the information in a library's collection should occur before the library's physical location is closed." EPA says it is only half finished with the digitalization and it'll take at least another two years.

More likely is that the closings were designed to eliminate public availability to information that could curtail some business activities. In January, blogs run by Cox Newspapers indicated that EPA had halted the closings. Spokesperson Emond says that's not the correct characterization because there were no more closings planned anyway. Well, OK...

EPA Administer Stephen Johnson was questioned by the Senate Committee on Environment and Public Works in February 2007 about recent changes including a revised policy minimizing scientific input in determining air pollution standards, an attempt to raise the reporting threshold for toxic chemicals and the closing of the five libraries which removed scientific and health documents from public access. Johnson denied trying to roll back environmental safeguards, but committee chair Senator Barbara Boxer wasn't convinced. "Nobody's fooled by this," she said; "EPA has gone too long without meaningful oversight," and these changes "benefit polluters' bottom line and they hurt our communities."[14]

Restricting Testimony before Congress. New Pentagon guidelines described in an April 2007 memo to Congress places unprecedented restrictions on Pentagon testimony. The military reserves the right to prevent testimony by lower-ranking officers, enlisted men and civilian employees. Congressional testimony will be confined to the rank of colonel (navy captain) or above, or to civilians appointed by Bush. Congress claims these guidelines are illegal. Congressional subpoenas, of course, are not affected.

Failing to Report Annual Classification Activity. President Bush signed Executive Order 13292 in March 2003 that, among other things, requires all executive branch agencies to accept oversight regarding the handling of classified material. This includes submitting annual reports to the Information Security Oversight Office (ISOO) of the Federal National Archives and Records Administration and allowing inspections by that office.

Cheney's office complied with the old reporting and inspection requirements, but when EO13292 was issued, Cheney stopped reporting claiming his office is exempt. ISOO unsuccessfully pressed for coöperation, pointing out Cheney's office may be a national security risk without oversight. The leak that Valerie Plame was a CIA operative is a case in point. When ISOO complained to Atty. Gen. Gonzales, Cheney allegedly tried to abolish ISOO. Finally ISOO went to the House Committee on Oversight and Government Reform.

Chairperson Henry A. Waxman fired off an eight-page letter to Cheney in June 2007 demanding answers to why he felt exempt from the executive order, what steps his office takes to ensure safeguarding classified information, and if he actually sought to retaliate against the National Archives by having ISOO shut down. Next day the White House announced that not only was Cheney's office exempt from oversight, but so was the president's, claiming Bush never intended their offices be required to report. Waxman and ISOO argued the executive order is clear, all agencies must comply and it doesn't compute that offices handling the highest of security information should be exempt. They insisted that not having oversight could risk very serious national security breaches. White House spokesperson Tony Fratto had to admit the order didn't specifically exempt the president or vice president, adding it "does take a little bit of inference."[15]

It takes a lot more than inference. It's a real stretch. EO13292 specifically states: "'Agency' means any 'executive agency' as defined in 5U.S.C.105; and 'military department' as defined in 5U.S.C.102; and *any other entity within the executive branch that comes into the possession of classified information*" (emphasis added).[16] The Bush administration got its tail caught and is trying to wiggle out. Tom Blanton, director of the National Security Archive at George Washington University, (not to be confused with the National Archives) asks: "If the president and vice president don't take their own rules seriously, who else should?" Blanton notes that "a substantial number of [White House] e-mails had disappeared in recent years, at a time when investigators wanted to review them for possible evidence of inappropriate leaks of classified information."[17]

★ ★ ★ ★ ★

I have only presented a few examples of government secrecy which are far from comprehensive. Secrecy abounds in virtually every aspect of the Bush administration – from the Valerie Plame leak to the firing of US attorneys; from war justification to unaccountability on reconstruction. No other administration in American history has had such a penchant for keeping its operations out of public view. The examples given do illustrate how the workings of government have been hidden. Now I will show how the law to open government has been undermined.

Squelching the Freedom of Information Act

The Bush administration has steadily impeded citizens' access to documents needed for informed and participatory democracy. The steady erosion of the Freedom of Information Act is particularly dangerous to an open government.

The Freedom of Information Act (FOIA)

This act, passed by Congress in 1966 which became effective in 1967, established the principle the public should have broad access to government records. The FOIA did recognize a need for secrecy in some cases and exempted nine categories of records from release. These include those classified for national security and those that involve trade secrets, personnel issues or medical records. A Clinton administration executive order mandated that FOIA operate on a "presumption of disclosure." Atty. Gen. Janet Reno ordered that when in doubt, release it and she informed US agencies that in the case of a lawsuit, the Justice Department "would defend an agency withholding information only when the agency reasonably foresaw that disclosure would harm an interest protected by an exemption."[18]

Eight years later the Bush administration reversed that openness. The month after 9/11, Atty. Gen. Ashcroft issued a memorandum suggesting when in doubt, don't release it. The Ashcroft memo also added a "sensitive but unclassified" category to the exemption-from-disclosure list and promised legal cover for officers who withheld information ("sensitive but unclassified" will be discussed later).

The Bush administration then pursued more exemptions. Two prominent examples are:

NSA Operational Files. In 2003 the administration sought and achieved legislation exempting NSA "operational files" from the FOIA. In the past these files, although classified, were usually provided with classified parts blacked out. Valuable information was still received. Now requests are simply refused.

Vehicle Safety Defect Information. The administration issued regulations blocking this information from release. An inexcusable delay by Ford, Firestone and the National Highway Transportation Safety Administration (NHTSA) regarding tire defects was linked to 270 highway deaths. Congress passed legislation in October 2000 requiring NHTSA to issue reporting requirements assuring prompt notification by manufacturers of known or potential safety defects. It still honored the right to withhold confidential business information. In July 2003 NHTSA amended its reporting policy to withhold reported safety defects from FOIA release because it would cause competitive harm to the company. This hides safety information that caused the Ford/Firestone investigation in the first place. Profits again triumph over human welfare. More examples will be discussed below.

Other means were used to undermine the FOIA system. Denying a fee waiver is one. Many individuals and organizations can't afford the cost of FOIA searches, which are often significant. In 1986 the FOIA was amended to provide two conditions for waiving the fee if the information is not to be used for commercial purposes: (1) if it is to be used by an institution, whose purpose is scholarly or scientific research; if the requestor is a representative of the news media only copying fees may be charged; or (2) fees must be waived or reduced if disclosure of the information is in the public interest and likely to contribute significantly to public understanding of government operations or activities.

The Bush administration has used several tactics to challenge or deny fee waiver requests. One is to challenge the "preferred status" of the requester – such as, how the information requested is going to contribute significantly to public understanding of the operations or activities of the government. When denying fee waiver requests for this reason, the government is deciding what the public should know.

The administration also narrowed the definition of "representative of the news media." Freelance writers and non-fiction book authors have had fees denied because publishing books and articles is not publishing or broadcasting news to the public itself. Thus, one who pursues these activities is not representative of the media. Such reasoning is usually rectified by appeal but can cause months delay – which often dilutes the usability for the information requested.

Public interest research centers and educational organizations that publish material on privacy, open government, free speech and other civil rights issues have not fared well. A request by an entity describing itself as an educational organization that disseminates information was denied because it was not both organized and operated to disseminate information. In this case the fee-waiver request was still denied on appeal.

There have been cases of sequential fee-waiver denials. One challenge is used until it has been overruled after months of appeals. Then the government comes up with a new challenge and the delay continues. In one case an environmental advocacy organization requested documents from the National Institute of Environmental Health Sciences. Fee waiver was denied because the information would not be widely distributed and the organization could not educate people beyond those who feel the same. After over ten months of appeals the challenges were overturned. Then the government came up with a new challenge, saying the group had not demonstrated how the information would significantly improve public understanding of government activities beyond what it already knows or reach people who aren't already informed.

Inappropriate use of exemption requests can cause long and often critical delays. Frivolous exemption claims, even though the government knows they are frivolous, still take months to resolve. Another trick is to mark documents improperly, such as reports marked "pre-decisional" or "deliberative" to make them exempt, even though the actual decisions or deliberations are long past.

And then there is simple bureaucratic foot dragging. The FOIA sets specific timeframes for responding and outlines specific notification of "unusual circumstances" if the deadlines can't be met, but the government simply fails to respond. Or it may respond and then take forever to find the information.

In one case I requested information from the US Navy and I was bumped around from one branch to another and from one regional office to another. It took months to obtain the information and then only because one sympathetic navy employee decided to "just send it anyway."

A July 2007 report by National Security Archive of George Washington University showed that the oldest pending FOIA requests date back to the 1980s – one from 1987, two from 1988, and three from 1999.[19] The US Justice Department has been the biggest roadblock to FOIA reform by Congress. Of all the government agencies from which National Security Archive made a FOIA request for their ten oldest unanswered requests in 2006, one-third did not respond. Ten agencies did not respond to similar requests in 2005. The law requires a response within 20 business days.

The administration's handling of FOIA requests is summed up by Jane E. Kirtley, professor of media ethics and law at the University of Minnesota: "The Bush Justice Department does not seem to view the FOIA as a law, like any other law, that must be enforced to promote the legislative goal of openness and accountability. Instead, it regards the exemptions as loopholes to be interpreted as broadly as possible in order to thwart the public's right to know what its government is up to."[20]

Sensitive but Unclassified Information

White House Chief of Staff Andrew Card issued a memorandum in March 2002 specifically instructing agencies to review their records handling procedure to assure they are protecting from release any records categorized as "sensitive but unclassified." Since there was still no definition for this term, the agencies were left to flounder with compliance to the memo and how they would process FOIA requests. This category was also addressed in the Ashcroft memo described above.

This new, all-pervading category was officially defined by the State Department in 2005: "Sensitive but unclassified (SBU) information is information that is not classified for national security reasons, but that warrants/requires administrative control and protection from public or other unauthorized disclosure for other reason."[21] It must meet one of nine criteria which include "inter- or intra-agency communications, including e-mails that form part of the internal deliberative processes of the US government, the disclosure of which could harm such processes."[22] That is the type of material used by whistleblowers to prove their claims and the type of information that reveals misdeeds and corruption in government. These semi-secrets are being stamped with various labels at the rate of 125 a minute by federal agencies seeking to mask their activities.

It is important to note that SBU does not have the same authority to conceal information as does a national security classification. The implementing document states: "Designation of information as SBU is important to indicate that the information requires a degree of protection and administrative control but the SBU label does not by itself exempt information from disclosure under the FOIA [5 U.S.C. 552(b)]. Rather, exemption is determined based on the nature of the information in question."[23] In other words, to deny release of the information under the FOIA the "nature of the information in question" must meet the criteria for exemption under the FOIA. Denying information with the sole justification that it is "sensitive but unclassified" is a bluff, but a bluff that cannot be easily challenged.

Many aspects of government which do not fall under the heading of national security do have to be guarded; however this type of protection has been greatly expanded by the Bush administration. Ambassador Thomas E. McNamara told a House subcommittee in May 2006 that over 60 types of markings come under the heading of sensitive but unclassified. OpenTheGovernment.org has identified 50 in its 2006 report.[24] They include "Controlled but Unclassified," "Controlled Unclassified Information," "Defense Information," "For Official Use Only," "Official Use Only," "Limited Official Use Only,"

"Law Enforcement Sensitive," "Sensitive Unclassified" and more. This report quotes a Library of Congress researcher who noted: "Key terms often lack definition, [and] vagueness exists regarding who is authorized to apply markings, for what reasons, and for how long. Uncertainty prevails concerning who is authorized to remove markings and for what reasons." Confusion begets caution, and caution begets secrecy.

Critical Infrastructure Information

Additional guidance given to agencies in the March 2002 Card memo was to exempt from release information voluntarily submitted to government from the private sector which could fall under the protection of Exemption 4 of the FOIA, which reads: "This section does not apply to matters that are trade secrets and commercial or financial information obtained from a person and privileged or confidential."[25] A US Navy guidance document for implementing the FOIA states: "This exemption requires protection of certain trade secrets and commercial or financial information received from a private source when disclosure is likely to cause substantial competitive harm to the source."[26] Although the Card memo urged application of Exemption 4 to the utmost, it was not all-inclusive. The administration needed something more powerful to serve its agenda.

The Homeland Security Act was introduced in Congress in 2002, the same year the Card memo was issued. When the Act became law in November, it contained a major new justification for keeping information from the public called the Critical Infrastructure Information Act of 2002.[27] "The term 'critical infrastructure information' means information not customarily in the public domain and related to the security of critical infrastructure or protected systems."[28] A protected system is defined as any service, physical, or computer-based system, process, or procedure that directly or indirectly affects the viability of a facility of critical infrastructure.[29]

Bush issued Homeland Security Presidential Directive 7

(HSPD-7) in December 2003 directing the Department of Homeland Security (DHS) to establish policies, guidelines and methodologies to protect 17 designated sectors of critical infrastructure which are "agriculture and food; banking and finance; chemical; commercial facilities; commercial nuclear reactors, materials, and waste; communications; dams; defense industrial base; drinking water and water treatment systems; emergency services; energy; government facilities; information technology; national monuments and icons; postal and shipping; public health and health care; and transportation systems."[30] Whew! What is left in life to talk about?

The Homeland Security Act exempts critical infrastructure information from disclosure under the FOIA – that is a lot of information removed from public review since some 85% of America's critical infrastructure is owned and operated by private entities – and that critical infrastructure takes in almost our entire lifestyle. Hiding those 17 sectors from public view casts a thick veil of secrecy over DHS's principle activities.

The original Homeland Security bill introduced in Congress exempted FOIA disclosure of "infrastructure vulnerabilities or other vulnerabilities *to terrorism*," which seems reasonable and adequate (emphasis added). But when the bill was reported out of the House Select Committee on Homeland Security to the Republican-controlled Congress, the FOIA exemption was significantly expanded. The Congressional Research Service (CRS) explains that "protections now extended to a broad and newly defined category of information – *critical infrastructure information* voluntarily submitted to the DHS with an express statement of expectation of protection from disclosure" (emphasis in original). This report explained the final bill included protections long-sought by industry, to wit:

> [I]t provided exemption from disclosure under FOIA; it provided that covered information would not be used directly in civil actions; it provided that critical infrastructure information would not be used or disclosed by any federal employee

[whistleblower] except to further criminal investigation or prosecution or to disclose the information to Congress or the [Government Accountability Office]; it established that critical infrastructure information provided to a state or local government by DHS may not be made available pursuant to any state or local law requiring disclosure of information or records [state-government freedom of information requests]; and it provided that communications of critical infrastructure information would not be subject to the requirements of the Federal Advisory Committee Act.[31]

Two significant problems emerge from this secrecy. First, the terrific amount of information removed from oversight by citizens, whistleblowers who encounter problems, fraud or hazards will be gagged in reporting them to the media or the public. Information on potential pipeline routes, chemical plant leaks and other areas of public welfare will no longer be available—or most likely not until it's too late for remedial action. No one needs an expansive interpretation of what constitutes an "infrastructure vulnerability" to see how much knowledge can be hidden from the public.

The second problem is that information voluntarily shared with DHS is exempt from public disclosure, even for civil lawsuits. Of course there are caveats as to what constitutes "voluntary" information. It must be *offered*—if DHS requests the information it's not voluntary. Information a company or institute provides DHS that DHS is required to provide another agency (such as reporting required by federal/state/local health, safety or environmental laws) is not protected from disclosure. If a whistleblower gets the information by some other means than through DHS, it is not a violation of the exemption although it may be restricted by other laws. Likewise, if governments or private parties obtain information through a channel other than DHS it can be used in a civil case.

For DHS to withhold voluntarily-submitted information on critical infrastructure information, the entity providing the information must expressly state it expects the information to be protected from disclosure. Nevertheless, allowing manufacturers and businesses to voluntarily report critical infrastructure information to DHS, even with the above restrictions and ostensibly to promote infrastructure security, is dangerous. Once voluntarily submitted, this information cannot be shared with the public nor used in a lawsuit, even by a government watchdog agency. An expansive interpretation of the Critical Infrastructure Information Act could allow what a Heritage Foundation commentator described: "One need not be a Harvard law graduate to see that, without clarification of what constitutes vulnerabilities [of infrastructure], this loophole could be manipulated by clever corporate and government operators to hide endless varieties of potentially embarrassing and/or criminal information from public view."[32]

An example is the generically-engineered food industry which now occupies about 100 million acres nationwide. Only the Animal and Plant Health Inspection Service of the Department of Agriculture knows where those crops are grown and they won't tell because farmers say it will compromise their confidential business information. For organic farmers it is imperative to know where biologically altered crops are growing. If their farms are cross pollinated by the wind or birds, or some genetically altered seeds find their way into their organic farm, they cannot be certified "organic."[33] People who object to eating genetically engineered food also have a right to know how widely spread these crops are. More than 50 of these biologically altered foods have been approved by the Food & Drug Administration and it is estimated they are in 70% of all processed foods in grocery stores.

Lobbyists also thrive under the Critical Infrastructure Information Act. Even their routine communications can be excluded from public release. If a corporate lobbyist met with DHS to suggest changes in immigration and customs regulations under the guise of protecting the agricultural infrastructure – which may be the pressure behind Bush's desire for a guest worker program to provide a cheap labor force—that meeting could be withheld from disclosure. The Federal Advisory Committee Act does not apply.

This Critical Infrastructure Information Act has been called a "get-out-of-jail-free card, allowing companies worried about potential litigation or regulatory actions to place troublesome information in a convenient 'Homeland Security' vault."[34] It has been proposed that this anti-disclosure provision be extended to all government agencies. At least humor sometimes applies: David Brancaccio of PBS Television called DHS for their address. The receptionist was hesitant. She stalled and stonewalled. Pressed a little harder she finally blurted out, "Our physical location is something I am not obligated to give."[35]

Shutting Down the Presidential Records Act

Bush signed Executive Order 13233, "Further Implementation of the Presidential Records Act" in November 2001. The 1978 Act, passed in the wake of Watergate, allows former Presidents to restrict public access to their records for up to twelve years after they leave office, after which access was governed only by the Freedom of Information Act.

Under Bush's order, "former presidents or their designated representatives may veto the release of their presidential papers, as may the sitting president—a decision that vested George W. Bush with authority to block release of his father's papers, or even those of Bill Clinton." They can veto release of their records even if the sitting president disagrees. Any challenge from the requester must be resolved by court action with the Justice Department representing the former president gratis. President Steven Hensen of the Society of American Archivists asks: "How can a democratic people have confidence in elected officials who hide the records of their actions from public view?"[36]

This executive order also allows former vice presidents to block release of their records. However, in this case either the sitting president or the former president under which the vice president served must authorize the claim. Another provision allows a former president to appoint a designated representative who has the power to veto release of records on his behalf—even after the former president's death. If no representative has been designated, the former president's family becomes the designated representative. This automatic designation of the family to oversee presidential records after death or disability is illegal according to the Presidential Records Act, which states: "Upon the death or disability of a president or former president, any discretion or authority the president or former president may have had under this chapter shall be exercised by the archivist unless previously provided by the president or former president in a written notice to the archivist."[37]

One huge benefit for the Bush family from this executive order is that Texas A&M University hosts the George H.W. Bush Presidential Library and it is believed that papers in there, as well as in the Reagan Presidential Library, reveal much about the Iran-Contra scandal and how the president and vice president at that time, as well as others, were involved in it. This order keeps those papers secret in perpetuity.

The 1978 Presidential Records Act allowed some records opened five years after the president left office and all records declassified twelve years after. Reagan records were to be declassified in 2001, but Thomas Blanton, director of George Washington University's National Security Archive, told Congress Alberto Gonzales (then White House counsel) stalled release of the 68,000 pages of Reagan records that had been cleared and ready to go until Bush could issue Executive Order 13233. In concluding his testimony, Blanton pointed out that congressional action could remove the bad features of this executive order: **"We need to rescind the veto power the order gives to former presidents and their descendants; we need to eliminate the order's invention of a new vice president privilege; and we need to restore the 30-day notification process that worked so well in the 1990s"** (boldface in original).[38]

National Security Archive sued for release of Reagan's presidential records. Federal District Judge Colleen Kollar-Kotelly ruled in October 2007 the US Archivist should not rely on Executive Order 13233 to delay release of those records. The case is still pending at the time of this writing.

Hobbling the Federal Advisory Committee Act

The Federal Advisory Committee Act (FACA) of 1972 is the legal foundation defining how federal advisory bodies operate. It places special emphasis on open meetings and accountability, public involvement, balanced viewpoints and reporting. If all members of the advisory group are federal employees, FACA does not apply, but if only one member is *not* a government employee, that committee is bound by the Act.

Section 5 of FACA provides that committee members must be "fairly balanced in terms of the points of view represented and the functions to be performed," and to have provisions in place "to assure that the advice and recommendations of the advisory committee will not be inappropriately influenced."[39] Section 10 mandates each "advisory committee meeting shall be open to the public," that except for national security concerns "timely notice of each such meeting shall be published in the *Federal Register*," and interested persons "shall be permitted to attend, appear before or file statements with any advisory committee" subject to reasonable rules. Section 10 also provides that, except for exemptions specified in the FOIA, "the records, reports, transcripts, minutes, appendixes, working papers, drafts, studies, agenda or other documents which were made available to or prepared for or by each advisory committee shall be available for public inspection and copying."

When the Homeland Security bill was introduced to Congress, the Bush administration proposed that advisory committees to Homeland Security be exempted from the FACA. It didn't get the blanket exemption proposed but something just as effective. The final act granted the secretary of Homeland Security power to exempt individual committees from FACA on a case-by-case basis as long as a notice of the committee is published in the *Federal Register*. So, one by one, every advisory committee to DHS can be exempted from openness, accountability and reporting requirements. When one considers the number of agencies that have been rolled together to form DHS, that is a big chunk of government engulfed in secrecy.

Another exemption to FACA was established by Medicare amendments signed in December 2003 providing for an advisory committee to implement a competitive acquisition program for medical equipment and supplies. "In particular, the committee is to offer advice on establishing data collection requirements and 'the development of proposals for efficient interaction among manufacturers, providers of services, suppliers...and individuals.'"[40] This is exactly the interaction causing such high prices in the medical profession, yet the proceedings of that committee are exempted from FACA requirements.

There will be many reruns to Cheney's energy task force. At the administration's urging, there was language in the Pentagon's 2004 Authorization Bill that allows Department of Energy contractors to be considered federal employees for FACA purposes. That means representatives from the oil and gas industry can provide consultation to the DOE in secrecy. That is like Lockheed Martin engineers being considered federal employees so they can lobby for what missiles they want to sell. I've had firsthand experience in that area during pre-FACA days.

In some instances the Bush administration has deliberately sidestepped FACA requirements or outright violated them. Cheney's energy task force is the most obvious example. Another is the President' Commission on Intelligence on Weapons of Mass Destruction established in February 2004 – also known as the WMD Commission – and set up to investigate intelligence failures regarding weapons of mass destruction in Iraq. In Executive Order 13328 establishing that commission, Bush exempted it from FACA requirements. A 30 June 2004 White House notice in the *Federal Register* announced a WMD commission's meeting, noting the administration refused to apply FACA.

There are three other techniques used to circumvent FACA. (1) The President's Commission to Strengthen Social Security, established by Executive Order 13210 to advise on changes to the Social Security System, has worked mainly through subcommittees which conducted their business in closed meetings. The commission's position was that only when it met as a full committee were they subject to FACA. (2) The Energy Project Streamlining Task Force established in May 2001 by Executive Order 13212 was composed of federal employees and thus not subject to FACA – but it tended to serve as a conduit through which the energy and petroleum industries could make recommendations to the president. This task force also pressured government agencies in the field in such areas as speeding up the issuing of permits. (3) In April 2004 the White House Office of Management and Budget advised federal agencies on the technique of avoiding FACA by hiring an outside contractor to hold peer reviews of government science and activities.

Changed Rules on Classifying New Documents and Declassifying Old

By presidential orders issued since 1940, there are three levels of national security classification: CONFIDENTIAL (could cause damage to national security), SECRET (expected to cause serious damage if revealed), and TOP SECRET (could cause exceptionally grave damage). Some agencies (DOE, DOD, CIA, and NSA) use different classification levels within their own areas of responsibility.

In 1997 the government was spending $22 to keep secrets for every dollar spent toward opening up secrets. In 2005 that ratio had increased to $134 spent creating new and securing old secrets for every dollar spent declassifying. All in all, the government spent $7.7 billion in 2005 to classify 14.2 million documents – a huge jump from $3.4 million used to classify 6.5 million documents in 1997. These figures do not include CIA activity because its totals are themselves classified.

Using an executive order, Bush added to the list of who can stamp documents secret. Now such purely domestic agencies as the Department of Agriculture, Department of Health and Human Services, the Environmental Protection Agency and the Office of Science and Technology Policy can wield the national security stamp. Bush also implemented a new national space policy whereby more government surveillance would be accomplished by commercial satellites. This gave the administration control over the distribution of photos taken from those commercial satellites. Executive Order 13292 ordered all agencies and entities in the executive branch to report annually the number of documents classified. The National Archives and Records Administration received reports from over 80 agencies that had a collective total of 15.6 million classification decisions in 2004 – almost double the 2001 aggregate.

Looking at it from the other end, in 1997 there were 204 million pages declassified and made available to the public at a cost of $150 million. In 2005 that total had shrunk to a paltry 29.5 million pages with a correspondingly lower cost of $57 million. These figures for classifying and declassifying documents include 41 federal agencies. The president, vice president and CIA are not included in these figures. Millions of 25-year-old classified documents were scheduled to be de-classified and released by 17 April 2003, but the month before Bush signed Executive Order 13292 delaying their release until the end of 2006. In the meantime, EO13292 allowed FOIA officers to reclassify information that had been declassified. This EO also removed a provision that says don't classify if there is significant doubt. The Bush policy is to classify information even when the need to do so was in significant doubt giving the government more leeway to classify "sensitive" (i.e. embarrassing) information and to reclassify material that had been "inappropriately declassified."

America in Peril

The Defense Department classified the entire March 2004 investigation report of Maj. Gen. Antonio Taguba, which detailed the unlawful treatment of Iraqi prisoners of war in US custody. One reporter who had reviewed a widely disseminated copy of the report raised the issue in a Defense Department briefing with Gen. Peter Pace, [then] vice chair of the Joint Chiefs of Staff and Secretary Rumsfeld. The reporter noted that "there's clearly nothing in there that is inherently secret, such as intelligence sources and methods of troop movements," and asked: "Was this kept secret because it would be embarrassing to the world, particularly the Arab world?" Gen. Pace responded that he did not know why the document was marked secret. When asked whether he could say why the report was classified, Secretary Rumsfeld answered: "No, you'd have to ask the classifier."[41]

The Information Security Oversight Office (ISOO) of the Federal National Archives and Records Administration reported over 20 million decisions to classify government secrets during 2006 – with serious shortcomings in the process.

Reclassification of Documents in the Public Domain

It came to public attention in February 2006 that a secret program at the National Archives was removing thousands of historical documents from public access – documents that had been available for years and had already found their way into the files of historians and others. This program was started in 1999 as a backlash by the CIA and other agencies to President Clinton's 1995 presidential declassification order.

Suspicions rose in December 2005 when an Oregon historian, Matthew M. Aid, discovered some 50 documents he had previously copied had been removed from the shelves. Most were from the Korean War and the early cold war. Aid said: "The stuff they pulled should never have been removed. Some of it is mundane and some of it is outright ridiculous." Aid and other researchers filed a complaint with the archives' Information Security Oversight Office. When J. William Leonard, director of the office, checked 16 secret documents and determined they should not have been reclassified, he ordered an audit of the reclassification program. Leonard told reporters: "If those sample records were removed because someone thought they were classified, I'm shocked and disappointed. It just boggles the mind."[42]

This audit, conducted in April 2006, revealed that ten agencies had been conducting a major reclassification program. The names of the agencies cannot be revealed but as of September 2006 they had reclassified at least 25,315 records that had previously been available to the public—some reports put the number as high as 55,000. OpenTheGovernment.org felt the audit showed 64% could probably qualify for reclassification, but there were 24% which definitely should not have been reclassified and another 12% were questionable.

Leonard of the National Archives does not have authority to declassify them—the agency that originally classified must sign off on declassification. Meanwhile, researchers and historians are concerned that documents in their personal files might technically put them in violation of the Espionage Act with the associated serious penalties. This secret reclassification program at the National Archives has also used a bureaucratic quirk to exempt itself from reporting to ISOO. The intelligence agencies involved claim the documents were never properly declassified so reclassifying them is not something that needs to be reported. Thus making them inaccessible to public access is not really reclassification. Right!

The Bush administration made its imprint on internet content as well. Following 9/11, government agencies were ordered to purge all potentially sensitive information from their websites. At least 15 federal agencies complied, and hundreds of thousands of pages were deleted. OMB [Office of Management and Budget] Watch noted in an October 2002 paper: "It is no longer possible for families and communities to get data critical to protecting themselves—information such as pipeline maps (that show where they are and whether they have been inspected), airport safety data, environmental data and even documents that are widely available on private sites today were removed from government sites and have not reappeared."[43]

According to a March 2007 study by the National Security Archive at George Washington University, federal agencies seem to be ignoring the Electronic Freedom of Information Act of 1997 and are not properly using the internet to make government documents available to the public. The study examined 91 federal agencies and 58 of their component agencies, and found:

- Only 22% followed the law properly.
- Only a third of the agencies and components provided the required index to help find records on their website.
- 75% did not provide online forms for FOIA requests.
- Many links to records were wrong or didn't exist.

Libraries suffered a similar fate. The *Los Angeles Times* reported in November 2001 that the Government Printing Office ordered some 1,300 libraries nationwide "to destroy government records that federal agencies say could be too sensitive for public consumption." One example is a federal directive telling libraries to destroy a CD on a survey of dams and reservoirs. When the public uses reading rooms at federal agencies they "must now make an appointment and be escorted by an employee to ensure that information is not misused."[44]

The student newspaper at the University of Michigan, *The Michigan Daily*, made a cogent observation: "While it is frightening that the government would consider such Orwellian information controls, it is even scarier that the general public is not much more upset about it. Many Americans, buying into the rhetoric of 'safety' are all too eager to exchange their rights for a sense of false security."[45] This concern has motivated me to write this book.

In December 2006 *The New York Times* was blocked from publishing an article containing unclassified information on why engagement in dialogue with Iran would be fruitful. Written by Flynt Leverett, former senior director for Middle East affairs at the National Security Council, and Hilary Mann, former foreign service officer who participated in US discussions with Iran from 2001 to 2003, it was submitted to the CIA's Publication Review Board because the authors were former federal employees. Leverett had written over 20 articles that passed the prepublication review process with absolutely no changes and without the board consulting the White House. This time it was different. New procedures were apparently in force. The CIA asked the White House for permission to clear the article. That resulted in large portions being censored out. The CIA told the authors "that they had concluded on their own that the original draft included no classified material, but that they had to bow to the White House."[46]

Leverett and Mann said the deleted portions did nothing more than discuss US-Iranian relations during Bush's first term—issues that had been publicly discussed in the media which the authors and others had written about many times. These issues had also been openly discussed by Secretary of State Condoleezza Rice, former State Secretary Colin Powell, former Deputy State Secretary Richard Armitage, former State Department Policy Planning Director Richard Haass and former Special Envoy to Afghanistan James Dobbins. Now the information could not be published. Orwell's Ministry of Truth is at work.

Past deployment numbers of strategic nuclear missiles have also been re-designated "secret" and redacted (censored out) in government documents released to the public. This is information the US had to declare to the Soviet Union in compliance with various treaties which has always been publicly available and still is on some websites. I have published the information many times. William Burr, senior analyst at George Washington University's National Security Archive said it "would be difficult to find more dramatic examples of unjustifiable secrecy than these decisions" to reclassify the inventories of strategic weapons during various stages of the cold war. Director of the Archive, Thomas Blanton, added: "It's yet another example of silly secrecy."[47]

Censoring Information Released to the Public.

It started on the afternoon of Bush's inauguration in January 2001. Newly appointed White House Chief of Staff Andrew Card ordered federal agencies to freeze more than 300 pending regulations issued by the Clinton administration which affected issues such as health and safety, the environment and industry. Ostensibly this freeze would allow new appointees to review the regulations but what happened was to prevent review by the citizens for it was decided such review would not be in the public interest.

In January 2004 a St. Louis *Post-Dispatch* article began: "Under a new proposal, the White House would decide what and when the public would be told about an outbreak of mad cow disease, an anthrax release, a nuclear plant accident or any other crisis."[48] This proposal would give the White House Office of Management and Budget[49] control over health, safety and environmental information released by the various government agencies, so individual federal agencies will no longer release their own public warnings based on scientific determination. Citizens will no longer be immediately warned by the Food and Drug Administration (FDA) that hormone replacement therapy could cause breast cancer in women; or that anti-arrhythmic drugs are useless and in fact dangerous; or that a certain batch of green onions from Mexico are causing a hepatitis outbreak. These warnings will first wind their bureaucratic way through the White House to be screened for potential political effects or undue hardship on industry.

Former deputy commissioner of the FDA Michael Taylor warned it is dangerous to have OMB involved in sending out warnings on imminent health hazards: "OMB's proposal says it gets to weigh in on any agency statement that would have a significant impact on an industry.... Should the FDA commissioner have to go to Graham [OMB's administrator of the Office of Information and Regulatory Affairs] for permission to warn people about tainted green onions?... Speed is often essential. If you discover that a heart valve is defective and killing people and can't issue a recall until the White House has weighed in on the issue, people could die."[50]

An issue surfaced in 2007. Critics were pressuring for tighter controls on fresh-cut produce such as shredded lettuce, sliced tomatoes and peeled carrots because destroying the protective skin makes contamination easier. Cutting them in such large batches allows contagion to spread farther. In March the FDA floated a draft of guidelines pertaining to fresh-cut vegetables which proposed the produce industry use safety checks similar to those in the meat industry. Critics called the draft unacceptable because compliance was only voluntary (the meat industry has mandatory rules and periodic government inspections). Caroline Smith DeWaal, food safety director at the Center for Science in the Public Interest, said: "The FDA is still not addressing the underlying problem, which is, there are no enforceable standards in place for the fresh-cut produce industry."[51] Before circulating that draft it first had to have OMB approval.

Another incident involved the Department of Health and Human Services. Former Surgeon Gen. Richard H. Carmona told Congress in July 2007 that the administration repeatedly overrode scientific evidence with its political decisions. On numerous issues – such as stem cell research, teen pregnancy, sex education, prison health care, the effect of second-hand smoke, mental health and global health issues – his reports had been delayed and watered down to give politics priority over science. Dr. Carmona said: "Anything that doesn't fit into the political appointees' ideological, theological or political agenda is ignored, marginalized or simply buried."[52] There were 18 pages of executive branch e-mails released to Congress to substantiate Carmona's testimony. He served his four-year term from 2002 to 2006 but was not asked to serve another.

The political appointee Carmona referred to is William R. Steiger, head of the office of global health affairs at HHS. He blocked Carmona's 2005 report covering all the contemporary issues of public health which tied poverty and the environment to the global health issue. Steiger wouldn't release the report because it didn't hype Bush's health policies. Carmona refused to make the change because it would tarnish the surgeon general's office to make the political pitch. The report has never been released but the *Washington Post* acquired a copy.

When Dr. Julie Gerberding, director of the Center for Disease Control (CDC) under HHS, was scheduled to testify to Congress in October 2007, she was censored by the White House. Originally a 12-page study explaining the effect of climate change on the spread of disease, her report was cut in half. A CDC official speaking anonymously said the original draft was eviscerated by heavy-handed changes in Washington. Explicit findings on how global warming will increase the spread of insect-carried diseases and otherwise impact health conditions were deleted. Although the White House claimed only deletions that disagree with scientific findings were removed, Congressional committees ridiculed the notion. The International Panel on Climate Change report agreed with what had been cut out.

Besides taking charge of all public warnings, the proposed policy lets the OMB manage all scientific and technical reviews. These so-called peer reviews cover all major plans, guidelines, proposed regulations and announcements prepared by various agencies. Industry is delighted because previous peer reviews often resulted in tighter control over products and processes.

OMB says Congress mandated it take a greater role in supervising the agencies. What Congress required in the Information Quality Law was that OMB oversee the quality of information released by federal agencies. It didn't tell OMB to censor and release that information. Winifred de Palma of Public Citizen explained: "OMB has no statutory or other expressed legal authority to impose this type of control on the agencies. If the plan is implemented, it will mean that political considerations, and not public health, will be the administration's primary public concern in deciding whether to release health and safety information to the public in emergency situations."[53]

Things went from proposal to reality in January 2007 when Bush issued Executive Order 13422 giving White House control over federal agencies responsible for health, safety and the environment. The order empowers OMB's Office of Information and Regulatory Affairs (OIRA) to make agencies change proposed and existing regulations to align with the president's priorities. Federal regulations on everything from warning labels on containers to occupational safety can be preëmpted by White House policy. Environmental, health and safety regulations are a lower priority than political-economic considerations.

The new order goes even further than rules and regulations. It allows OIRA to oversee "guidance" documents prepared by the agencies, which explain how the rules and regulation will be enforced. These documents are often more significant in enforcing federal standards and drawing up contracts than the regulations themselves because they elaborate how tasks should be accomplished. OMB has always had some control over government agencies but guidance documents were frequently used to circumvent bureaucratic decisions and reflect the statutory function of the agency.

That will no longer be the case. Each agency must now establish a regulatory policy office to evaluate guidance material according to political-economic criteria. A political appointee will head that office to be a gatekeeper in evaluating regulations and guidance documents for costs and benefits and see if the problem justifies government intervention. If the gatekeeper thinks a free-market environment will correct the problem there'll likely be no government intervention.

An example surfaced in March 2007. In the autumn of 2006 the FDA advisory board recommended disapproval of the new antibiotic cefquinome to treat a pneumonia-like disease in cattle. The American Medical Association, many other health groups, and most of the FDA's own scientists warned it could build up an immunity in humans (who eat the meat and drink the milk) to a potent antibiotic of the same family needed to treat some highly-resistant bacteria. The wording of "Guidance for Industry Document #152" favored the pharmaceutical companies and the drug was approved.

Executive Order 13422 is a direct response to what industry demands. Public Citizen called this new order "an appalling arrogation of power" because it grasps more executive power while dodging congressional oversight. Rick Melberth of OMB Watch added: "They don't want regulations to impact the regulated industries that are friends of theirs. This is one way they can make that process slow down. It's a perfectly logical extension of their approach to regulation."[54]

At a January 2007 hearing the House Committee on Oversight and Government Reform heard about coverups regarding global warming. Scientists and advocacy groups said 46% of 1,600 government scientists interviewed—who work at seven federal agencies from NASA to the EPA—were instructed not to reference issues about global warming in scientific reports and avoid public statements that would pressure the administration for mandatory controls. They were told not to use terms like "climate change" or "global warming." 43% of them said their published works had been changed so drastically the meaning was lost. 38% said they knew first-hand of global warming material being purged from websites and printed reports.

No detail was too small in the climate coverup campaign. NASA scientist Drew Shindell told of a dispute over what a report on measuring the rapid warming in Antarctica should be titled. Finally, said Shindell, "word came back from above that it should be 'Antarctic Climate Change.' I thought it was so watered down it would be of little interest to anybody." Rick Piltz, former senior associate at the US Climate Change Science Program who resigned his position because of censorship pressure, was astounded by the amount of political interference in a technical subject and testified, "There were a very large number of edits that came in at the 12th hour after all the earlier science people had signed off." He described a case where White House appointee Phil Cooney wanted 400 last-minute changes which drastically changed the essence of the report.

Cooney was an American Petroleum Institute lobbyist who was appointed head of the White House Council on Environmental Quality in 2001. After resigning that position in 2005, he was hired by Exxon-Mobil. Piltz described one EPA report from which Cooney excised a key part on the dangers of climate change, calling it "speculative musing." Piltz warned the House committee on the dangers of such interference: "If you know that what you are writing has to go through a White House clearance before it is published, people start writing for the class. An anticipatory kind of self-censorship sets in."[55]

In December 2006, environmental groups were pressuring Bush to put polar bears on the endangered species list because global warming is melting the icebergs on which they hunt seals. Early in 2007 an internal memo circulated in the Alaska division of the US Fish & Wildlife Service instructed employees and scientists not to discuss "climate change," "polar bears" or "sea ice" in their travels around the Arctic unless authorized to do so. There were also samples of how to prepare travel requests with a cover note marked "Foreign Travel – New Requirement – Please Review and Comply, Importance: High," which read:

> Please be advised that all foreign travel requests (SF1175 requests) and any future travel requests involving or potentially involving climate change, sea ice and/or polar bears will also require a memorandum from the regional director to the director indicating who'll be the official spokesperson on the trip and the one responding to questions on these issues, particularly polar bears.

The new travel requests, which require the employee's signature, have a phrase saying the employee seeking permission to travel "understands the administration's position on climate change, polar bears and sea ice and will not be speaking on or responding to these issues."[56]

The Union of Concerned Scientists sent a survey to climate specialists working for the government and received responses from 279 – of whom 58% said they had experienced censorship to eliminate words like "climate change" and "global warming," to alter their reports to change the meaning of their findings or to falsify their findings through official statements. They also had to remove or delay on-line reports and comply with new and strange requirements. The climate scientists reported 435 incidents of political censorship over a five-year period. In some cases the employee or scientist resigned rather than dilute the message in their report.

Self censorship is also taking place under the tacit threat of budget cuts or losing their jobs. The Smithsonian Institution, although ostensibly autonomous in its decisions on what to exhibit, is mostly taxpayer funded and has an annual budget of $1.1 billion. To prevent offending the Bush administration or Congress in 2007 they toned down the exhibit on how global warming is affecting the Arctic region, according to Robert Sullivan, former associate director in charge of natural history exhibits. He said: "It just became tooth-pulling to get solid science out without toning it down.... The obsession with getting the next allocation and appropriation was so intense that anything that might upset the Congress or the White House was being looked at very carefully."[57]

James Hansen, director and top climate scientist of Goddard Institute for Space Studies of NASA, testified before the House Oversight and Government Affairs Committee in March 2007. Critical of government censorship regarding global warming, he said: "This is the United States. We have freedom of speech here." Republican committee member Darrell Issa responded saying he thought it was reasonable Hansen shouldn't speak publicly on views contrary to those of the administration. Hansen replied: "I am concerned that many scientists are increasingly engaging in political advocacy and that some issues of science have become increasingly partisan.... When I testify to you as a government scientist, why does my testimony have to be reviewed, edited and changed by a bureaucrat in the White house?"[58] Sitting beside him was one of those bureaucrats, Philip Cooney. Documents released from this hearing showed hundreds of cases where Cooney had altered scientific reports to play down human contributions to global warming.

Notes for Chapter 6

1. Ewen, Stuart, *PR! A Social History of Spin* (Basic Books, NY, 1996), p. 152.
2. After World War II, Lippmann returned to a more liberal viewpoint. During his 30-year syndicated column he upset both parties by opposing the Korean War, McCarthyism, and the Vietnam War. Born in 1889, he died in 1974.
3. *Secrecy and the Bush Administration*, a report prepared for Representative Harry A. Waxman, 14 Sep 2004.
4. GAO-03-894; "Energy Task Force: Process Used to Develop the National Energy Policy," Aug 2003.
5. Environmental Media Service; "Cheney Rejects Requests for Information about Energy Task Force," 15 Jul 2002, at http://www.ems.or
6. *Mercury News*; "Cheney's Got a Pal on the Court – ruling in His Case," San Jose (CA) *Mercury News* 20 Jan 2004.
7. Savage, David G. and Richard A. Serrano, "Scalia Was Cheney Hunt Trip Guest; Ethics Concern Grows," *LA Times*, 5 Feb 2004.
8. *Mercury News*; "Democrats Question Scalia-Cheney Trip," San Jose (CA) *Mercury News* 23 Jan 2004.
9. Savage and Serrano, op. cit.
10. Cornwell, Susan; "Supreme Court to Hear Cheney Energy Task Force Case," *Reuters*, 15 Dec 2003.
11. 5 U.S.C. 2954 – "Information to Committees of Congress on Request."
12. The House Committee on Government Operations was renamed in 1995 to the Committee on Government Reform and Oversight; then in 1999 it became the Committee on Government Reform. In 2007 it was again renamed to the Committee on Oversight and Government Reform.
13. Moraff, Christopher, "Why are EPA Libraries Closing?" *In These Times*, 1 Feb 2007.
14. Werner, Erica (AP), "Democrats Rip EPA Chief over Reforms," *Yahoo! News*, 6 Feb 2007.
15. Meyer, Josh, "Bush Claims Oversight Exemption too," *LA Times*, 23 Jun 2007.
16. Executive Order 13292: "Further Amendment to Executive Order 12958, as Amended, Classified National Security Information," signed by George W. Bush on 25 Mar 2003, Section 6.1(b).
17. Meyer, op cit.
18. GAO-03-981; "Freedom of Information Act: Agency Views on Changes Resulting from New Administration Policy," Sep 2003.
19. See Knight Open Government Survey, *40 Years of FOIA, 20 Years of Delay: Oldest Pending FOIA Requests Date Back to the 1980s*, conducted by the National Security Archive of George Washington Univ., 2 Jul 2007.
20. *Secrecy and the Bush Administration*, op. cit.

21. 12 FAM 541 "Scope of Sensitive but Unclassified Information," US Dept. of State Foreign Affairs Manual Volume 12–Diplomatic Security, Section 541, 4 Nov 2005.

22. Ibid., Section (b)(9)

23. Ibid., Section (c)

24. See McDermott, Patrice and Emily Feldman, "Secrecy Report Card 2006: Indicators of Secrecy in the Federal Government," released by OpenTheGovernment.org, 3 Sep 2006.

25. 5 U.S.C. 552–"The Freedom of Information Act," as amended in 2002.

26. "SSC San Diego FOIA/Privacy Program," Space and Naval Warfare Systems Center, San Diego, CA.

27. Codified as 6 U.S.C. 131 et seq., it is in Subtitle B of Title II of the Homeland Security Act of 2002 (sections 211-215).

28. 6 U.S.C. 131 et seq., "Critical Infrastructure Information Act of 2002."

29. Ibid., Section 6(a) and (b).

30. GAO-07-706R – "Critical Infrastructure Protection: Sector Plans and Sector Councils Continue to Evolve," a report by GAO, 10 Jul 2007.

31. CRS Report RL31762–"Homeland Security Act of 2002: Critical Infrastructure Information Act," 28 Feb 2003, prepared by Gina Marie Stevens, American Law Div.

32. Secrecy and the Bush Administration, op. cit.

33. Federal authorities say contamination of organic farms "'does not necessarily" lead to decertification–which may allay negative public opinion but it is hardly assuring to an organic farmer.

34. Schmitt, Christopher H. and Edward T. Pound, "Keeping Secrets," US News & World Report, 22 Dec 2003.

35. Moyers, Bill; NOW, PBS Television transcript, episode on government secrecy 12 Dec 2003, at http://www.pbs.org/now/printable/transcript246_full_print.html

36. Lewis, Charles; "Secrecy as Policy," Center for Public Integrity, 30 Jan 2004. from The Buying of the President 2004: Who's Really Bankrolling Bush and His Democratic Challengers–and What They Expect in Return, at http://www.alternet.org/print.html?story=17700

37. 44 U.S.C. 2204, "Restrictions on Access to Presidential Records."

38. Blanton, Thomas S., testimony before Subcommittee on Information Policy, Census and National Archives of the Committee on Oversight and Government Reform, US House of Representatives, 1 Mar 2007.

39. 5 U.S.C. App.1, "Federal Advisory Committee Act."

40. Secrecy and the Bush Administration, op. cit.

41. Ibid.

42. Shane, Scott, "US Reclassifies Many Documents in Secret Review," NY Times, 21 Feb 2006.

43. Lewis, op. cit.

44. Lichtblau, Eric, "Rising Fears That What We Do Know Can Hurt Us," LA Times, 18 Nov 2001.

45. "Information Please: Government Censorship must Not Continue Unchallenged," 21 Nov 2001.

46. Leverett, Flynt and Hillary Mann, "What We Wanted to Tell You about Iran," NY Times, 22 Dec 2006.

47. Lee, Christopher, "Cold War Missiles Target of Blackout," Washington Post, 21 Aug 2006.

48. Schneider, Andrew, "The Office of Management and Budget Wants to Have the Final Say on Releasing Emergency Declarations to the Public," 11 Jan 2004.

49. The OMB was created in 1970 to evaluate all budget, policy, legislative, regulatory and management issues originating from various government departments and agencies.

50. Schneider, op. cit.

51. Bailey, Brandon, "Critics Attack FDA's Guidelines for Cut Produce, Call Them Weak," *San Jose Mercury News*, 13 Mar 2007.

52. Alonso-Zaldivar; "Ex-Surgeon General Faults White House," *LA Times*, 11 Jul 2007.

53. Schneider, op. cit.

54. Chen, Michelle, "Executive Order Expands Presidential Power over Agencies," *New Standard* (Syracuse, NY), 24 Jan 2007.

55. Shindell and Piltz quoted in Goldenberg, Suzanne, "Bush Administration Accused of Doctoring Scientists' Reports on Climate Change," *Guardian* (London), 31 Jan 2007.

56. *Fish & Wildlife* quotes in Revkin, Andrew C., "Memos Tell Officials How to Discuss Climate," *NY Times*, 8 Mar 2007.

57. Zongker, Brett (AP), "Smithsonian Toned down Exhibit on Arctic," *Yahoo News*, 21 May 2007.

58. Havemann, Joel, "Scientist Accuses White House of 'Nazi' Tactics," *LA Times*, 19 Mar 2007.

7

Pseudo-Patriotism and Covert Propaganda

The conscious and intelligent manipulation of the organized habits and opinions of the masses is an important element in democratic society. Those who manipulate this unseen mechanism of society constitute an invisible government which is the true ruling power of the country.... We are governed, our minds are molded, our tastes formed, our ideas suggested, largely by men we have never heard of. This is a logical result of the way in which our democratic society is organized. Vast numbers of human beings must coöperate in this manner if they are to live together as a smoothly functioning society.... In almost every act of our daily lives, whether in the sphere of politics or business, in our social conduct or ethical thinking, we are dominated by the relatively small number of persons...who understand the mental processes and social patterns of the masses. It is they who pull the wires which control the public mind.

–Edward L. Bernays, *Propaganda* (1928)

"Patriotism" has become a buzz word with many connotations. Most usage implies what I call pseudo patriotism, like saluting the flag and following the leader. These practices are superficial but not intrinsically bad. It is when they represent the extent of a person's patriotism that they are troublesome. True patriotism includes loyalty to country but not to the extent of suppressing others. Mohandas Gandhi wrote: "It is not nationalism that is evil; it is the narrowness, selfishness, exclusiveness which is the bane of modern nations which is evil. Each wants profit at the expense of, and rise at the ruin of, the other."[1] To practice this evil a leader must have the people's support. No form of propaganda is more effective for rallying the masses behind the leader's agenda than creating a cult of pseudo patriotism.

America's Cult of Pseudo Patriotism

In their book *Age of Propaganda*, Pratkanis and Aronson devote a chapter to describing how to become a cult leader. Most people think of cults as forms of religion but that is not a complete definition. They can also be centered on race, politics, the occult, and more. It is merely a pattern of social relationships within a larger group. America's Cult of Pseudo Patriotism is political and is mustering support for the War on Terror with all its spinoffs.

Earlier I illustrated how the War on Terror is really *Pax Americana* to establish a global empire in which American interests are first priority and are met to the fullest. It was kicked into high gear by the 9/11 attack and has maintained momentum through the fear of terrorism, putting human rights on the back burner, and mustering citizen support through an ingenious propaganda campaign.

Most people believe they would never be fooled by propaganda. In the introduction to the French sociologist Jacques Ellul's book, translator Konrad Kellen explains that many are deluded by propaganda "because of their firm but entirely erroneous conviction that it is composed only of lies and 'tall stories,'" thinking something true is not propaganda. However, modern propaganda uses "many different kinds of truth – half truth, limited truth, truth out of context." People also mistakenly think they are not being propagandized when they hear something they already believe. But a paramount aim of propaganda is "to intensify existing trends, to sharpen and focus them, and, above all, to lead [people] to *action* (or...to non action...to prevent them from interfering)" (emphasis his).

Don't think because you're educated you aren't vulnerable to propaganda. Kellen says education is necessary. "In fact, education is largely identical with what Ellul calls 'pre-propaganda.'" Ellul believes intellectuals are more susceptible because (a) they read the most information, (b) they are compelled to have an opinion which makes them easy prey to the misinformation offered by propaganda, and (c) they feel capable of judging things for themselves.[2]

Let us look at two techniques outlined by Pratkanis and Aronson that nourish America's Cult of Pseudo Patriotism — the "granfalloon" and the "rationalization trap."

A Granfalloon

We have all been in situations where a group divides into teams. Whether they are friends or strangers, team members soon develop a spirit and camaraderie with their teammates. In pitting themselves against the opposing teams they become the "in" group and their opponents the "out" group. American novelist Kurt Vonnegut coined the word "granfalloon" for such proud and sometimes meaningless groupings of people, calling it "a seeming team that was meaningless in terms of the ways God gets things done."[3] Machinations of this type are also an "emotionally powerful persuasive technique. In this procedure... complete strangers are formed into groups using the most trivial, inconsequential criteria imaginable."[4]

Pratkanis and Aronson describe two psychological processes for granfalloons: cognitive and motivational. Cognitively they know they are part of a group and through this feeling of belonging, group members are inculcated to view the world in a prescribed manner. Similarities among group members are emphasized and personalized. Co-members are called by their names or titles and are shown respect. Simultaneously, the "out" group is depicted in a pejorative manner. Its members are given labels and described as of common ilk with no personality differences. They are stereotyped.

It is this cognitive nature of a granfalloon that cult leaders use to motivate members. By getting members to link their self esteem to the group, the leaders manipulate behavior – in essence saying: "You are on my side (never mind that I created the teams), now act like it and do what we say." They don't speak that bluntly but this is the message conveyed. That is the motivational aspect.

The granfalloon concept can be expanded to the larger society and the nation. Mass media reaches the crowd and the individual simultaneously. This psychological mass, that Ellul calls the lonely crowd, is an innate characteristic of modern society which is exploited to the fullest: "The most favorable moment to seize a man and influence him is when he is alone in the mass; it is at this point that propaganda can be most effective."5 It is precisely this loneliness which motivates an individual to "belong." The granfalloon is imposed as the answer – inviting the individual to become a member of the "in" group.

In America today this granfalloon is the Cult of Pseudo Patriotism. People are distracted from being true patriots with an allegiance to democracy based on the rights, freedoms and obligations spelled out in the US Constitution and the Declaration of Independence. Democracy is an ideology – a set of ideals and goals accepted by the peoples that are cherished, relevant and believed rather than proved. The Cult of Pseudo Patriotism, on the other hand, is a myth. The difference between a myth and an ideology, according to Ellul, is threefold:

> *First,* a myth embeds its roots deeper and more permanently, providing a basic role for the person in society as a whole.
> *Second,* a myth is more intellectually fragmented, stimulating emotion rather than reason, and is viewed as something hallowed rather than a concept – sentimental rather than pragmatic – and is more impelling than an ideology.

Third, the myth, being emotional, is more persuasive in motivating action. Ultimately the myth dominates people's thinking to the point where they build their lives around it.

That precisely defines the Cult of Pseudo Patriotism—an emotional yet unrealistic concept of America and Americans. To feed that myth the leader must create the cult as a granfalloon which cultivates the us-against-them mentality. The basic ideology of Constitutional democracy is already a widespread belief in America, so the cult leader's propaganda builds on that. In this "war on terror," the myth begins when the people feel their freedom, lifestyle and national interests are being threatened. Never mind how exploitative that lifestyle is, or how deep the national interests plow in other countries; cult members view preserving those interests and lifestyle as part of America's destiny. Any threat to that perceived freedom stokes emotional fury.

Virtually all Americans have heard of the atrocities committed in Afghanistan and Iraq. They know, intellectually, that the war against Iraq was perpetrated through lies and deception. But their emotions are somewhere else. Cult members nourish the myth that America stands for democracy for all people and that human rights is the cornerstone of US foreign policy, so they feel the community of nations should respect America and thank Americans for their contribution to a just world order. In the conflict between knowledge and emotions, ideology and myth, the latter always seems to triumph.

As the translator Konrad Kellen said, modern propaganda consists of many different kinds of truth—half truth, limited truth, and truth out of context—and that it aims to intensify existing trends. This is exactly what George W. Bush was doing when he exhorted the graduating class at Concordia University in Wisconsin to "promote 'a culture of life' in America as part of a lifetime commitment to serve the weak, the vulnerable, and 'the most easily forgotten.'" He extolled the virtues of America and justified the Iraq war: "Where there is tyranny, oppression and gathering danger to mankind, America works and sacrifices for peace and freedom. The liberty we prize is not America's gift to the world; it is the almighty God's gift to all humanity."[6]

That is how granfallooners in the Cult of Pseudo Patriotism like to be stroked. God is on our side, says the leader. Granfalloons are easy-to-start propaganda devices. Once started the members strive for a social identity by strictly following the bidding of the cult leaders, but the resulting convoluted view of what goes on in government and the world creates a false social identity for cult members. Granfalloons quickly develop "out" groups on which to blame problems – "we" have the correct answer and "they" are the evil ones. When faced with the lies that got us into the war on Iraq, granfallooners quickly justify that war by emphasizing the evils Saddam Hussein wrought. Never mind international law, never mind the atrocities and horrors the US invasion created, never mind the disdain in which our former allies now view us, the important thing is that we got rid of Saddam. The Iraqi people are now better off, they say. The rules of the granfalloon are that members believe America did the right thing.

It is the Cult of Pseudo Patriotism that today allows America to be steered down the path of world domination, preëmptive force, international criminal atrocities and *Pax Americana*. Yet the granfallooners in that cult are ordinary people who love their family and want a decent way of life. They merely suffer from a distorted concept of patriotism and rely too much on the delusion that America's leadership is always just. They are literally chasing a myth and the solution is not an easy one. Serious reëvaluation, introspection and prayer are called for. Sincere criticism of the road America is now traveling is warranted. To facilitate an opening of minds and constructive communication on *all sides* of the political-religious spectrum, Mohandas K. Gandhi suggests:

It is a bad habit to say that another man's thoughts are bad and ours only are good and that those holding different views from ours are the enemies of the country.[7]

Rather than Kurt Vonnegut's granfalloon who as an apparent team is "meaningless in terms of the ways God gets things done," we who take our spiritual feelings seriously, whatever our religion, should contemplate the ways God gets things done.

Manufacturing Consent Through a Rationalization Trap

According to Webster, rationalize means to "devise superficially rational, or plausible, explanations or excuses for (one's acts, beliefs or desires), usually without being aware that these are not the real motives." This tendency to rationalize can be manipulated by the clever propagandist. As we have noted, democracy is an ideology – an intellectual ideal which may or may not hold up in practice. Intellectual perceptions are not good at motivating people to action. Emotion is the powerful motivator. Propaganda adds the emotional spin to sustain the mythical momentum on people's emotions to stimulate action.

There are many examples of what stimulated support for World War II. Songs are good motivators such as "Remember Pearl Harbor" and "Praise the Lord and Pass the Ammunition." Others followed: "There's a Star Spangled Banner Waving Somewhere," "Johnny Got a Zero," "Coming in on a Wing and a Prayer," "The Ballad of Roger Young," among others. They all provoked pseudo patriotic feelings and strengthened the granfalloon.

Then came the movies with their powerful visibility to glamorized the war and stimulate emotions – *From Here to Eternity, South Pacific, Midway, The Battle of the Bulge, Mr. Roberts, G.I. Joe,* and over forty more. From the Korean War came *The Bridges of Toko Ri, Battle Circus, Bamboo Prison, Men of the Fighting Lady.* Songs and movies were supplemented by posters, slogans, mottos and sensational media reporting. A Vietnam-era movie was *The Anderson Platoon* and songs like "The Battle of the Green Berets," "Yellow River" and "The Fighting Side of Me" – which inspired the slogan "America! Love it or Leave it."

> Yeah, walkin' on the fightin' side of me.
> Runnin' down the way of life,
> Our fightin' men have fought and died to keep.
> If you don't love it, leave it:[8]

That still-popular slogan does not ask logical questions or seek germane answers. It does not provoke constructive criticism of a straying government or look for meaningful dialogue that could make democracy stronger. In short, it does not define that "way of life" our soldiers and sailors thought they were fighting to preserve. Such simplified thinking does not encourage opposing viewpoints – but it does fuel emotions to justify the brute, militant solution. That is the rationalization trap.

A similar slogan, "My Country, Right or Wrong!" was even more irrational. But it is a concise description of pseudo patriotism for it confounds the distinction between country and government. Is it right to *not* question wrong behavior? Over 300 American youth were dying in Vietnam each week. Were they dying for a just cause? Should we have known for sure? Most of us didn't ask those questions until the body count got too high and personal grief surpassed pseudo patriotic emotions. The Vietnam War is now recognized as a political-moral debacle. Try as we might to make it seem otherwise, it is not a glorious feeling to have supported that war.

Desert Storm, the first Gulf War, brought the taste of blood again to American lips. Flag manufacturers hit a bonanza as the pseudo patriotic fervor rose. The slogan from that round of violence was "Support Our Troops." During World War II it was "Support Our Boys," which was synonymous with getting behind the war effort. The Desert Storm version was designed for the same purpose.

So what should be our reaction to such slogans? We cannot dismiss supporting our young people who are caught in the morass, but most of us have a difficult time rationalizing support for the killing in war, the atrocities committed on prisoners, the indiscriminate bombing of cities and mosques, and the shooting of civilian families. How cam we express our objections without putting down our youth in battle fatigues? An advice column in the *San Jose Mercury News* says the issues are acts, not thoughts. "Support Our Troops" is an ambiguity used to move our sympathetic thoughts to sympathetic action. "The right to urge your government toward what you consider wise policies (current or future ones) should not be inhibited by calls for national unity."[9]

Now we have the War on Terror, and the subsequent wars in Afghanistan and Iraq. Flag manufacturers are again back in business. Old slogans have been resuscitated and an ancient one resurfaced—"United We Stand"—which goes back to the birth of our nation and the 1768 patriotic ballad by John Dickinson, *The Liberty Song*. The fourth verse goes:

Then join hand in hand, brave Americans all,
By *uniting we stand*, by dividing we fall;
In so righteous a course let us hope to succeed,
For heaven approves of each generous deed.

That motto reappeared during the Civil War as a rallying cry for the Union Army. The early 20th century labor unions adopted it to call for solidarity. In 1942 the motto was used to kick off the World War II war bond campaign. "United We Stand" is a powerful cultural stereotype that worked well in the emotional aftermath of 9/11, providing security as a collective belief. Old stereotypes are easy to understand and cling to, helping people identify themselves behind a cause in a manner they did not have before the crisis.

Many words symbolizing ideologies can be used in patriotic jargon. I will discuss two—*Freedom* and *Patriot*—and will italicize these buzz words wherever they're used in a quotation.

Freedom brings to mind a familiar stereotype dear to all Americans, reminding us of something good, something that should be and that is part of our heritage. It is an ideology. The war in Afghanistan is called "Operation Enduring *Freedom*" and the Iraq fighting is "Operation Iraqi *Freedom*." Wars are invariably categorized as a fight for freedom. When Vice President Dick Cheney spoke to the World Economic Forum in January 2004, he warned that "the world continues to face the unremitting threat from a sophisticated global network of terrorists opposed to the values of *freedom* and openness." The headline about Cheney's speech was "Spread of *Freedom* Needed to Combat Terrorism, Cheney Says."[10] The word is used generously to connote the good – our team. There is no argument that terrorism must be stopped, but conjuring up ideologies in a misleading manner while military carnage continues unabated only inflames more people to terrorist activities. Propaganda is the antithesis to a solution.

Another example is titled "Bush Says US Has Responsibility to Lead Fight for *Freedom*." The introductory paragraph tells us Bush "said much of his foreign policy is based on his belief that America has a mission to promote *freedom* around the world." The news release quotes Bush as telling the country's governors: "A lot of my foreign policy is driven by the fact that I truly believe that *freedom* is a gift from the Almighty to every person, and that America has a responsibility to take a lead in the world, to help people be free."[11] In that speech freedom is not only an ideology but a mandate from God. It is hard for the propagandee not to go along with this idea.

The word "Patriot" has also wiggled its way to the forefront since 9/11. First was the *Patriot* Act – which sounds like the right way to go. In the emotional wake of that attack Americans couldn't allow the terrorists to throw down the gauntlet with impunity. The *Patriot* Act was indeed needed. Never mind that it restricted our freedom, we have sacrificed

America in Peril

before. Never mind that it upset human rights and due process of law; we couldn't take a chance terrorists might slip through the cracks. So the *Patriot* Act was eagerly accepted—at least by those who weren't detained or prosecuted under its authority.

To keep the rationalization trap active, and sustain the emotions of 9/11, Bush designated September 11th as *Patriot* Day. At the second annual observance of *Patriot* Day in 2003, Defense Secretary Rumsfeld said:

> A *patriot* is one who loves his land, prizes its principles and cherishes its creed. A *patriot* so reveres the ideals of his home country that he is willing to lay down his life that those ideals endure. Throughout our history, from the earliest days of our nation up to the present time, America has been blessed with *patriots*, men and women willing to give of themselves that this nation, and the *freedom* upon which it was founded, might live.[12]

Wow! Those words are appealing. But when placed against the backdrop of how the Bush administration has administered our domestic and foreign affairs and alienated the world community, those words are hypocritical. Yet they motivated the listeners to tout themselves as "patriots" and rationalize their support for the present government—the rationalization trap in its most profound sense.

In 2002 an organization called "Together for *Freedom*" helped the Pentagon put on a public relations webcast. An April Pentagon news release titled "Service members to discuss *Patriotism* and *Freedom*," said: "The Department of Defense will participate in a nationwide discussion about *patriotism* and *freedom* through a webcast...broadcast from Bertie Backus Middle School in Washington, DC." The webcast was broadcast on April 30th through satellite TV to 14 participating middle schools located in California, Michigan, Illinois, Florida, Texas, Maryland, Virginia, New Jersey, Pennsylvania and Washington DC. But all schools across the country and Defense Department schools overseas could tune in and hear Rumsfeld say: "I commend the Together for *Freedom* organization for initiating a national dialogue about the meaning of *freedom* and the importance of *patriotism*, and increasing support for our troops at home and abroad."[13]

What is this organization "Together for *Freedom*?" Its website seems no longer to be available, but it was ostensibly a "non-profit organization dedicated to promoting *patriotic* initiatives so that America's strength and spirit will endure."[14] And who was one of the cofounders of this organization? None other than Doro Bush Koch, the president's sister – and the organization bears all the characteristics of a front organization for the neoconservative agenda – in this case to target youth for military service.

When ABC television reporter Cokie Roberts moderated this "Celebration of *Patriotism*" webcast she announced: "We're going to be talking to thousands of middle school students simultaneously about *freedom* and *patriotism* and what it means to kids today." B1B bomber pilot and panelist, Lt. Kathryn M. Gries, told the children, "Every opportunity is available to women on the war fighting team." When asked what *freedom* meant to her, she responded: "*Freedom* means you can choose what you want to do," adding she was able to become a bomber pilot because of *freedom* in America.[15] Does that make sense to you?

The panel also had representation from the army, navy, marines and others willing to present the Pentagon's message. Each one hyped the military and disparaging the conditions "over there." After the webcast, "Together for *Freedom*" cofounder Doro Bush Koch explained they selected middle school children because "they're just the right age before they're making important decisions and choices in their lives. So we thought it was a good time to educate them on *patriotism*."

Yes, the middle school years are a very impressionable age. There is no question on how their thoughts were being guided by that propaganda. Taking advantage of vulnerable young kids in this heavy-handed manner is the most vicious application of the rationalization trap. All these songs, mottos, slogans, posters, patriotic jargon and stereotyped words are aimed at one goal – to stir up strong emotions to perpetuate the myth of pseudo patriotism. They provide the necessary, and usually limited, information for a person to rationalize compliance with the administration's corrupt policies.

Another form of propaganda is just as devious – which comes at us through the media.

Covert Propaganda – Prepackaged News Stories

According to the GAO, seven federal departments account for most of the spending on public relations and advertising.[16] Between October 2002 and March 2005 they spent $1.62 billion for 343 media contracts. The GAO report did not say how many were prepackaged news stories.

Prepackaged news stories, also called Video News Releases (VNRs), are prepared on tape or disk with both audio and visual elements prepared by a PR firm and given to television news agencies. They usually contain three parts: The first consists of video clips called the "B-roll" with the information needed for a news agency to put together its own report. The second is a collection of statements and facts about the VNR supplier that helps the news agency with its own report. The third part is a prepackaged news story or "story package" – usually a 90-second segment including scripts for the station's news anchor to lead into and conclude the story. Since prepackaged news stories have all the characteristics of a regular news clip prepared by real reporters, the stations tend to use them instead of preparing their own. The only problem is they look like independent reporting whereas they are actually prepared propaganda.

VNRs with story packages have become popular in the corporate world because they are almost always used as-is, so corporations and their PR agencies can tailor these stories to suit corporate needs. For a private corporation this is deceptive and ethically unsound, but not illegal. Journalism scholars "began questioning the effect of this third-party material" because of the false implication "that news was derived from a neutral source."[17]

Government Restrictions on Covert Propaganda

It is another matter for the government to prepare VNRs with prepackaged news stories that do not tell the viewer—either in the story or the anchor scripts—what agency produced it. US Comptroller Gen. David M. Walker explained:

> The purpose of this letter is to remind agencies of the constraints imposed by the publicity or propaganda prohibition on the use of prepackaged news stories... prepackaged news stories can be utilized without violating the law, so long as there is clear disclosure to the television viewing audience that this material was prepared by or in coöperation with the government department or agency....The current publicity or propaganda prohibition states: "No part of any appropriation contained in this or any other act shall be used for publicity or propaganda purposes *within the United States not heretofore authorized by Congress*" [emphasis added]. Consolidated Appropriations Act, 2005, Pub. L. No. 108-447, div. G, title II, §624, 118 Stat. 2809, 3278 (Dec. 8, 2004). (The language of the prohibition has remained virtually unchanged since 1951.)[18]

This same report explained the two exceptions allowing appropriated funds to be used for publicity and propaganda: (1) broadcasting outside the US, as done by the Voice of America, and (2) if authorized by Congress. The first is not applicable and the latter was deemed irrelevant by the GAO in the cases discussed below, although the culpable agencies tried to raise that excuse.

Hyping Bush's Medicare Prescription Drug Plan

During the campaign to promote Bush's Medicare Prescription Drug, Improvement and Modernization Act of 2003, the Center for Medicare and Medicaid Services (CMS) sent out flyers and prepackaged news releases. CMS is part of the Department of Health and Human Services (HHS) and the flyers were legal because they showed CMS issued them. The prepackaged news stories were another matter. GAO claimed CMS's "use of appropriated funds to pay for the production and distribution of prepackaged news stories that were not attributed to CMS violated the restriction on using appropriated funds for publicity and propaganda purposes.... In neither the story packages nor the lead-in anchor scripts did HHS or CMS identify itself to the television-viewing audience as the source of the news report. Further, in each news report, the content was attributed to an individual purporting to be a reporter but actually hired by a HHS contractor."[19]

Using fake reporters posing as a independent journalists adds to the deception. The HHS contractor was Ketchum, Inc. and according to their contract, the firm was hired to assist with a "full range of social marketing activities to plan, develop, produce, and deliver consumer-based communications programs, strategies, and materials" – in other words, to sell Bush's plan to the public.

Ketchum subcontracted to Home Front Communications, a public relations firm in the DC area that specializes in making VNRs. Three VNR packages were reviewed and approved by HHS and CMS – two in English and one in Spanish. The English packages had someone called Karen Ryan as moderator. She runs her own PR firm but she is not an independent reporter in the CMS story packages. The Spanish-language script was narrated by Alberto Garcia.

The news anchor's lead-in script implied an independent reporter is narrating. In one script the lead-in said "Karen Ryan explains." The other lead-in notes "There have been a lot of questions" about the new Medicare prescription drug plan and "Karen Ryan helps sort through the details." The Spanish-language anchor lead-in is the same except Alberto Garcia "helps sort through the details." All three story packages ended with "In Washington, I'm Karen Ryan reporting," or "I'm Alberto

Garcia reporting."

CMS contended such misleading story packages are "standard practice in the news sector" and a "well-established and well-understood use of a common news and public affairs practice." But GAO replied "our analysis of the proper use of appropriated funds is not based upon the norms in the public relations and media industry" and claimed the story packages prepared by CMS "raise concerns as to whether they constitute 'covert' propaganda.... The critical element of covert propaganda is the concealment of the agencies role in sponsoring the materials.... [T]he target audience could not ascertain the information source." The 41 million Medicare beneficiaries—the target audience—did not know "Karen Ryan and Alberto Garcia were paid with HHS funds for their work." GAO concluded: "Because CMS did not identify itself as the source of the news report, the story packages...violate the publicity or propaganda prohibition."

Illegal Means to Promote Bush's Anti-Drug Program

The GAO was also asked to investigate VNRs produced and distributed during 2002 to 2004 by the White House's Office of National Drug Control Policy (ONDCP) because it was thought ONDCP may have used appropriated funds for covert propaganda to promote the administration's anti-drug campaign. In January 2005 GAO reported that seven of the eight VNRs discovered contained story packages which did not identify ONDCP as the producer and distributor, so were covert propaganda.

ONDCP contracted with Fleishman-Hillard for the PR work. They in turn subcontracted Gourvitz Communications and Harbour Media to produce and distribute the VNRs. The seven illegal story packages included narration by unseen "announcers" variously identified as Mike Morris, Karen Ryan (again) and Jerry Cosini. The lead-ins contained phrases as "Mike Morris has the story" and "Mike Morris has more." None of the narrators were affiliated with a news agency at the time the story packages were produced and distributed.

GAO concluded "ONDCP's prepackaged news stories violate the ban on covert propaganda.... ONDCP designed and executed its prepackaged news stories to be indistinguishable from news stories produced by private sector television news organizations." Also, "ONDCP's prepackaged news stories reached more than 22 million households without disclosing... the products they were watching, which 'reported' on the activities of a government agency, were actually prepared by that government agency.... This is the essence of the 'covert propaganda' violation."[20]

Comptroller Gen. Walker became so concerned about these blatant violations he wrote a letter to all federal departments and agencies calling attention to the prohibitions on covert propaganda: "It is not enough that the contents of an agencies communication may be unobjectionable. Neither is it enough for the agency to identify itself [only] to the broadcasting organization."[21]

The Bush administration bristled. Joshua B. Bolton, then director of the White House Office of Management and Budget, disagreed with GAO's interpretation and was backed up by Steven G. Bradbury, then the Justice Department's principal deputy assistant attorney general. They contended it is the Justice Department's Office of Legal Council, not the GAO, which makes legal interpretations that are binding on federal agencies – which is bureaucracy in its most blatant form. Who can better convey the intention of Congress in legislation passed by Congress than the investigative arm of Congress? The Justice Department has a reputation for finding interpretations that meet a predetermined agenda.

To illustrate his point, Bradbury wrote: "Our view is that prohibition does not apply where there is no advocacy of a particular viewpoint, and therefore it does not apply to the legitimate provision of information concerning the programs administered by the agency." But Walker denounced that disclaimer as both contrary to appropriations law and unethical: "This is more than a legal issue. It's also an ethical issue and involves important good government principles, namely the need for openness in connection with government activities and expenditures. We should not be seeking to do what's arguably legal. We should be doing what's right." Nevertheless, White House spokesperson Scott McClellan repeated that same day: "As long as they are providing factual information, it's OK."[22]

Summary on Prepackaged News Stories

These 90-second government-produced prepackaged news stories are more common than what meets the eye – and some were clearly not just providing factual information. One produced by the State Department about the fall of Baghdad has an Iraqi-American saying "Thank you, Bush. Thank you, USA." A spot touting "another success" in the "drive to strengthen aviation security" prepared by the Transportation Security Administration, has a PR expert posing as a reporter calling the drive "one of the most remarkable campaigns in aviation history."[23] A third story package was put together by the Agricultural Department to tell how the administration is determined to open markets for American farmers (i.e. corporate farmers).

Other cases have come to light. The Environmental Protection Agency paid Cable TV's Weather Channel to produce several two-minute news stories on ozone depletion and ultraviolet radiation, but the stories did not reveal they were paid for by the government. The Department of Education also got into the act by using "appropriated funds to produce and distribute a prepackaged news story regarding programs under the No Child Left Behind Act of 2003."[24]

At least 20 federal agencies have produced and distributed hundreds of prepackaged news stories over the past four years and "many were subsequently broadcast to local stations across the country without any acknowledgment of the government's role in their production." In some cases, it is fair to report, the culpability is with the news stations which have on occasions edited out reference to the government, but in "most cases, the 'reporters' are careful not to state in the segment that they work for the government."[25] Still, the Bush administration is determined to continue using prepackaged news stories without revealing they are government-produced.

Prepackaged news stories and fake reporters are not the only place where the Bush administration is using deception. There is also the practice of embedding reporters in the media.

Covert Propaganda – Embedding Media Pundits

Paying sympathetic reporters to clandestinely champion specific items on the Bush administration agenda is another form of illegal covert propaganda. Four such cases have come to public attention.

Armstrong Williams on Education

Armstrong Williams, a conservative Black commentator, was paid $240,000 by the Department of Education to provide favorable publicity for Bush's No Child Left Behind bill. His contract was awarded through Ketchum, Inc. – the same firm that produced story packages featuring Karen Ryan and Alberto Garcia. Williams is a syndicated newspaper columnist as well as a television and radio show host, so he was also being paid by Sinclair Broadcasting Co. which is well known for championing the Bush administration's agenda. In May 2004 it refused to air "Nightline" when Ted Koppel read the names of all the US soldiers killed in Iraq. It also presented a skewed anti-Kerry documentary on the eve of the 2004 presidential election.

One of Williams' guests was then-Education Secretary Rod Paige, also Black, whom Williams interviewed flattering Bush's education program without revealing to the audience he was being paid to do just that. Later Williams had a similar interview with Vice President Dick Cheney, to whom he pitched softball questions such as why the media was always trying to tie him to Haliburton.

When the scam was discovered, Sinclair Broadcasting claimed ignorance about Williams being paid by the government. Williams admitted to bad judgment but said he wouldn't give the money back, claiming his business ethics were not in question and he was comfortable with the facts he delivered. The FCC chairperson, Michael Powell, ordered an investigation in early 2005. Although the FCC did not charge Williams with wrongdoing, it did issue letters to 77 TV stations warning them of license revocation if they failed to reveal the sources of VNRs. A Justice Department investigation did not determine Williams was guilty of wrongdoing, but did fine him $34,000 for not fulfilling all of his contractual requirements.

The spotlight focused on the Department of Education, but an internal investigation "found no evidence of unlawful or unethical behavior in connection with Mr. Williams's contract but criticized top department officials for 'poor management decisions' and lax oversight."[26] The Insp. Gen.'s report didn't mention covert propaganda or Williams' hyping Bush's signature education initiative. Neither was there any consultation with those in the Education Department who were critical of hiring Williams.

GAO was not so easily swayed and reported that because the Department of Education "took no steps to assure that its role in sponsoring that commentary was disclosed to the targeted audiences," its role "constituted covert propaganda in violation of the fiscal year 2004 publicity and propaganda prohibition." In addition, because the department used funds appropriated for another purpose it "also violated the Antideficiency Act, 31 U.S.C. 1341."[27]

Maggie Gallagher Upholding Bush's Marriage Initiative

Another journalist was found on the Bush payroll the same month the Armstrong Williams scam surfaced. Maggie Gallagher, columnist for Universal Press Syndicate, in 2002 wrote approvingly on Bush's marriage initiative, saying it "would emphasize the importance of marriage to poor couples [and] educate teens on the value of delaying childbearing until marriage."[28] She called Bush a "genius" at playing "daddy" to the nation: "Mommies feel pain. Daddies give you confidence that you can ignore the pain and get on with life."[29] That's fine, except she didn't tell her readers she had a $21,000 contract with the HHS to promote that initiative and make the Bush administration look good.

Gallagher claims her relationship with HHS was along the lines of an academic doing independent research. Admitting she regretted not disclosing the government contract, she implied she forgot and was sorry. *National Review Online* editor Jonah Goldberg retorted: "She's doing better than I thought if she doesn't remember getting paid $21,000.... In the wake of the Armstrong story, she showed poor judgment by not coming clean about this."[30]

In an early January press conference Bush disclaimed any knowledge of payments to Armstrong and Gallagher, but did acknowledge inadvertent breaches of ethics by his administration and ordered that hiring journalists to push administrative agendas would cease. This is something he still has not done with regards to VNRs. Bush avoided the question of whether there were any more such contracts but his press secretary, Scott McClellan, said the White House was not aware of any. That statement wasn't quite accurate.

Michael McManus Also Upholds the Marriage Initiative

The day after Bush admonished his cabinet secretaries not to hire journalists and commentators to create a favorable image for the administration's political agenda, another well-known conservative journalist surfaced on the government payroll. Michael McManus, author of the syndicated column "Ethics & Religion" which appears in some 50 newspapers, was paid about $10,000 to promote Bush's marriage initiative. HHS contracted

Ketchum, Inc. who in turn subcontracted McManus who then plugged the ideological agenda in his columns without telling his readers he was paid to do just that.

HHS, of course, says it was implementing Bush's order to stop hiring journalists to further the administration's programs. Dr. Wade Horn, assistant secretary for children and families, insisted his department didn't pay people like Gallagher and McManus to write those articles—but rather because they are marriage experts. He said it's a complicated world and people with expertise also write columns. Such dissembling didn't fly for attorney Tim Casey who called Gallagher and McManus "ideological sympathizers who propagandize," and identified them as members of the "extreme religious right."[31]

Neither were Democrats on the House Committee on Government Reform taken in by Horn's excuses. They wrote a letter to Bush demanding he immediately provide a listing of all past and current instances of employing covert propaganda of any type. They received no reply.

James Guckert and Gannongate

White House news conferences are tricky affairs. An embarrassing question from a reporter can kick off all kinds of undesirable publicity. Even when reporters are carefully screened and their number limited, it is neither politically possible nor desirable to have all attendees look like a partisan assemblage. Therefore some reporters critical of government are admitted. Consequently, it is helpful to the administration's public image to have a strongly supportive person in the press corps who can be called upon to defuse tense situations. Jeff Gannon was one such person—at least that is the name he was registered under. Early in 2005 it was discovered he was a plant. His real name is James D. Guckert and he claimed to be a reporter for TalonNews.com, a website which touted the delivery of accurate and unbiased news. But Talon News appears closely connected with GOPUSA which has a stated purpose of bringing the conservative message to America.

Gannon/Guckert claimed Talon News was separate and independent from GOPUSA, yet both GOPUSA and Talon News are operated by Texas Republican activist Bobby Eberle, a Republican delegate in 2000. Eberle created Talon News in April 2003 because he feared GOPUSA appeared to have political bias. Talon News seemed to have a less political bias than GOPUSA because it boasted a more impartial mission statement. That may influence some people, but since both were owned by the same person, it didn't inspire much confidence of Talon News' unbiased state. Then there's that slight problem – Gannon/Guckert was first admitted to the White House press corps in February 2003 – before Talon News was created – when he was still working for the blatantly partisan GOPUSA. The thought occurred that Talon News might have been created to give him cover.

Besides, Talon News and GOPUSA hardly qualify as news organizations – which is why Gannon/Guckert couldn't obtain Capitol Hill press credentials – a prerequisite for a permanent White House pass. Refused status because his news organization failed to qualify, he entered time and again for two years by obtaining temporary one-day passes which are usually reserved for occasional out-of-town reporters. He also attended invitation-only White House Christmas parties for the press in 2003 and 2004. When White House Press Secretary Scott McClellan was asked how a GOPUSA reporter was cleared to enter the briefings, he replied: "The staff assistant went to verify that the news organization existed."[32]

With today's level of security, especially in the nation's capital, one wonders how a bogus reporter can walk around the White House with credentials bearing a phony name. Gannon/ Guckert managed to do this for two years. Guckert made a ridiculous declaration that he adopted a fake name because it was easier to pronounce and remember. Veteran White House correspondent Bruce Bartlett said "If Gannon was using an alias, the White House staff had to be involved in maintaining his cover."[33]

During the 2004 presidential campaign, Gannon/Guckert laced his softball questions with phrases such as the Democrats being "divorced from reality." He also linked Democratic candidate John Kerry with Jane Fonda who made the controversial trip to Hanoi and "questioned why anyone would dispute Bush's National Guard service."[34]

Gannon/Guckert's downfall came during a January 2005 news conference when Bush selected him, over many more-experienced reporters, to pose a question – which was: "Senate Democratic leaders have painted a very bleak picture of the US economy. Harry Reid was talking about soup lines, and Hillary Clinton was talking about the economy being on the verge of collapse. Yet, in the same breath, they say that Social Security is rock solid and there's no crisis there. How are you going to work – you said you're going to reach out to these people – how are you going to work with people who seem to have divorced themselves from reality?"[35]

That leading question went out live over national TV and was picked up by bloggers on the lookout for suspicious behavior in the White House. The manner in which that question led into Bush being able to defend his unpopular Social Security initiative was not missed by critical observers who started investigating Mr. Jeff Gannon and uncovered his charade. The result was Gannongate.

Congress became concerned, especially after so much other misuse of the media for covert propaganda. Representatives John Conyers, Louise Slaughter, Bennie Thompson, Charles Rangel and Henry Waxman announced in March 2005 they had authored and sponsored a resolution of inquiry into Gannongate which would require the Justice Department and the Department of Homeland Security (which has jurisdiction over the Secret Service that screens reporters) to turn over all documentation regarding James Guckert's (a.k.a. Jeff Gannon) regular access to the White House.[36]

Representatives Slaughter and Conyers had previously and repeatedly sent requests to the White House and DHS for all records regarding Gannongate but had received no response. Slaughter announced: "We cannot allow the White House to stonewall the United States Congress and the American people on an issue of such importance. This is a matter of national security and unethical White House media manipulation." Conyers added: "We had hoped that the half dozen congressional and senate requests for information would have been sufficient.... We hope that this resolution gets to the bottom of whether any processes were abused in favoring Mr. Guckert, a fake reporter from a fake news organization."[37]

In a sardonic stonewall, DHS sent a letter saying: "Thank you for submitting your Freedom of Information/Privacy Acts (FOI/PA) requests, received by the United States Secret Service, on March 8, 2005.... We wish to inform you that a search for files responsive to your requests is being conducted. When the results of the search are known, you will be notified." This mocking reply from a lower government official to a legislative inquiry prompted Slaughter to comment that she is "deeply disappointed that the President and the White House continue to stonewall Congress and the American People by not providing any details on the nature of their relationship with this disgraced, discredited 'reporter,'" Conyers added: "It is a sad day when US Representatives have to make FOIA requests to get simple answers to important questions."[38]

Obviously, releasing the information would be more ruinous to the president's image than suspicions of foul play. Stonewalling distracts people from knowing facts that would be more damaging than what they are imagining.

★ ★ ★ ★ ★

So goes the engineering of opinion in America today. It is part of the neoconservative agenda. Another part is to put away those people who might threaten that agenda—which is the topic of the next chapter.

Notes for Chapter 7

1. Kripalani, Krishna, *All Men Are Brothers: Life and Thoughts of Mahatma Gandhi as Told in His* Own Words, (India: Navajivan Publishing House, 1960/1968), p. 153 .

2. Ellul, Jacques, *Propaganda: The Formation of Men's Attitudes*, (NY; Alfred A. Knopf, 1965).

3. Vonnegut, Kurt, *Cat's Cradle*, (NY; Delta Books, 1963), p. 90.

4. Pratkanis, Anthony R. and Elliot Aronson, *Age of Propaganda: The Everyday Use and Misuse of Persuasion*, (NY, W.H. Freeman, 2000), p. 216.

5. Ellul; op. cit., pp. 8-9.

6. Hutcheson, Ron, "Bush: US Values Support Iraq War," Knight Ridder article in the San Jose (CA) *Mercury News*, 15 May 2004.

7. Kripalani; op. cit., p. 219.

8. Haggard, Merle, "The Fighting Side of Me," 1969.

9. Cohen, Randy, "Everyday Ethics," San Jose (CA) *Mercury News*, 26 Apr 2003.

10. *Washington File*, "Spread of Freedom Needed to Combat Terrorism, Cheney Says," US State Department website, 24 Jan 2004, at http://usinfo.state.gov/

11. *Washington File*, "Bush Says US Has Responsibility to Lead Fight for Freedom," US State Department website, 23 Feb 2004, at http://usinfo.state.gov/

12. *Defense Link*, "Patriot Day Observance," US Dept of Defense, 11 Sep 2003, at http://www.defenselink.mil/

13. *Defense Link*, "Servicemembers to Discuss Patriotism and Freedom," US Dept of Defense, 24 Apr 2002, at http://www.defenselink.mil/

14. Compaq News Release; "Middle School Students to Engage in National Discussion of Patriotism Via Interactive Webcast," 1 Apr 2002 at http://www.prdomain.com/companies/c/compaq/news_releases/200204apr/pr_20020401_webcast.htm/_

15. Williams, Rudi (American Forces Press Service); "Service Members Discuss Freedom on National Webcast," dcmilitary.com, 3 May 2002 at http://www.dcmilitary.com/army/pentagram/7_17/national_news/16367-1.html/

16. They are Commerce, Defense, Health & Human Services, Homeland Security, Interior, Treasury and Veterans Affairs.

17. B-302710 – GAO decision, signed by Anthony H. Gamboa in the matter of DHHS Centers for Medicare & Medicaid SERVICES – VNR, 19 May 2004.

18. B-304272 – "Prepackaged News Stories," David M. Walker, Comptroller General of the US, letter to heads of all government departments and agencies, and others concerned, 17 Feb 2005.

19. B-302710, op. cit.

20. B-303495 – GAO decision, signed by Anthony H. Gamboa, in the matter of Office of National Drug Control Policy – VNR, 4 Jan 2005.

21. B-304272, op. cit.

22. Lee, Christopher, "Administration Rejects Ruling on PR Videos," *Washington Post*, 15 Mar 2005.

23. Barstow, David and Robin Stein, "Under Bush, A New Age of Prepackaged TV News," *NY Times*, 13 Mar 2005.

24. B-304228 – "DOE – VNR and Media Analysis," Anthony H. Gamboa letter to Senators Frank R. Lautenberg and Edward M. Kennedy, 30 Sep 2005.

25. Barstow and Stein; op, cit.

26. Kornblut, Anne E., "Inquiry Finds Radio Host's Arrangement Raised Flags," *NY Times*, 16 Apr 2005.

27. B-305368 – "DOE – Contract to Obtain Services of Armstrong Williams," Anthony Gamboa letter to Senators Frank R. Lautenberg and Edward M. Kennedy, 30 Sep 2005.

28. Boehlert, Eric, "Right-Wing Pundits: We're Not on the Bush Payroll," *Salon.com*, 27 Jan 2005.

29. Dowd, Maureen; "Love for Sale," *NY Times*, 27 Jan 2005.

30. Boehlert, "Right Wing Pundits...," op. cit.

31. Boehlert, Eric, "Third Columnist Caught with Hand in the Bush Till," *Salon.com*, 27 Jan 2005.

32. Boehlert, Eric, "Gannongate: It's Worse Than You Think," *Salon.com*, 23 Feb 2005.

33. Rich, Frank, "When Real News Debunks Fake News," *Intern'l Herald Tribune*, 19 Feb 2005.

34. Savage, Charlie and Alan Wirzbicki, "White House-Friendly Reporter Under Scrutiny," *Boston Globe*, 2 Feb 2005.

35. Boehlert, Eric, "Fake News, Fake Reporter," *Salon.com*, 10 Feb 2005.

36. These representatives were then the ranking minority members of the House Committees on Judiciary (Conyers), Rules (Slaughter), Government Reform (Waxman), Homeland Security (Thompson) and Ways and Means (Rangel).

37. Slaughter, Louise M., "Reps. Conyers, Slaughter, Thompson, Rangel and Waxman Author Resolution of Inquiry on Gannongate," Slaughter press release, 3 Mar 2005.

38. Lyerly, Kathy J., FOIA officer, US Secret Service, letter to Slaughter, 4 Apr 2005. Published in "Homeland Security Department to Provide Details on Gannon," Slaughter press release, 4 Apr 2005.

8

Farewell Due Process, *Vale Habeas Corpus*

Equal and exact justice to all men, of whatever state or persuasion, religious or political; peace, commerce, and honest friendship with all nations, entangling alliances with none.... Freedom of religion, freedom of the press, and freedom of person under the protection of habeas corpus, *and trial by juries impartially selected. These principles form the bright constellation which has gone before us, and guided our steps through an age of revolution and reformation.*   – Thomas Jefferson, *First Inaugural Address*

A writ of *habeas corpus*, commonly known as The Great Writ, dates back centuries – predating the US Constitution and even the Magna Carta of 1215. Although thought to have Anglo Saxon beginnings, its exact origin is uncertain. Today its most common use is a court order that a prisoner be told the reason for confinement. It is also used to produce evidence of the charge so this can be challenged. A.V. Dicey wrote: "The *Habeas Corpus* acts declare no principle and define no rights, but they are for practical purposes worth a hundred constitutional articles guaranteeing individual liberty."[1]

Article I, Section 9 of the US Constitution reads: "The privilege of the writ of *habeas corpus* shall not be suspended, unless when in cases of rebellion or invasion the public safety may require it." Then came 9/11.

The Penttbom Roundup: Mass Arrests in the US

Fifteen of the 19 suicide hijackers on 9/11 were from Saudi Arabia. Yet immediately after the attack 140 Saudi nationals – including relatives of Osama bin Laden – were hustled out of the US on a special flight. That rushed evacuation, certainly approved by the White House, had private planes flying individuals from ten different cities to collect them for the evacuation flight while most aircraft were still grounded. The FBI allegedly interviewed bin Laden's relatives at the airport to assure no connection with 9/11. Dale Watson, former head of counterterrorism at the FBI, said there were no serious interviews or interrogation of the Saudis. Senator Schumer said it was too soon to know what questions to ask and that it was just another example of coddling the Saudis. Immediately after the Saudis had been safely packed out of the country, a massive sweep began for those of Arab ancestry, the Muslim faith or who were just plain suspicious.

By November 5, 2001, the government announced 1,182 people had been picked up as part of the Pentagon/Twin Towers Bombing (PENTTBOM) investigation – said to be the largest criminal investigation in US history. A senior law enforcement official said "just 10-15 of the detainees are suspected as terrorist sympathizers, and the government has yet to find evidence indicating that any of them had knowledge of the Sept. 11 attacks or acted as accomplices."[2] Using the Bush administration's unique interpretations of the Bill of Rights and international law, these unfortunate victims were held indefinitely without charges, without access to a lawyer, family or a court hearing. The government was also preparing to interview some 5,000 young Middle-Eastern men visiting America on temporary visas.

Three days later Ashcroft's Justice Department said it would no longer publicize the number of people being detained. That was followed by Bush's November 13th Military Order creating military commissions (discussed later). FOIA requests for a list of those jailed, filed by a coalition of 20 Arab-American and human rights organizations, were turned down by the FBI. Even members of Congress had no success.

Amnesty International's March 2002 report stated: "These detentions have been surrounded by extreme secrecy, which creates the potential for abuse. Our research confirms that basic rights have been violated, including the rights of humane treatment, to be informed of the reasons for detention, to have prompt access to a lawyer, to be able to challenge the lawfulness of the detention and to be presumed innocent until proven otherwise." It referred to claims "of cruel treatment including prolonged solitary confinement, heavy shackling of detainees during visits or when they are taken to court, and lack of adequate exercise."[3]

Alien "Special Interest" Detainees

"Special interest" refers to an alien detainee not yet cleared of terrorist connections by the FBI. On October 26, 2001, Ashcroft signed a rule allowing the government to keep such prisoners even after an immigration court orders deportation or release. It says the Immigration and Naturalization Service (INS) simply has to appeal the judge's order to the Board of Immigration Appeals. If the board sides with the judge, the INS can still hold the "special interest" immigrant by appealing directly to the attorney general. The rule went into effect on the 29th but was not entered in the *Federal Register* until the 30th, thus eliminating the normal comment time before becoming effective. Cleveland immigration lawyer David W. Leopold said: "With this rule change the government can lock someone up on very little or even no evidence and throw away the key until they decide to let him go.... [I]t just takes immigration judges out of the mix, bypassing their role entirely."[4]

Immigration judges are under the executive branch, not the judicial branch, and the immigration courts they preside over, as well as the Board of Immigration Appeals, come under the director of the Executive Office for Immigration Review. At that time – before the Department of Homeland Security existed – the director of that executive office reported to the attorney general, as did the INS. There were no checks and balances. The attorney general ruled all.

This "special interest" rule was used to the ultimate. Hundreds of foreigners were detained for trivial immigration violations normally resolved with paperwork and held for such things as having too much cash, possessing box cutters (the weapon reportedly used by the 9/11 hijackers) or inquiring about airplanes and flight training. Of the 1,182 from the original dragnet, Ashcroft said 548 were aliens held for immigration violations, but he declined to release names. They were from 47 different countries including 16 from Saudi Arabia. Many were held for minor visa violations – most for overstaying the time limit. Even those who admitted violations and agreed to leave the country remained in jail if they were of "special interest."

By mid-January 2002, the number detained for immigration violations, traffic stops or merely because of a neighbor's suspicion had risen to some 725. A month later the Justice Department admitted 327 – mostly Arab or Muslim – including 87 who had been ordered deported but still held as "special interest" detainees were still in custody. By June 2002 government figures showed 74 being held on immigration charges. Still unknown is how many of the original number had been secretly deported or how many released.

We do know of one unusual airlift arranged by the Justice Department on 26 June 2002. A Portuguese jet took off from Louisiana with 131 deported Pakistani detainees who had been held for months. 170 were originally to have been on board but 39 remained detained because of "special interests." None appeared to have a link to terrorism although 35 had criminal charges against them. About 300 Pakistanis were detained after 9/11. A secret program was started in early 2002 to deport small numbers of Pakistanis on commercial jets but that bogged down in May. Then this airlift of a larger number was chartered. Glenn A. Fine, inspector general for the Justice Department, reported in June 2003 that "we found significant problems in the way the detainees were handled," and called the conditions under which 762 special interest detainees were confined "unduly harsh."[5] That number probably includes only those at the federal Manhattan Detention Center in Brooklyn and Passaic County Jail in Paterson, NJ.

The statutory requirement to charge detainees within 72 hours or release them stretched to a hold-until-cleared policy for months without bail. The FBI was averaging 80 days to run clearance checks. Fine's "deplorable conditions" included restrictive and inconsistent telephone access, seriously limiting detainees' ability to obtain legal help, falsely telling family members and lawyers the detainee was not at a particular facility, physical and verbal abuse, cells illuminated 24 hours a day, being locked in cells 23 hours a day, put in handcuffs and leg irons when moved, and failing to be properly informed on the process for filing complaints.

Fine made 21 suggestions for improvement. Ashcroft did not back down. One congressional official stated: "What [Fine's] report does is it gives a semblance of an independent review criticizing the department over what all the Democrats and civil rights groups have been complaining about. But it doesn't go so far as to say that Ashcroft broke the law."[6]

In October 2006, Ali Partovi still sat in Arizona's Florence Correctional Center. Immigration officials insisted he was the last of the "special interest" aliens held after 9/11. Originally arrested on Guam in the fall of 2001 for trying to enter the US on a fake passport so he could seek asylum, he pleaded guilty and was sentenced to 175 days in jail. When he completed that sentence he was turned over to Homeland Security as a "special interest" case. Up until then Partovi had filed seven lawsuits demanding restitution for civil rights abuses. DHS spokesperson Dean Boyd said they would like to release Partovi if he would return to Iran—the country from which he was originally seeking asylum. Understandably, he refused. Although not a suspect or charged with a crime, and not considered dangerous, he remained in jail after five years. This is America?

Court Rulings Regarding Secret Detentions and Hearings

Ten days after 9/11, chief immigration judge Michael J. Creppy sent a memo to all judges saying the attorney general had implemented additional security procedures for "special interest" cases in immigration courts. Known as the Creppy Memo, it said: "These procedures require us to hold the hearings individually, to close the hearing to the public, and to avoid discussing the case or otherwise disclosing any information about the case to anyone outside the Immigration Court."[7] Civil rights and media groups filed lawsuits to open "special interest" hearings to the public and press. Here are summaries of a few prominent cases:

North Jersey Media Group et al v. Ashcroft et al. In March 2002, State Superior Court Judge Arthur N. D'Italia in New Jersey called secret detentions odious to a democratic society and ruled state law requires the names of hundreds of people detained in state jails be released. The Justice Department was unimpressed. In April INS commissioner James Ziglar signed an unusual order barring state and local governments from releasing names of those detained in connection with 9/11.

Ziglar's order was challenged. Federal District Judge John Bissell in New Jersey ruled on May 29th that it was unconstitutional to hold immigration hearings in secret. He acknowledged some hearings should be closed but said they can be decided on a case-for-case basis and elaborated that continuing to bar the public and press from all hearings without justification "presents a clear case of irreparable harm to a right protected by the First Amendment."[8] Bissell added that closing the hearings was ineffective anyway because detainees and their lawyers were not prohibited from discussing the proceedings publicly.

On June 28 the US Supreme Court ruled that closed immigration hearings could continue while the government appealed all the lower court decisions against secrecy. This ruling did not decide the merits of the case, it was just a temporary stay during appeal. In the meantime, the number of detainees on immigration charges had been reduced to 74 people, all but 18 represented by lawyers. By October a three-judge panel (all conservative Reagan appointees) of the 4th US Circuit Court of Appeals unanimously reversed Bissell's decision and upheld the government's right to conduct immigration hearings in secret. The court's opinion stated that "unlike criminal or civil hearings, there was no history of immigration hearings being open to the public."[9] The New Jersey Media group requested a hearing before the entire 3rd Circuit but it was denied. The US Supreme Court declined to review the case in 2003, letting the circuit court decision stand.

Detroit Free Press et al v. John Ashcroft et al. Unlike the New Jersey case which sought to open all "special interest" hearings, this lawsuit focused on one detainee—Rabih Haddad from Lebanon. Federal District Judge Nancy Edmunds of Detroit ruled in April 2002 immigration hearings conducted in secret were unconstitutional:

> The subtext is all about the government's right to suspend certain personal liberties in the pursuit of national security. It is important for the public, particularly individuals who feel that they are being targeted by the government as a result of the terrorist attacks of Sept. 11, to know that even during these sensitive times the government is adhering to immigration procedures and respecting individuals' rights.[10]

A three-judge panel (Carter and Clinton appointees in the majority opinion—the third a temporary district judge) of the Sixth US Circuit Court of Appeals on August 26 upheld the lower court's decision and struck down the Creppy Memo for the Haddad case. It used the often quoted decision that democracies die behind closed doors. The government requested a hearing before the entire Sixth Circuit. Judge Edmunds ruled on September 17 that Haddad must have a bail-bond hearing before a different immigration judge or be released. That took place October 1 with many supporters and the press present. The judge closed the hearing despite Edmunds' ruling. Bail was denied and later that month asylum was denied. In January 2003 the Sixth Circuit denied the government's request that the entire court review its previous decision. On July 14 Haddad was taken from jail and flown back to Lebanon. The ruling on appeal was only regarding Haddad and not a binding precedent.

Center for National Security Studies, et al v. Department of Justice. This FOIA lawsuit filed by about 24 groups – including ACLU, the American-Arab Anti-Discrimination Committee and Human Rights Watch – resulted in another adverse ruling for the government. In August 2002 US District Court Judge Gladys Kessler in Washington DC gave the Justice Department 15 days to release the names of those detained in the post-9/11 terrorist investigation. (Later she put a stay on the order pending government appeal.) She opined: "Secret arrests are... profoundly antithetical to the bedrock values that characterize a free and open" society, reminding the executive branch of its responsibility to guarantee people's security and said "the first priority of the judicial branch must be to ensure that the government always operates within the statutory and constitutional constraints which distinguish a democracy from a dictatorship." Further: "Unquestionably, the public's interest in learning the identity of those arrested and detained is essential to verifying whether the government is operating within the bounds of law."[11] Kessler's ruling affected all "special interest" detainees who had been held under jurisdiction of immigration courts since 9/11. Regarding material witnesses (discussed below) the order allowed the government to maintain secrecy if a federal judge had agreed on a case-by-case basis.

The government appealed to the US Circuit Court of Appeals for the District of Columbia and oral arguments were heard November 18. In June 2003 the appeals court ruled two-to-one that the government was entitled to withhold names of INS detainees and material witnesses during the post-9/11 terrorism investigation – along with dates and location of arrest, detention and release; and the names of detainees' lawyers. The two favoring the government were Reagan and GHW Bush appointees. The dissenter was a Clinton appointee.

The US Supreme Court in January 2004, with no reason given, declined to hear the plaintiff's appeal of the circuit court's decision. Kate Martin, director of the Center for National Security Studies, deplored the judicial branch's blessing of "a secrecy regime in which arrests are off the public docket, people are held in secret, deported in secret, and two and a half years later, we still don't know their names."[12]

New Rules – Mandatory Registration of Selected Aliens

An immigration rule issued in late 2002 allowed INS to monitor legal US visitors. All male visitors 16 and older from certain countries, not having permanent status, were required to register with INS and be fingerprinted. Immigrants from Iran, Iraq, Libya, Sudan and Syria had to register by December 16, 2002. Those from Afghanistan, Lebanon, Eritrea, North Korea, Somalia, Tunisia, the United Arab Emirates and Yemen had until January 10, 2003. Those from Pakistan and Saudi Arabia were to register between January 13 and February 21.

Just like the sweep immediately following 9/11, immigrants were arrested on the least infraction even though they came voluntarily. The government won't say how many had been detained but estimates place the figure as high as 700 in the Los Angeles and San Diego areas. San Francisco and San Jose had over two dozen arrests. Southern California was home to some 600,000 Iranian exiles since the 1979 Islamic Revolution and they made up the bulk of those detained. Ramona Ripston, director of Southern California ACLU, said: "I think it is shocking what is happening. It is reminiscent of...the internment of Japanese Americans.... [P]eople went down wanting to coöperate and they were detained."[13] This same report quoted M.M. Trapici, 45, from Syria who went with a dozen friends in Orange County but came out of the INS office alone. He told reporters: "All my friends are inside right now. I have to visit the family of each one today. Most of them have small kids."

Many of those detained have applications for permanent status pending but bureaucratic delays caused their visas to expire before the process was complete. Others were delayed because they were a day or so late registering; others had minor visa violations. Nationwide, this voluntary registration had a bigger toll. BBC News reported in June 2003 that 82,000 teenage boys and men obeyed the government-mandated registration and, according to the latest count, 13,354 were set for deportation. A class-action lawsuit filed in the US District Court of Los Angeles on 24 December 2002 accused the INS and the attorney general of illegal arrests of hundreds of legitimate visitors. Plaintiffs were several American-Arab and Muslim organizations.

Jim Chaparro of DHS told *The New York Times* in June 2003 there was a major shift in priorities: "We need to focus our enforcement efforts on the biggest threats. If a loophole can be exploited by an immigrant, it can also be exploited by a terrorist."[14] How effective was this shift in priorities? Of those 82,000 who voluntarily registered, plus tens of thousands more screened at border crossings and airports, only eleven had by that time been found with any links to terrorism. Only one of *all* the aliens subjected to "special interest" detention since 9/11 had by June 2003 been convicted of a criminal terrorist charge — Karim Koubrriti, convicted in June 2003 in Detroit of conspiracy to support terrorism

★ ★ ★ ★ ★

Again Justice Department Insp. Gen. Glenn T. Fine enters the picture. In February 2007 he reported that federal prosecutors "counted immigration violations, marriage fraud and drug trafficking among anti-terror cases in the four years after 9/11 even though no evidence linked them to terrorist activity." The inspector general's auditors "looked at 26 categories of statistics – including numbers of suspects charged and convicted in terror cases and terror-related threats against cities and other US targets – compiled by the FBI, Justice's Criminal Division, and the Executive Office of US Attorneys."[15] Only two of the 26 sets reported as of 2005 were accurate. All unlawful activities uncovered during an antiterrorism operation were counted as terror-related. The audit found that the statistics compiled by US attorneys nationwide were most seriously flawed. US officials promised to change their counting procedures.

Criminals Caught in the Post-9/11 Dragnet.

The sweep of aliens snagged a few criminals with outstanding arrest warrants who were confined under the criminal justice system of the judicial branch, not an immigration court in the executive branch. Being a criminal does not equate to being a terrorist however. Information given to Congress indicated many were charged with such things as credit-card fraud and possession of false documents. The Bush administration blurred that distinction to hype the success of its detention program. In June 2005 Bush told the Ohio State Highway Patrol Academy that "federal terrorism investigations have resulted in charges against more than 400 suspects, and more than half have been convicted." Watch those words carefully. He mentions "terrorist investigations" which leads one to believe the suspects and convictions were terrorist-related. They were not, yet those statistics were misused repeatedly to falsify the administration's successes. "An analysis of the Justice Department's own list of terrorism prosecutions by the *Washington Post* shows that 39 people – not 200 as officials have implied – were convicted of crimes relating to terrorism or national security."[16]

In mid-June 2002 the Department of Justice announced 129 people had been held on criminal charges during the PENTTBOM investigation. There were still 73 in custody – all with legal representation. But the only one charged in connection with the

9/11 attacks was Zaccharias Moussaui who had been detained prior to the attacks.

Detainees Held On Material Witness Warrants

About a dozen from the initial dragnet were held on material witness warrants for possible testimony before a grand jury. Ashcroft declined to give the exact number. Such witnesses are not usually jailed but, according to an obscure 1984 federal law, a material witness in a criminal case can be held under maximum security if there is danger of flight. The prosecutor must first get a court order to do so and the witness is entitled to a court-appointed lawyer and a bail bond hearing.

There is no public evidence these formalities were observed, but they apparently weren't. In April 2002 a federal district judge in Manhattan ruled the Justice Department had misused a material witness statute to detain a student from Jordan suspected of ties to 9/11. A November 2002 *Washington Post* article claimed 44 or more had been arrested as material witnesses with at least seven being US citizens. Of those 44 plus, 29 had been released, 9 were still in custody and the status of the other six was unknown.

Summary and Results of Detentions

The Transactional Records Access Clearinghouse (TRAC) at Syracuse Univ. collects, researches and distributes data for public information. In 2006 TRAC issued a report on detainees referred for criminal action from 9/11 through September 2003.[17] Those cases were then tracked through May 2006. The month-by-month data on criminal referrals obtained through Justice Department FOIA requests and showed from 9/11 through September 2003 there were 6,472 "terrorist-related" referrals to federal prosecutors which included international terrorism, domestic terrorism, terrorism-related financing and various forms of "anti-terrorism arrests" such as immigration, identity theft and violent crimes. Of that number, 59 were determined not to be terrorist related. Another 1,122 were still pending as of May 2006 and federal attorneys declined to prosecute 3,140 cases for various reasons (which indicates an over-zealousness to arrest people). So 2,151 cases were actually filed for prosecution of which 381 were still pending. Of the remaining 1,770 cases – 415 were dismissed and another 26 were found not guilty.

Now we are down to 1,329 convictions. 399 received no prison sentence and 305 were sentenced to time served. Of the 625 that went to prison, 327 received less than a year, another 231 received less than five years, 53 received 5-20 years and 14 received 20-years-to-life. For those sentenced between 11 September 2001 and 30 September 2003 the median prison sentence was 28 days (half got more and half got less). For the remainder who were sentenced prior to 31 May 2006 the median prison sentence was 20 days.

That includes every offense which can loosely be construed as terrorist-related in any way. Looking more narrowly at the "international terrorism" category – the most severe form of terrorism – during that time period, 1,391 criminal referrals resulted in only 213 convictions of which only 123 went to prison. Six of those were considered dangerous enough to receive 20-years-to-life. Only an inefficient and uncaring government needs to disregard constitutional guarantees and civil rights in such a fashion to ostensibly protect the American public.

Enemy Combatants

The term "enemy combatant" is used by the Bush administrations to denote certain captives are not prisoners of war so thus do not qualify for prisoner-of-war protections offered by international law. Prisoners taken in Afghanistan or terrorists arrested elsewhere in the war on terror that are not part of a national army and wearing a uniform have been designated enemy combatants – they constitute part of the detentions in the US denied *habeas corpus* rights. Enemy combatant status will be discussed in greater detail later, as will military commissions, Guantanamo Bay and the right to *habeas corpus*.

Yasser Esam Hamdi

Yasser Esam Hamdi, a Saudi Arabian captured near Mazar-e Sharif in Afghanistan during November 2001, was 21 at the time. He was first sent to the military prison at Guantanamo Bay in Cuba, then it was discovered he was born in Louisiana and, therefore, a US citizen. He was then moved to a naval brig in Norfolk, Virginia in April 2002 and later transferred to the brig in Charleston, South Carolina. There he was put in solitary confinement as an enemy combatant for three years without being charged with a crime. He had no access to lawyers or anyone else from the outside. Neither did he have contact with other prisoners. The government asserts that anyone, even US citizens, whom Bush decrees to be an enemy combatant, does not have the right to see a lawyer.

Nevertheless, Public Defender Frank Durham challenged Hamdi's detention. US District Judge Robert Doumar of Norwalk agreed. In August 2002 the judge ruled the government could not hold war captives indefinitely without charges, bail or access to an attorney. A three-judge panel (with two GHW Bush or Reagan appointees in the majority opinion, the third a temporary district judge) of the Fourth US Circuit Court of Appeals in Richmond, Virginia reversed the district judge's decision and ruled enemy combatants could be held incommunicado without charge until the war is over, an event which could be decades away. Durham applied for *certiorari* to the US Supreme Court.

The Supreme Court combined Hamdi's case with that of another detainee at Guantanamo (*Rasul v. Bush*, 542 U.S. 466), also to be discussed later, and they ruled in June 2004 that Bush had the authority to detain enemy combatants, but those detainees still had a right to *habeas corpus* – which meant Hamdi would be allowed a trial during which his treatment and solitary confinement for three years would become public. This displeased the government so it decided Hamdi could return to Saudi Arabia under certain conditions: he was to renounce any claim to US citizenship; he was to promise not to collaborate with terrorists and not to visit Afghanistan, Iraq, Israel, Pakistan or Syria; and – most critically – he would not sue the US over his detention. As with Rabih Haddad, when things didn't go right for the government the detainee was just deported home. In October 2004 Hamdi was reunited with his family – and claims, even after his release, that he is innocent.

Jose Padilla

Government and the media have dubbed Jose Padilla the "dirty bomber." A US citizen born in Brooklyn, he grew up in Chicago where he was convicted as a gang member. Later he moved to southern Florida where he converted to Islam. Then he traveled to the Middle East, from which point the stories vary. Padilla's defense lawyers claim his conversion to Islam straightened him out. The prosecution asserts Padilla went to the Middle East to join ranks with forces hostile to the US, took up arms in Afghanistan and later escaped to Pakistan. There he was allegedly recruited by Al Qaeda to continue terrorism in the US by blowing up apartment buildings and the like. He flew from Zurich to Chicago in May 2002.

Arriving at Chicago's O'Hare airport, Padilla was arrested by the FBI on a material witness warrant issued by a US District Court in New York and taken to New York. There he filed a motion to vacate the warrant, but while that motion was pending, Bush declared Padilla an enemy combatant on June 9 and ordered him into military custody. He was moved to the naval brig at Charleston, South Carolina. Padilla's lawyer filed a *habeas corpus* petition in the New York federal court which was denied, but in December 2003 the US Second Circuit Court of Appeals reversed the lower court's decision and ordered Padilla released. (A Reagan appointee joined a Clinton appointee in the majority opinion.) The Pentagon petitioned the US Supreme Court for *certiorari*.

The Supreme Court decided Padilla's case on June 28, 2004,

the same day it granted *habeas corpus* in the *Hamdi* and *Rasul* cases. The decision for Padilla, however, was quite different. The Court sidestepped responsibility on a procedural technicality by ruling the court in New York had no jurisdiction over a detainee in South Carolina and reversed the circuit court's decision and sent the case back to go through proper channels.

Padilla's attorney started all over again. In February 2005 US District Court Judge Henry Floyd in Spartanburg, South Carolina ruled Padilla must be charged with a crime or released. That ruling was reversed by the US Fourth Circuit Court of Appeals in September 2005 (Two Clinton appointees joined a GHW Bush appointee in the majority opinion.) Now it was Padilla's lawyer's turn to petition the Supreme Court.

In November 2005, just before the Supreme Court deadline for the administration's briefs to show Bush has the power to detain enemy combatants in the US indefinitely, the government hastily charged Padilla with several federal crimes and added him to an existing case in Miami. Bush ordered him released from military custody and imprisoned under the attorney general, thus preventing a possible Supreme Court ruling granting *habeas corpus* to a US citizen detained as an enemy combatant. Consequently, the Supreme Court ruled that since Padilla had been transferred out of military custody and charged, the appeal for *habeas corpus* was moot.

Padilla was transferred during January 2006. His "enemy combatant" charge was downgraded to conspiracy in sending supplies to terrorists in Bosnia and Chechnya. Padilla's attorneys claimed he was unfit to stand trial because of three years and seven months of complete isolation in a 9 x 7-foot cell with natural light blacked out. He had no mirror, clock, radio, TV or calendar; a steel platform for a bed (no mattress, sheet or pillow); a slot in the door through which to slide his food; and was kept awake with loud music, cold temperatures, and the light on 24 hours a day. For significant stretches of time he had no reading material, not even the Koran. His attorneys said

Padilla was also routinely subjected to prolonged stress positions and was given drugs as a "truth serum." They produced brig photos of Padilla in chains while wearing blackout goggles and soundproof ear coverings. (I will discuss the forms of torture in more detail in the next chapter.)

Two psychiatrists and a clinical psychologist agreed Padilla suffers from post-traumatic stress disorder and is psychotically disorganized. They diagnosed depression, paranoia, anxiety, memory lapses, short attention span and inability to concentrate. When Padilla first went into the Charleston brig a military psychologist reported he had no mental health concerns.

An army field manual defines sensory deprivation as "an arranged situation causing significant psychological distress due to a prolonged absence, or significant reduction, of the usual external stimuli and perceptual opportunities." It warns that sensory deprivation "may result in extreme anxiety, hallucinations, bizarre thoughts, depression, and anti-social behavior. Detainees will not be subjected to sensory deprivation."[18] Padilla, after over 3 years of isolation, is now experiencing all the symptoms warned against. Nevertheless, US District Judge Marcia Cooke allowed the trial to continue, although she dismissed the conspiracy charge which could have brought a life sentence. The remaining two material-support conspiracy counts could bring 20 years – or 15 more years if he were given credit for time served. Padilla's trial began in Miami on 17 May 2007 after two weeks of jury selection. Two other Muslim men went to trial with him.

Notice how the government flip-flops at its convenience. Padilla – dubbed the "The Dirty Bomber," with all its strong propaganda connotations – was first declared one of the world's worst. Then when it looked like the administration might be embarrassed, he was transferred to a civilian court to stand trial on lesser offenses. During that trial the prosecution presented no evidence of Padilla's involvement in planning or executing a terrorist plot. In August 2007 the jury found Padilla guilty.

Sentencing was set for December 5. Padilla's lawyers are expected to appeal.

Ali Saleh Kahlah al-Marri.

Ali Saleh Kahlah al-Marri, 37, is a citizen of Qatar who came to the US with his wife and five children to obtain a masters degree at Bradley University in Peoria, Illinois. He was detained in December 2001 during the PENTTBOM dragnet. Later he was charged with credit-card fraud and other criminal offenses which were later dropped. In January 2003 he was charged with making false statements to the FBI along with using fake identification for a bank loan. He pleaded innocent and his trial was set for July 2003. But in June Bush designated him an "enemy combatant" and had al-Marri transferred to the naval brig in Charleston.

Al-Marri is the only "enemy combatant" arrested in the US that has been detained since December 2001. He has been subject to cruel treatment, kept in solitary confinement and held incommunicado with the outside world. In 2004 his lawyer petitioned for *habeas corpus*. The federal district court in Spartanburg, South Carolina refused this petition in August 2006. The case was appealed to the US Court of Appeals for the Fourth Circuit which found in June 2007 that the Military Commissions Act doesn't apply to a legal US resident. They stated: "To sanction such presidential authority to order the military to seize and indefinitely detain civilians, even if the president calls them 'enemy combatants,' would have disastrous consequences for the constitution – and the country.... For in the United States the military cannot seize and imprison civilians, let alone imprison them indefinitely."[19] The court's contention was that the powers granted to the president by Congress in September 2001 applied only to those who had taken up arms against the US.

The Appeals Court three-judge panel (two Clinton appointees in the majority opinion, the third a temporary district judge) ordered al-Marri released or charged with a crime in civilian court. The government could also start deportation proceedings or hold him as a material witness in grand jury proceedings. At the time of this ruling, al-Marri had been imprisoned over five years, four of which were in solitary confinement in the naval brig.

The administration requested the full Fourth Circuit review the panel's decision. In August they granted the government's request and heard arguments in October. The court seemed divided during the hearings but no decision has been issued at the time of this writing.

Immigrant Detentions – Fastest Growing Incarceration Rate

As noted, immigrants are under the jurisdiction of courts controlled by the judicial department of the executive branch. Those detained while awaiting deportation or for other reasons are kept in a mish mash of institutions ranging from county jails, private institutions or federal facilities. The number of immigrants detained per year rose from 95,000 in fiscal year 2001 to 283,000 in 2006. On any given day more than 27,500 noncitizens are held indefinitely while immigration officials decide what to do with them and immigration detention has become the fastest growing form of incarceration in the country.

From 2004 until June 2007 there were 62 immigrants that died while in custody. The cause has been attributed to improper independent oversight of immigrants detained and unsatisfactory provisions for medical care. One grandmother, a legal permanent resident of the US for 30 years, but detained in a regional jail because of a three-year-old drug possession conviction, died seven weeks after being jailed because she could not take her blood-pressure medicine. Another woman, a 60-year-old cook with pancreatic cancer, was held in a private prison after being swept up in a raid. She pleaded for help for weeks but was not hospitalized until she stopped eating and her eyes yellowed. She died the next day – 11 September 2006. A 50-year-old man who had been a taxi mechanic in Washington for 17 years was held in a regional jail because of a mix up on an old deportation order. He could not get the medication for his serious kidney ailment and died in December 2006.

No agency is charged with accounting for immigration deaths while in custody. Secrecy and confusion abound. Many are discovered through family, friends and former detainee witnesses. Civil liberties lawyers compiled a list of 20 deaths, including them in a briefing paper to the UN special rapporteur on human rights. Thomas Hogan, warden of York County Prison in Pennsylvania, one of the largest housing immigrant detainees, said in a court affidavit: "The Department of Homeland Security has made it difficult, if not impossible, to meet the constitutional requirements of providing adequate health care to inmates that have serious need for care."[20] The immigration agency adopted detention standards in 2000 but they are informal and unenforceable. Citing a need for flexibility, the DHS has resisted upgrading these standards to regulations.

During 2006 the number of immigrant detentions grew by over 32%. Immigration authorities tout cutting the average length of stay per detainee from 89 days to 35 days—an improvement but most likely done for logistic and space purposes. How would we privileged Americans feel if we were held for a month without access to medical necessities and *habeas corpus*?

TRAC made a study of immigration arrests from FOIA data received from immigration courts and their report released in May 2007 showed that of 814,073 cases filed by the DHS during the preceding three years, there were only 12 that were terrorism related. That is only 0.0015%. Furthermore, out of those same number of cases, there were only 114 (0.014%) that were charges of national security violations—a pretty sad showing for a cabinet department whose primary mandate is to protect the American public from terrorism.

It is not my purpose to argue the guilt or innocence of any detainee, only to emphasize that whoever they are, guilty or innocent, they deserve to be treated humanely and afforded the same constitutional rights we hold so dear. I will next look at the subject of military commissions and "enemy combatants" more thoroughly and how *habeas corpus* and basic human rights are denied foreign prisoners outside the borders of this country.

Notes for Chapter 8

1. Dicey, Albert Venn; *Introduction to the Study of the Law of the Constitution*, at http://www.constitution.org/cmt/avd/law_con.htm/

2. Wilgoren, Jodi, "Swept up in a Dragnet, Hundreds Sit in Custody and Ask 'Why?'" *NY Times*, 25 Nov 2001.

3. Amnesty International News Release; "USA: Post 11 September Detainees Deprived of Their Basic Rights," 14 Mar 2002.

4. Firestone, David, "Order Boosts Federal Power to Hold Detained Foreigners," *San Jose Mercury News*, 28 Nov 2001.

5. DOJ Press Release—"The September 11 Detainees: A Review of the Treatment of Aliens Held on Immigration Charges in Connection with the Investigation of the September 11 Attacks," 2 Jun 2003.

6. Lichtblau, Eric, "Ashcroft Defends Detentions as Immigrants Recount Toll," *NY Times*, 5 Jun 2003.

7. Memo sent to all immigration judges and court administrators: "Cases Requiring Special Procedures," 21 Sep 2001.

8. Fainaru, Steve, "US Judge Rejects Closed Hearings for Terrorist Suspects," *San Jose Mercury News*, 30 May 2002.

9. "Post 9-11 Secrecy Lawsuits Work Way up Legal Ladder," ACLU of NJ website, n.d.

10. Fainaru, op. cit.

11. Moritsugo, Ken and Cassio Furtado, "US Told to Identify Sept. 11 Detainees," *San Jose Mercury News*, 3 Aug 2002.

12. Greenhouse, Linda, "Justices Allow Policy of Silence on 9/11 Detainees," *NY Times*, 13 Jan 2004.

13. Serjeant, Jill, "Hundreds of Muslim Immigrants Rounded up in California," Findlaw website, 18 Dec 2002.

14. BBC News; "US Threatens Mass Expulsions," 10 Jun 2003.

15. Jordan, Lara J., "Audit: Anti-Terror Case Data Flawed," *Yahoo! News*, 21 Feb 2007.

16. Eggen, Dan and Julie Tate, "US Campaign Produces Few Convictions on Terrorism Charges," *Washington Post*, 12 Jun 2005.

17. TRAC Report: "Criminal Terrorism Enforcement in the United States During the Five Years since 9/11/01 Attacks," prepared in 2006.

18. Richey, Warren, "US Gov't Broke Padilla Through Intense Isolation, Say Experts," *Christian Science Monitor*, 14 Aug 2007.

19. Sampson, Zinie Chen, "Court Rules in favor of Enemy Combatant," *San Jose Mercury News*, posted on website 11 June 2007.

20. Bernstein, Nina, "New Security as Immigrants Die in Custody," *NY Times*, 26 Jun 2007.

9

Military Commissions:
Tribunals or Kangaroo Courts?

We must be ever-vigilant against those who would strong-arm the judiciary into adopting their preferred policies. It takes a lot of degeneration before a country falls into dictatorship, but we should avoid these ends by avoiding these beginnings.

— Justice Sandra Day O'Connor[1]

Coming from a recently retired Supreme Court justice, Sandra Day O'Connor's warning is especially significant. Minimizing the judicial branch's checks and balances over the president is dangerous. Particularly threatening is how the administration has circumvented due process — the focus of this chapter.

Military Commissions by Presidential Decree

Very few actual terrorists were apprehended after 9/11. Minneapolis FBI agents suspected French citizen Zacarias Moussaoui prior to 9/11 and had him picked up on an immigration violation. After 9/11 he was charged and convicted as a terrorist conspirator. British citizen Richard Colvin Reid — the notorious shoe bomber who on December 22, 2001, tried to blow up American Airlines Flight 63 en route from Paris to Miami — was also convicted on terrorism charges. Both are now serving life sentences in Federal ADX Supermax prison in Florence, Colorado. American citizen John Walker Lindh was captured in Afghanistan. In a plea bargain he admitted helping the Taliban and is now serving a 20-year sentence at the same federal prison in Colorado.

Those were a few cases tried in US courts. But with hundreds of alleged terrorists captured in Afghanistan, Bush issued a military order to establish an expedient but dictatorial system for trying noncitizen suspects in an off-shore prison.

Bush's Military Order

Bush issued his military order in November 2001 to establish military commissions. It stated that Bush, alone, would decide who is subject to prosecution. A list of offenses ended with a catch-all phrase to try a detainee if "it is in the interest of the United States that such individual be subject to this order." Former deputy attorney general and Harvard law professor Philip Heymann said there are 18 million aliens living in this country, most of them legally, but "whenever the president suspects that one of them may have been a terrorist in the past, or is a terrorist, or has aided a terrorist, or has harbored a terrorist," no matter how long ago, that person can be sent to trial "before three colonels" who can convict with a "two-thirds vote."[2]

Justification for detention was spelled out with a list of possible charges that ended with a phrase opening the door to anything: the prisoner shall be "detained in accordance with such *other* conditions as the Secretary of Defense may prescribe" (emphasis added). To justify his military order, Bush cited former use of military commissions, especially during World War II to prosecute eight German saboteurs who landed from submarines on the beaches of Long Island and Florida. No mention was made that those commissions had congressional approval.

Regarding detainee's treatment and rights, Bush issued a

memorandum proclaiming his "authority as commander-in-chief and chief executive" and determining "that none of the provisions of Geneva[3] apply to our conflict with Al Qaeda in Afghanistan or elsewhere" and that "Taliban detainees are unlawful combatants and, therefore, do not qualify as prisoners of war."[4] By choosing the term "unlawful combatant" Bush claims to have sidetracked international law. That term was coined by the Supreme Court in its 1942 decision upholding trial by military tribunal of the eight World War II spies mentioned above. They had penetrated our homeland for a belligerent mission in civilian clothes—a violation of the laws of war—thus were "unlawful combatants."

Bush then, through some twisted logic, started calling the detainees merely "enemy combatants" until they were deemed "unlawful." but he still contended they were not eligible for POW privileges although he'd abide by the Geneva Conventions anyway. The Bush logic is indefinite detention without recognizing POW protections. If any were later deemed "unlawful enemy combatants," they would be tried before military commissions, but would still be detained indefinitely even if acquitted of the "unlawful" charge.

Civil rights groups and legislators rose in opposition, citing numerous binding cases of international law such as the International Covenant on Civil and Political Rights (ratified by the US in 1992) and the 1949 Geneva Conventions (ratified by the US in 1955), accusing the administration of offering a lower standard of justice to foreigners. They abhorred such unfettered power for the president, calling the parallel judicial system inconsistent with checks and balances and contrary to fundamental principles of justice.

Other governments raised similar objections. European Union (EU) officials warned that support for the US in the war on terror could be restricted by their obligation to human rights treaties. Extradition of captives to the US could become a problem if the death penalty is possible because all EU countries have banned capital punishment. The Spanish government had already refused to extradite eight Al Qaeda suspects unless the US guarantees they won't face execution.

Then the Pentagon released detailed procedures for military commissions.

Rumsfeld's Military Commission Order No. 1.

To implement Bush's military order, Defense Secretary Rumsfeld issued Military Commission Order No. 1 in March 2002. Its main provisions, as told by Rumsfeld, are commented on below:

1. *Defendants will be presumed innocent until proven guilty.* Everything is controlled by the executive branch. Rumsfeld's order says commission members are appointed "from time to time," which allows handpicking for specific cases. The executive branch assigns the chief prosecuting attorney and the chief defense attorney. Members of commissions are military officers steeped in a code of obedience who can be subtly controlled or risk their careers (which I will illustrate later). There is no guarantee innocence will be presumed.

2. *Defendants will not be required to incriminate themselves or testify against themselves.* They may already have done this through "coercive interrogation techniques" which can be admitted as evidence.

3. *Through legal counsel they will be able to discover information and to obtain witnesses and evidence.* Government- appointed Judge Advocate General (JAG) corps lawyers are the only defense lawyers who will see all the evidence and even they can't discuss secret or sensitive material with their client. Evidence may be introduced without revealing the source or how it was obtained, allowing hearsay evidence to be admitted or evidence obtained through torture.

4. *Trials will be public, proceedings will be open and defendants will be present to the maximum extent possible.* A Pentagon fact sheet gives four reasons to close a trial: to protect a) classi-

fied or sensitive information; b) the physical safety of participants; c) intelligence or law enforcement sources, methods and activities; and d) the catch-all national security interests. At the government's convenience trials can be closed and defendants excluded. Civilian defense lawyers can also be excluded.

5. *Defendants cannot be tried twice for the same offense.*

6. *Defendants will receive military legal counsel at US expense and will also be able to hire (at their own expense) their own defense counsel.* They will be assigned JAG lawyers. Defendants may engage civilian lawyer but, in practice, only when the lawyers donate their time. A security clearance requires an FBI background check for which the lawyer must pay.

7. *The standard for conviction must be "beyond reasonable doubt" and will require a two-thirds vote of the military commission.* Commission members are chosen by the defense secretary or their designate—all are military officers subject to "consequences" and overseen by higher ranks. There is no way of assuring "beyond a reasonable doubt" will be respected.

8. *Imposition of the death penalty requires a unanimous vote of a seven-member commission.* This is more specific than Bush's military order in requiring both a seven-member commission and a unanimous vote for a capital cases.

9. *There will be an automatic post-trial process for appeal and review.* This consists of a three-member review panel—all military officers or civilians commissioned according to the Uniform Code of Military Justice. Only one need have experience as a judge. This panel is chosen by the executive branch and their decision is only a recommendation. The final decision on everything lies with the President, who accused the detainee in the first place. The only thing final is that a "not guilty" verdict cannot be changed. There is no recourse to independent civilian courts as provided for in courts-martial.

★ ★ ★ ★ ★

Bush's military order and Rumsfeld's Military Commission Order No. 1 are not limited to violations of laws of war. Rumsfeld's order specifically states that military commissions "shall have jurisdiction over violations of laws of war *and all other offenses triable by military commission*" (emphasis added). To find what these "other offenses" are, we turn to Bush's military order which defines the term "individual subject to this order" as "any individual who is not a United States citizen with respect to whom I determine from time to time in writing that it is in the interest of the United States that such individual be subject to this order." Simply stated, what Bush says, goes. To understand military commissions and the type of evidence that can be admitted, we need to understand the American government's definition of torture.

The American Style of Torture

It started with the CIA – and probably is still with the CIA although the Army seems to have replaced the Agency for International Development (AID) as the front organization. When Alfred McCoy, author of *A Question of Torture*, saw the now-notorious Abu Ghraib prison photos first broadcast in April 2004, he said: "I did not see snapshots of simple brutality or a breakdown of military discipline.... [T]hat iconic photo of a hooded Iraqi with fake electrical wires hanging from his extended arms shows, not the sadism of a few 'creeps,' but instead the two key trademarks of the CIA's psychological torture. The hood was for sensory disorientation. The arms were extended for self-inflicted pain. It was that simple; it was that obvious."[5]

McCoy pointed out that shortly after World War II the Office of Strategic Services (OSS) launched "Operation Paperclip" to recruit German scientists who had experimented with truth serum (mescaline) on Jewish prisoners. The National Security Act of 1947 metamorphosed the OSS into the CIA and the Central Intelligence Agency Act of 1949 permitted the CIA to operate secretly and be funded with the so-called black budget. During the 1950s the CIA led a billion-dollar-a-year secret research program using various drugs to extract information from people. Truth serums were a failure but the contracts led to two key discoveries that became the groundwork for the American form of psychological torture.

One was made by Canadian psychologist Dr. Donald O. Hebb at McGill University who induced a state similar to psychosis in only two days by simply depriving the subject of sensory stimulation. The subjects merely sat isolated in a comfortable cell with their senses inactivated by use of painted goggles, ear muffs, surgical masks over nose and mouth and thick gloves or cardboard tubes covering the hands. In just a couple days the subject began to lose touch with reality. McCoy also described two neurologists at Cornell Medical Center who used techniques developed by the Soviet KGB which showed it wasn't beatings, hot cigarettes, pulling out fingernails, electric shock and other extreme forms of physical abuse that proved effective. What worked best were stress positions: "simply forcing the victim to stand for days at a time...while the legs swelled, the skin erupted in suppurating lesions, the kidneys shut down, hallucinations began."

These two techniques – sensory deprivation and self-induced pain – became the central elements of the CIA's psychological torture.[6]

The 1963 Kubark Manual

As the US was getting involved in Vietnam, the CIA compiled all of its torture techniques into a secret guidebook entitled *KUBARK Counterintelligence Interrogation, July 1963*. Kubark was the CIA's code name for itself. Part IX of that handbook, called "Coercive Counterintelligence Interrogation of Resistant Sources," explains coercive techniques available but warns there is no blanket authorization for their use. The principle ones are arrest, detention, deprivation of sensory stimuli, threats and fear, debility, pain, heightened suggestibility and hypnosis, and drugs. These techniques are summarized in Appendix D. The Kubark manual was released to the public in January 1997.

From 1962 to 1974 the CIA used a division of US AID as a front organization for work in Third World countries including South Vietnam, Brazil, Uruguay, Iran and the Philippines. Torture went from research to application and fatalities became less important. During the infamous Phoenix Program in Vietnam there were 26,369 prisoners killed in the CIA's 40 Provincial Interrogation Centers.

The 1983 CIA Interrogation Training Manual

When US involvement in Central America picked up during the 1980s, the CIA published its *Human Resource Exploitation Training Manual – 1983* which was cobbled together from the Kubark manual, notes and lesson plans from training courses in Honduras and military intelligence field manuals written in the 1960s. The declassified version, also released in January 1997, had many revisions apparently made in July 1984. A prologue was added giving lip service to coercive techniques being "prohibited by law" and "neither authorized nor condoned."

The remainder of the manual was corrected by marking out certain words and phrases and writing revised language in by hand, with the crossed-out material still legible. A sentence reading "While we do not stress the use of coercive techniques, we do want to make you aware of them and the proper way to use them," has been changed to read: "While we deplore the use of coercive techniques, we do want to make you aware of them so that you may avoid them." Similar corrections are inserted by hand throughout the manual, but the original information is still readable. The section on coercive techniques is similar to the Kubark manual (see Appendix D).

If the CIA were truly sincere in not wanting their Latin American trainees – especially the Honduran death squad ELACH responsible for "disappearing" some 200 people during the 1980s – to use coercive techniques, they could have simply removed that entire section without disturbing the rest of the manual's flow.

The Army's Project X

In 1965 the Army's assistant chief of staff for intelligence (G-2) commissioned a top secret program dubbed "Project X" which began at the US Army Intelligence Center and School at Fort Holabird, Maryland. The first document was a guide for clandestine operations and used at the US Intelligence School on Okinawa to train Vietnamese. CIA officers from the Phoenix Program may have helped prepare some lesson plans. Objectionable material from Phoenix found its way into Project X.

The US Army Intelligence Center and School moved to Fort Huachuca, Arizona, early in the 1970s. Project X material continued to be used for training and went into lesson plans for foreign officer training. In 1975 Fort Huachuca was directed to prepare unclassified lesson plans for the School of the Americas (SOA) at Fort Benning, Georgia (renamed Western Hemisphere Institute for Security Coöperation in 2000). The working group chose Project X material because it had already been cleared for foreign use. Those new SOA lesson plans taught torture, blackmail, assassinations, executions, paying bounties for enemy dead, false imprisonment and even kidnapping a subjects' family to coerce them into revealing information.

In February 1982 Capts. Victor Tise and John Zindar updated those SOA lesson plans which were originally prepared from Project X material. In 1987 the 470th Military Intelligence Brigade stationed in Panama compiled those lesson plans into seven Spanish language manuals that were used in Colombia, Ecuador, El Salvador, Guatemala and Peru. By 1989 perhaps a thousand copies of those manuals were distributed to students from Bolivia, Colombia, Costa Rica, Dominican Republic, Ecuador, Guatemala, Honduras, Mexico, Peru and Venezuela. The seven manuals are: *Handling of Sources, Revolutionary War & Communist Ideology, Counterintelligence, Terrorism & the Urban Guerilla, Interrogation, Combat Intelligence* and *Analysis I.*

These manuals were withdrawn from use in 1991, but copies had proliferated. *Covert Action Quarterly* said "techniques of control contained in the manuals were actively adopted by Latin American militaries, particularly in the 1970s and 1980s; in Chile's and Argentina's 'dirty wars' in which thousands of dissidents disappeared; by military dictatorships in Brazil, Paraguay, and Uruguay; in the Central American wars where tens of thousands of civilians were killed; and in the Andean countries where human rights violations still abound."[7]

The United Nations Convention Against Torture.

The "Convention Against Torture and Other Cruel, Inhuman or Degrading Treatment or Punishment" was adopted by the UN General Assembly in December 1984 and entered into force in June 1987.

Article 1 of that Convention defines torture as "any act by which severe pain or suffering, *whether physical or mental*, is intentionally inflicted on a person for such purposes as obtaining from him or a third person information or a confession.... It does not include pain or suffering arising only from, inherent in or incidental to lawful sanctions" (emphasis added).

Article 15 prohibits information derived from torture from use in courts or any other proceedings: "Each State Party shall ensure that any statement which is established to have been made as a result of torture shall not be invoked as evidence in any proceedings, except against a person accused of torture as evidence that the statement was made."

Article 16 invokes the same prohibition against cruel, inhuman, or degrading treatment as for torture: "Each state party shall undertake to prevent...other acts of cruel, inhuman or degrading treatment or punishment which do not amount to torture as defined in article 1."

When Ronald Reagan signed this Convention he attached a list of reservations which essentially relegated the Convention only to outlawing physical torture. These US reservations are given in their entirety in Appendix E but here is an outline of some of the key aspects:

Regarding Article 1, the US considers an interrogation technique as torture only if it is "specifically intended" as such. This seems to allow torture if it is meant to extract information, not to cause severe physical or mental pain. The US also considers that people must be in US custody or physical control to be liable for torturing them. That exonerates the CIA when it kidnaps people and turns them over to another country to extract information by torture—called "extraordinary rendition." The US interprets Article 1 "sanctions" as including "judicially-imposed sanctions and other enforcement actions authorized by US law or judicial interpretation" which allows judges, including military judges, to allow evidence obtained by "enhanced interrogation techniques."

Regarding Article 16, the US considers itself bound only to Amendments V, VIII, and XIV of the US Constitution, which are more general and less restrictive regarding torture (see Appendix F). Taken together, Reagan's Reservations exempt the US type of psychological torture.

When the Convention was ratified by the Senate in October 1994, all the Reservations imposed by the Reagan administration were also ratified. Subsequently, the War Crimes Act of 1996 (18 U.S.C. 2441) was signed into law. It defines war crimes according to the Geneva Conventions of 1949, Protocol II as modified in 1996, and certain articles of the annex to the Hague Convention IV of 1907. In January 1998 statute 18 U.S.C. 2340 was enacted to define torture with 18 U.S.C. 2340a defining torture outside the US. These statutes require "specific intent" to inflict severe physical or mental pain or suffering to be guilty of torture. The Justice Department built on such intent in its August 2002 memo.

The Justice Department's August 2002 Memo

To allay CIA concerns about legal actions related to interrogation techniques, Asst. Atty. Gen. Jay S. Bybee, head of the office of legal counsel, sent a 50-page memorandum to the

White House[8] outlining the standards of conduct under 18 U.S.C. 2340-2340A, stating that "for an act to constitute torture as defined in Section 2340, it must inflict pain that is difficult to endure. Physical pain amounting to torture must be equivalent in intensity to the pain accompanying serious physical injury, such as organ failure, impairment of bodily functions, or even death." Regarding psychological torture, for "purely mental pain or suffering to amount to torture under Section 2340, it must result in significant psychological harm of significant duration, e.g. lasting for months or even years."[9]

The memo concluded that mental harm was limited to the specific acts listed in the statute, so anything else the interrogator can think of is legal. It did express reservations regarding the United Nations Convention Against Torture: "Executive branch interpretations and representations to the Senate at the time of ratification further confirm that the treaty was intended to reach only the most extreme conduct." But regarding specific intent, the memo says even if the interrogator "knows that severe pain will result from his actions, if causing such harm is not his objective, he lacks the requisite specific intent...a defendant is guilty of torture only if he acts with the express purpose of inflicting severe pain or suffering on a person within his custody or physical control." It opined that "international decisions regarding the use of sensory deprivation techniques...make it clear that while many of these techniques may amount to cruel, inhuman, or degrading treatment, they do not produce suffering of the necessary intensity to meet the definition of torture."

Section V encompassed everything: "As Commander-in-Chief the President has the constitutional authority to order interrogations of enemy combatants to gain intelligence information concerning the military plans of the enemy." So it was this memo which laid the legal foundation for the CIA's "enhanced interrogation techniques."

Officials at Guantanamo then requested clarification of the

methods they were using. In a November 27, 2002, Action Memo, Defense Secretary Rumsfeld approved all Category I and II techniques as well as the fourth in Category III (see Appendix G for categories). On that same day the FBI released a legal analysis saying seven of the techniques Rumsfeld had just approved violated the US Constitution.[10] The following January Rumsfeld rescinded his November memo and appointed a Pentagon panel to investigate interrogation practices. Rumsfeld issued another memo April 16 which outlined 24 specific interrogation techniques with strict safeguards for use only at Guantanamo.

Alberto Gonzales took a lot of flack over the Bybee memo during his confirmation hearings for attorney general. Consequently, in December 2004, DOJ's Office of Legal Council issued a new memorandum repudiating the unbelievably high pain or mental agony threshold for torture and removed the "specific intent" evasion. It neither endorsed nor debunked the notion that Bush could order torture. But this memo was just a smokescreen. Two secret memos from the Office of Legal Council were discovered in October 2007: The first on 10 May 2005 authorized a combination of painful physical and psychological tactics for extracting information. The second on May 30 reaffirmed that the practices were legal. In November 2007 the DOJ inadvertently admitted that two memos were written on May 10th. Contents of the other one is unknown.

Congress passed the McCain torture bill in December 2005 which severely curtailed what the CIA could do. When Bush signed the bill on December 30 he added a signing statement that he would interpret the law in accordance with his constitutional authority and added that he would do so in a manner that protects the American people from further terrorist attacks.

The Supreme Court declared in 2006 that some CIA techniques were illegal because the prisoners are covered by the Geneva Conventions. Another executive order issued in July 2007 again outlined guidelines for the CIA. The concept of specific intent reappeared. The order forbids the use of willful and outrageous acts of personal abuse done for the purpose of humiliating or degrading the individual. Put simply, if you're not doing it just to humiliate or degrade the person, it isn't torture. Although the Justice Department rescinded its August 2002 torture memo in December 2004, it had been in effect over two years and the interrogation techniques it allowed were used on many captives. Later I will discuss how 14 of those key captives were sent to Guantanamo and how they seemed willing to confess to anything. But first we turn to military commissions, the resistance they met and an overview of the military justice system.

Bush's Military Commissions Meet Resistance

Bush's military commissions faced severe criticism and implementing them met resistance. The way the JAG corps is organized and how the military justice system operates is where the story begins.

Some Background Information – UCMJ and the JAG Corps

The Uniform Code of Military Justice (UCMJ) was created by Congress in 1950 to standardize the legal system for all branches of the service. The Judge Advocate General (JAG) of each branch of the service, who must be a lawyer, is charged with defense and prosecution under the UCMJ. In 1967 the JAG of each branch became autonomous in legal matters, perhaps similar to the medical corps and the chaplains corps. Each JAG is a two-star officer (major general or rear admiral) except for the marine corps, which has a brigadier general. The JAG oversees a corps of officer-lawyers who, in matters of law, report only to the JAG. However, under military commission rules JAG lawyers, both prosecution and defense, report up the regular military chain of command to the Defense Department general counsel (politically-appointed).

The Pentagon has for some time tried to put JAGs under

the regular military chain of command. Dick Cheney, as Defense Secretary in 1991, asked Congress to put a politically-appointed lawyer in charge of the JAG corps. Congress refused. A year later Cheney tried again with an internal Pentagon order. Congressional backlash squashed that. In May 2003 Cheney, as vice president, tried to replay the 1992 scheme by ordering Air Force JAGs to report to the Air Force general counsel (a politically-appointed civilian lawyer). Congress squelched that order. In October 2004, Congress passed a law prohibiting interference with the JAGs' autonomy. When Bush signed the law he issued one of his infamous signing statements "saying that the legal opinion reached by his political appointees would still 'bind all...military attorneys.'"[11]

In August 2001 when White House lawyers were drawing up Bush's military order, only one JAG corps representative was allowed to look at the draft and was not allowed to take notes. Suggestions offered by the JAGs weren't used. When Rumsfeld's 2003 Pentagon torture study report was released, the two-star JAGs warned such a policy would undermine the Geneva conventions and put interrogators at risk of prosecution for war crimes, but the civilian lawyers ignored the warning. Later we will see how JAG corps lawyers were similarly ignored when the White House was preparing proposed legislation for the Military Commission Act of 2006.

More on the Military Justice System

Courts-martial are presided over by a military judge; the equivalent of a jury is a panel of officers—five for a general court-martial, three for a special court-martial. At the defendant's request, one-third of the panel must be enlisted men. In summary courts-martial for minor offenses a single officer decides the verdict which can't exceed a month confinement. In any of these courts-martial, JAG lawyers act as defense counsel and prosecutor.

There are several tiers of appeal under the UCMJ. The commander convening courts-martial reviews all cases but cannot increase the sentence or change an acquittal to guilty. Next the court of criminal appeals—a panel of three military appellate judges—reviews cases involving capital punishment or punitive discharge. If it confirms a death penalty, the case must go before the court of appeals for the armed forces—five civilian judges appointed by the president and affirmed by the Senate for 15-year terms. This court of appeals also hears cases ordered by the JAGs and considers appeals from the court of criminal appeals. The final appeal is to request *certiorari* from the US Supreme Court to review the case.

The Lawyer Backlash

Civilian lawyers hesitated to participate in the planned military commissions because of the restrictions placed on them. Besides not being able to properly defend a client, they thought their coöperation would lend credibility to a system they deemed corrupt. Lawrence Goldman, president of the 11,000-member National Association of Criminal Defense Lawyers, said in 2003: "The rules regulating counsel's behavior are just too restrictive to give us any confidence that counsel will be able to act zealously and professionally," adding that lawyers could be "lending their legitimacy to what would otherwise be a sham proceeding." Neal R. Sonnett, chair of the American Bar Association's task force on treatment of enemy combatants, added: "If lawyers participate in the process and lend it an air of legitimacy without being able to contribute effectively, then we would fall into a trap that lawyers shouldn't fall into."[12]

Civilian lawyers didn't like agreeing to have conversations with their clients monitored for national security reasons and balked at having to report certain information their client might tell them. They would also have to pay for their security background check, would have to provide their own transportation to and from Guantanamo and be unable to speak with their client by telephone. Even when civilian counsel received

America in Peril

security clearance, they still could be excluded from certain proceedings and evidence.

Rules were later relaxed somewhat and civilian defense lawyers could bring in other lawyers, even from a foreign country, for the defense team. The gag rule was also relaxed so civilian lawyers could consult with others on a confidential basis – although public announcements had to be cleared with the military. Eavesdropping on lawyer-client conferences required stronger justification, prior approval and lawyers notified ahead of time. These small alterations were necessary to entice civilian lawyer participation.

JAG lawyers and military judges also had gripes. Salim Achmed Hamdan, a defendant at the first military commission hearing in August 2004 had a JAG attorney, Navy Lt. Cdr. Charles Swift, who had already challenged military tribunals with a *habeas corpus* petition to a federal civilian court. At this hearing Swift challenged four members of the commission panel on their impartiality. Two had served in the 2001 invasion of Afghanistan. The third had a member of his reserve regiment, a firefighter, killed in the World Trade Center collapse. Prosecuting JAG attorneys eventually joined Swift's challenge and those three were eventually dismissed. The fourth panel member challenged was the presiding officer who had political connections and stayed on. Swift said removal of the three without removing the presiding officer made little difference in the fairness of the panel.

Lt. Col. Sharon Shaffer, deputy chief judge for the Air Force, delayed her assignment to represent a detainee at Guantanamo. She made a motion in September 2004 that the Pentagon drop military commissions altogether, labeling them a relic of World War II, suggesting they be replaced with modern courts-martial that have evolved under the Uniform Code of Military Justice. Military defense lawyer Maj. Yvonne Bradley (Air Force) declined to participate in proceedings in April 2006, saying the military commission structure forces her to violate legal ethics. She also echoed the objection made by almost all defense lawyers – that the commissions are operating outside established laws and without clear and fair standards. Marine Col. Ralph Kohlmann, presiding officer on the commission, ordered her to "zealously" represent her client and warned her "you will disobey at your peril."[13]

Two e-mails written to their supervisors in March 2004 by JAG prosecuting attorneys were leaked to ABC News. One from Maj. Robert Preston said; "I consider the insistence on pressing ahead with cases that would be marginal even if properly prepared.... Surely they don't expect that this fairly half-arsed effort is all that we have been able to put together after all this time." Preston said he "cannot continue to work on a process he considers morally, ethically and professionally intolerable."[14] He was transferred less than a month later.

The other e-mail was from Capt. John Carr who said: "When I volunteered to assist with this process...I expected there would at least be a minimal effort to establish a fair process and diligently prepare cases against significant accused. Instead, I find a half-hearted and disorganized effort by a skeleton group of relatively inexperienced attorneys to prosecute fairly low-level accused in a process that appears to be rigged." Then he elaborated on the "rigged" accusation: "You have repeatedly said to the office that the military panel will be hand-picked and will not acquit these detainees and that we only needed to worry about building a record for the review panel." Carr has also departed from Guantanamo.

Revision to Military Commission Order No. 1.

In the face of so much criticism, and after the JAG e-mails became public, Rumsfeld made some changes and revised Military Commission Order No. 1 in August 2005 with two main changes: The presiding officer, still a military judge, was now separated from the other members to take on the role of judge in interpreting the law and ruling on the proceedings. The remaining members act as a jury to interpret the facts of the case and determine the verdict or, in the case of a sentencing hearing, make sentencing decisions. The presiding officer is not present when the others are deliberating. The other modification allows defendants to be present at trial at all times except when classified information needs to be discussed and the presiding officer determines exclusion will not prejudice a fair trial. If the defendant not having access to the classified information will jeopardize a full and fair trial, the presiding officer must exclude that information from the trial. Since the Pentagon makes all decisions, this appears to be merely a cosmetic change.

There was still no provision that granted *habeas corpus* or allowed any intervention of a civilian court.

"The Great Writ" vs. U.S. Courts

Article I, Section 9 of the US Constitution reads: "The privilege of the writ of *habeas corpus* shall not be suspended, unless when in cases of rebellion or invasion the public safety may require it." The International Covenant on Civil and Political Rights, ratified by the United States on 8 June 1992, spells it out in more detail:

Article 9:
1. Everyone has the right to liberty and security of person. No one shall be subjected to arbitrary arrest or detention. No one shall be deprived of liberty except on such grounds and in accordance with such procedure as are established by law.
2. Anyone who is arrested shall be informed, at the time of arrest, of the reasons for the arrest and shall be promptly informed of any charges against them.
3. Anyone arrested or detained on a criminal charge shall be brought promptly before a judge or other officer authorized by law to exercise judicial power and shall be entitled to trial within a reasonable time or to release. It shall not be the general rule that persons awaiting trial shall be detained in custody, but release may be subject to guarantees to appear for trial, at any other stage of the judicial proceedings, and, should occasion arise, for execution of the judgment.

4. Anyone who is deprived of liberty by arrest or detention shall be entitled to take proceedings before a court, in order that that court may decide without delay on the lawfulness of the detention and order release if the detention is not lawful.
5. Anyone who has been the victim of unlawful arrest or detention shall have an enforceable right to compensation.

That says *every* person is guaranteed those rights, not just Americans. Yet Rumsfeld's Military Commission Order No. 1 permits holding prisoners at Guantanamo indefinitely without charge with no provision for *habeas corpus*, or any other procedure, to challenge why they are held. To top that off, as attorney general of the United States, Alberto Gonzales had the audacity to tell the Senate Judiciary Committee "the Constitution doesn't say every individual in the United States or every citizen is hereby granted or assured the right to *habeas*, it doesn't say that. It simply says the right of *habeas corpus* shall not be suspended except by..."[15] Basically he is claiming you don't necessarily have the right to it, but once granted it can't be taken away. That extremely expansive and grossly erroneous interpretation coming from an attorney general is frightening. I will now show how the legal actions and ramifications of that interpretation are being applied to detainee policy.

Rasul v. Bush (2004). This important Supreme Court decision handed down in June held that: "United States courts have jurisdiction to consider challenges to the legality of the detention of foreign nationals captured abroad in connection with hostilities and incarcerated at Guantanamo Bay." Lower courts had dismissed the case claiming they did not have jurisdiction over a base in Cuba. But the 6-3 majority of the Supreme Court said the federal district court's jurisdiction "extends to aliens held in a territory over which the United States exercises plenary and exclusive jurisdiction, but not ultimate sovereignty."[16] The ruling was based on statute 28 U.S.C. 2241, "Power to Grant Writ," a law passed by Congress not on the Constitution. Congress has the power to change that.

Executive Branch Responses to the Rasul Decision

Hoping to head off a flurry of lawsuits following the Supreme Court's ruling in *Rasul*, and ostensibly to meet the Geneva Conventions requirement for a "competent tribunal" to determine "enemy combatant" status, Bush tried another tactic to keep Guantanamo proceedings out of civilian courts.

Combat Status Review Tribunals. These tribunals commenced in July 2004. All detainees were assigned a personal representative – a military officer but not a lawyer – to help them understand their legal options. Then the detainees could supposedly challenge their detention before a panel of three military officers who would decide if the detainee is an enemy combatant. The detainee would be present for all the proceedings except when the tribunal was deliberating.

Lawyer Rachel Meeropol of the Center for Constitutional Rights said: "The Supreme Court upheld the rule of law over unchecked executive authority. The review procedures for the detainees set up by the Department of Defense are inadequate and illegal, and they fail to satisfy the court's ruling." Jeffrey E. Fogel, legal director at the center wrote Rumsfeld: "Without access to a lawyer the Supreme Court's decision in *Rasul* would be meaningless. The right to *habeas corpus* has always included the right to legal assistance."[17]

Amnesty International said: "All forms of evidence will be admissible, including from anonymous witnesses and testimony that may have been coerced. We are convinced that what the administration is planning is to have the courts restrict their review to the narrow record that emerged from this Combat Status Review Tribunal scheme."[18]

Transcripts of the Combat Status Review Tribunal hearings for 393 detainees were subpoenaed by two civilian defense lawyers. Aided by 29 law students from Seton Hall University in Newark, NJ, they determined that:

- "The government did not produce any witness in any hearing.
- "The military denied all detainee requests to inspect the classified

evidence against them.
• "The military denied all requests for defense witnesses who were not detained at Guantanamo."[19]

Prior to Combat Status Review Tribunals being completed, US District Judge Joyce Hens Green refused to dismiss the claims of 50 detainees challenging their confinement. In her January 2005 decision she said Combat Status Reviews "violate long-standing principles of due process by permitting detention of individuals based solely on their membership in anti-American organizations rather than on actual activities supporting the use of violence or harm against the United States."[20] She called the administration's broad definition of "enemy combatant" illogical because classified evidence she reviewed showed no evidence of any combat activity for many of them. In addition, she felt those who fought in Afghanistan's Taliban army were entitled to all of the Geneva Conventions protection provided POWs.

Two weeks before Green's ruling, US District Judge Richard J. Leon upheld the government's position and said the handful of claims he was ruling on should be dismissed. Apparently feeling that two conflicting lower court rulings canceled each other out, the administration continued Combat Status Review Tribunals. In March 2005 the last one was held for a total of 558 Pentagon detainees, of which 38 were released.

The CIA's 14 High Value Prisoners. These detainees, claimed to be the most important prisoners taken into custody since 9/11, were transferred to Guantanamo in September 2006 from secret CIA prisons. Their Combat Status Review Tribunals began in March 2007 with Abu Faraj al-Libbi and Ramzi bin al-Shibh being the first two. Another was held the next day for Khalid Sheikh Mohammed, 41, attributed with being the mastermind of the 9/11 attacks. Others would follow.

Although the previous 558 tribunals for Pentagon detainees had been open, these were closed to the public and media. Since lawyers don't participate in these tribunals, there were no civilian lawyers to keep out. Detainees were present if they chose to be. The only ones excluded were observers and the media. Legal critics felt the Bush administration did not want it revealed how these prisoners were treated under "enhanced interrogation techniques" or where those interrogations took place.

Sensational stories about the 9/11 mastermind began to roll off the presses that month telling of censored transcripts and confessions. According to the transcripts Khalid Sheikh Mohammed confessed in a rambling statement to planning the 9/11 attacks and 30 other plots, most of which failed or never happened. He said earlier statements were made under torture but not at Guantanamo. Redacted parts of the testimony are believed to be references to his treatment by the CIA. At the end he said his testimony was not coerced.

Supposedly, these tribunals were to determine enemy- combatant status, not prove guilt, but they also determined whether incarceration should continue and possibly trial by military commission. Confessions made during these tribunals, run by non-lawyers and non-judges, could play a role in later proceedings. There is no assurance that confessions made under coercion are not admitted. Mohammed was speaking through an interpreter so someone else was reading his statements which could have been from previous confessions. Mohammed referred to previous confessions extracted under torture. Those could be what was read into the record. Without observers and reporters present we have no way of knowing.

Even if Mohammed did confess to those 31 plots during the tribunal proceedings, his confession may still have been related to torture. As the number three person in Al Qaeda he must have gone through some pretty horrible treatment. Possibly the threat of being returned to a CIA prison elicited his confession. Or it could easily be his treatment warped his thinking. We don't know all these details which makes any confessions associated with torture highly suspect.

The Geneva Conventions are very precise in defining how prisoners should be treated and their combat status defined by a competent tribunal. The 1977 Protocol 1 addition to those conventions goes further to cover any conceivable circumstance. Article 75 starts out: "[P]ersons who are in the power of a Party to the conflict and who do not benefit from more favorable treatment under the Conventions or under this Protocol shall be treated humanely in all circumstances and shall enjoy, as a minimum, the protection provided by this Article."[21] The article first lists personal protections including protection from murder, torture of all kinds (physical or mental), corporal punishment, mutilation, outrages upon personal dignity (humiliating and degrading treatment, enforced prostitution and any other form of indecent assault), or the threat of any of these. There is also an ample list of legal protections regarding incarceration (see Appendix H for the entirety of Article 75). Princeton University International Law Professor Emeritus Richard Falk pointed out: "The USA has signed but not ratified Protocol 1, and is thus bound not to disturb the treaty provisions while seeking in good faith to have the agreement ratified."[22]

Bush's Military Order Struck Down

The flurry of appeals to federal courts continued. One that reached the Supreme Court was the knockout blow to Bush's military order—the *Hamdan* case (not to be confused with the *Hamdi* case discussed previously).

Hamdan v. Rumsfeld (2006). Salim Achmed Hamdan was captured by the militia in Afghanistan in 2001 and turned over to US forces and transferred to Guantanamo in 2002. Over two years later the Pentagon charged him with "conspiracy to commit...offenses triable by military commission." In his petition for *habeas corpus*, Hamdan asserted the military commission lacked authority to try him because 1) conspiracy is not a crime of war and 2) the commission violates the requirements of military and international law, including having the right to see the evidence against him.

Just as military commission hearings were commencing for Hamdan, the D.C. district court granted *habeas* ruling that Hamdan was protected by the Third Geneva Convention until he was found to be an "unlawful" combatant. The court also ruled that military commissions as set up by Bush's order violate both the Uniform Code of Military Justice and the Third Geneva Convention because they allow conviction based on secret evidence unavailable to the accused. Military commission trials came to a halt. All proceedings were shut down pending appeal.

A three-judge panel (all Bush or Reagan appointees) of the D.C. Circuit Court of Appeals unanimously reversed the district court's ruling in July 2005, saying the Geneva Conventions were not judicially enforceable and ruled that *Ex Parte Quirin*, 317 U.S. 1 (1942), which upheld Roosevelt's World War II military commission nullified any separation-of-powers objections to a military commission's jurisdiction. Finally, the appeals court found that Hamdan's trial before a commission violated neither the UCMJ nor the Geneva Conventions. Judge John G. Roberts, Jr., soon to become chief justice of the Supreme Court, was one of the judges voting for reversal. Military commissions got the green light to start up again.

As mentioned, Congress could pass legislation to override the law cited by the Supreme Court in the *Rasul* decision – and they did just that, passing legislation to override 28 U.S.C. 2241. Attached to the Defense Appropriations Act of 2006, which became law in December 2005, was Section 1005(e) entitled "Procedures for Status Review of Detainees Outside the United States" which became the Detainee Treatment Act of 2005. It provided that no court, justice or judge has the jurisdiction to consider a writ of *habeas corpus* filed by or for any alien detained at Guantanamo. This was obviously an attempt to coerce the Supreme Court to refuse *certiorari* for *Hamdan*. It didn't work. The Supreme Court accepted the case in November 2005. Then the government lobbied the Supreme Court to dismiss the case. That didn't work either.

The Supreme Court soundly reversed the appeals court in a 5-3 decision. Newly-appointed Chief Justice John G. Roberts recused himself. In its June 2006 decision, the court went to great lengths to explain each ruling. Itemized simply, they are:

1. The government argues unpersuasively that federal courts should abstain from intervening, as they can in courts-martial, because Hamdan is not a US service member.

2. The military commission at issue is not expressly authorized by any congressional act.

3. The military commission at issue lacks the power to proceed because its structures and procedures violate both the UCMJ and the Geneva Conventions.

Whoa! Military commissions were again put on hold.

But JAG defense lawyers don't win Supreme Court decisions overturning presidential orders without reprisals. Navy Lt. Cdr. Charles Swift was Hamdan's lawyer. Two weeks after the Supreme Court ruling, Swift was passed over for a promotion to full commander. The navy has an up-or-out rule that if you can't keep advancing they don't want you, so he may be forced to retire early. At least ten other JAG lawyers representing detainees at Guantanamo have been passed over for promotion.

When asked if he thought challenging the administration's policy was the reason he wasn't promoted, Swift said: "As a defense attorney, I don't like allegations without evidence." Then he added: "What you sought in any career was an opportunity to make a difference. I got that opportunity and for that I will be forever grateful."[23]

Nevertheless, the eagerness of JAG defense lawyers to represent their clients at Guantanamo zealously was severely dampened after they saw how it would threaten their careers. The Bush administration proposed in December 2007 that promotion of any of the 4,000 officer-lawyers in the JAG Corps must first be "coördinated" with politically-appointed Pentagon lawyers. A final decision was to come within a month.

Congress Gives Bush What He Wants

After the administration's setback in *Hamdan*, and in order once again to put military commissions back on track, the Bush administration began drawing up proposed legislation that would authorize the military commissions.

The Military Commission Act of 2006

Some legislators insisted military lawyers participate in drafting the proposed military commission legislation. In August 2006 Atty. Gen. Gonzales told Congress that "our deliberations have included detailed discussion" with military lawyers whose "multiple rounds of comments... will be reflected in the legislative package."[24] That was a stretch. Allowing secret evidence was mentioned only once when Gonzales met with the top military lawyers from the JAG Corps. The bill was actually being drafted by politically-appointed civilian lawyers in the Justice Department who met only once with a working group of JAG lawyers on July 28. That was followed up with some e-mail exchanges which stopped in a couple weeks and those exchanges involved mostly language and procedures.

Retired JAG attorneys expressed anger at the lack of consultation and said dismissal of JAG's experience has been a chief cause of troubles like Abu Ghraib. Former Air Force JAG, retired Maj. Gen. Nolan Sklute, said: "The [Justice Department] should have learned that a failure to involve the JAG community can lead to problems. If they are talking to the JAGs only about superficial matters...that indicates that this is about form instead of substance, and nobody has learned any lessons out of this."[25]

Top active-duty JAGs testified before a Senate hearing in August strongly criticizing the proposed legislation. Using hearsay evidence, evidence derived from coercion and excluding defendants and their civilian lawyers from trials sparked a "rare, open disagreement with civilian officials at the Pentagon, the Justice Department, and the White House" by the active-duty two-star JAGs. This was assented by Army JAG Maj. Gen. Scott C. Black who said: "I don't believe that a statement that is obtained under coercion–torture, certainly, and under coercive measures should be admissible." Regarding secret evidence that only the military defense lawyer can see, Air Force JAG Maj. Gen. Jack Rives, said: "It does not comport with my idea of due process for...defense counsel to have information he cannot share with his client." What will happen to US soldiers in the future was also a concern. Black said: "Reciprocity is something that weighs heavily in all the discussion that we are undertaking... The treatment of [US] soldiers who will be captured on future battlefields is of paramount concern."[26]

Nevertheless, the final bill passed by the Republican-controlled House and Senate in September 2006 and signed by the president the next month, now designated 10 U.S.C. 948a *et. seq.*, contains most of the administration's desires and even gives the president more authority in some cases than his previous military order did. Specifically it:

1. Amends the UCMJ to provide for military commissions to try alien unlawful enemy combatants engaged in hostilities against the US for violating the laws of war and any other offenses specifically identified in the Act. It authorizes the president to establish such commissions and also makes aliens in the US subject to military commissions, not just those at Guantanamo.

2. Broadens the definition of "unlawful enemy combatant" to a person who has: (1) engaged in or supported hostilities against the US or its allies in the war, or (2) been determined to be an unlawful enemy combatant by a combatant status review tribunal or other tribunal established under the authority of the president or the secretary of defense. This allows any tribunal the administration designates a "competent tribunal" to make up its own rules regarding who is an unlawful enemy combatant.

3. Prohibits a combatant subject to trial by military commission from invoking the Geneva Conventions for relief or

America in Peril

habeas corpus. It also denies any court or judge the jurisdiction to hear a request for *habeas corpus* from such a detainee. This presumably applies to all prisoners at Guantanamo even though they haven't yet been classed as "unlawful." It also applies to aliens in the US.

4. Prohibits, with limited exception, a statement made under torture from being admissible against the accused. This still leaves hanging the technical definition of torture, and whether or not the evidence can be shown to have been obtained by torture.

5. Conviction requires a two-thirds vote of commission members except: (1) a three-quarters vote is required for sentences exceeding ten years, and (2) a unanimous vote of a 12-member commission for a death sentence.

6. The final two steps of appeal are to the US Court of Appeals for the District of Columbia and then the US Supreme Court. The latter two are an accused's right if the sentence exceeds ten years or it is a capital case.

7. Lists 30 offenses triable by military commissions, including such universal things as perjury, obstructing justice and contempt. It also lists such vague offenses as "using treachery or perfidy" and the old standby, "conspiracy."

8. UCMJ provisions concerning contempt, speedy trial, self-incrimination warnings and pretrial investigations are not applicable to military commissions.

9. Authorizes the president to interpret the meaning and application of the Geneva Conventions and strips the courts of that jurisdiction.

10. Prohibits using cruel, inhuman or degrading treatment on any person in US custody or control, regardless of geographical location. Since this legislation pertains to military commissions, it is generally interpreted as not having any effect on CIA activity.

The Act grants immunity to all US officials involved with torture prior to 2005. Achieving this immunity has long been a goal of then Atty. Gen. Gonzales to avoid prosecution for war crimes and also protects against being sued by former detainees who were innocent.

The administration has given a little and gained a lot. Bush obtained solid statutory footing for his detainee treatment and trial procedures. Yale Law School Dean Harold Koh said "the image of Congress rushing to strip jurisdiction from the courts in response to a politically created emergency is really quite shocking, and it is not clear that most of the members understand what they've done."[27] Another Yale law professor, Bruce Ackerman, added that "it's not only about these prisoners. If Congress can strip the courts of jurisdiction over cases because it fears their outcome, judicial independence is threatened."[28]

George Washington University Law Professor Jonathan Turley, described the new law on the day Bush signed it, as "a huge sea change for our democracy.... What the Congress did and what the president signed today essentially revokes over 200 years of American principles and values."[29]

Military Commissions Again Instituted

By the next January the Pentagon had issued a 238-page guidance document for the Military Commission Act of 2006 which contained most of the same old rules. A detainee's lawyer still could not share classified information with his client but, after review and approval by the military commission judge, the detainee could view a summary of the classified document. Hearsay or other disputable testimony could be introduced if it was determined to have probative value to a reasonable person. Evidence obtained without a search warrant was also admissible—and the new rules still allowed evidence obtained by coercive treatment:

> Statements obtained by torture are not admissible, but statements in which a degree of coercion is disputed may be admitted if reliable, probative, and the admission would best serve the interests of justice. In addition, for such statements obtained after December 30, 2005, the methods used to obtain those statements must comply with the Detainee Treatment Act of 2005, enacted on that date.[30]

The Detainee Treatment Act of 2005 invokes the United Nations Convention Against Torture and Other Forms of Cruel or Degrading Treatment or Punishment. Evidence derived from any means of coercion prior to the date when the Act became effective, seems to be admissible, so all the court cases, legislation and publication of a new manual did not bar evidence previously obtained through torture.

The Military Commissions Act affected dozens of cases already filed in federal court on behalf of Guantanamo prisoners. Their lawyers requested time to present arguments that the Military Commissions Act of 2006 is unconstitutional. But what does the new law do for the detainees at Guantanamo who are not charged or even declared "unlawful enemy combatants?" Nothing. They have been decreed by combat status review tribunals as "enemy combatants," thus remain in custody for the duration of the war on terrorism – and in legal limbo indefinitely, with no right to *habeas corpus.*

In February 2007, to fulfill a technical step specified in this military act and replace his military order of 13 November 2001, President Bush signed an executive order authorizing the establishment of military commissions at Guantanamo. The trials were again back on track.

Unsuccessful Court Challenges to the Military Commissions Act

By December 2006, the constitutionality of the Military Commissions Act was being challenged in the court system.

Boumediene v. Bush. Lakhdar Boumediene and five other men from Algeria worked for charities in Bosnia and were accused of plotting to blow up the US embassy in Sarajevo in November 2001. They were all acquitted by a Bosnian court in January 2002 but were apprehended by the US as they left the courthouse. This case, consolidated with almost three dozen others, was before the appeals court when the military commissions act became law. The central issue boiled down to whether the act stripped the courts of hearing *habeas corpus* appeals or if the act itself is unconstitutional.

The US district court in Washington D.C. upheld the Military Commissions Act in December 2006, ruling that detainees at Guantanamo Bay have no right to *habeas corpus*. However, the judge also ruled the new act unconstitutional in denying *habeas corpus* appeals to over 12 million legal immigrants in the US. With that split decision the *Boumediene* case went to the court of appeals for D.C. There a three-judge panel ruled 2-1 in February 2007 to uphold the military commission act, but simply said federal courts have no jurisdiction in these cases. (Reagan and GHW Bush appointees were in the majority, the Clinton appointee dissented.)

The Supreme Court on 2 April 2007 declined to hear the case in a 6-3 decision. Justices John Paul Stevens and Anthony M. Kennedy said they joined the four conservative justices because the prisoners had not exhausted all available remedies under the law. The Detainee Treatment Act of 2005 which entitled detainees to combat status review tribunals also provided the determination of that tribunal could be appealed to the US Court of Appeals for D.C. Defense lawyers called this a sham because it was the same appeals court that just denied *habeas corpus* to Boumediene and five others – the reason it was appealed to the Supreme Court in the first place.

Al Odah v. United States. This case, filed on behalf of Khaled A.F. al Odah and others, was denied *certiorari* at the same time and for the same reasons as *Boumediene v. Bush.*

Hamdan v. Gates and *Khadr v. Bush.* Both Khadr and Hamdan ran into the same difficulty with the US District Court for D.C. They applied for *certiorari* with the US Supreme Court where their cases were combined. This, too was denied because they had not exhausted all legal means.

The 29 June 2006 Supreme Court decision in the case of *Hamdan v. Rumsfeld* struck down Bush's military order establishing military commissions, but now since Congress passed the Military Commissions Act of 2006, Hamdan's JAG attorney had again gone through the appeals process up to the Supreme Court. The case of Canadian Omar Khadr is similar. Khadr was 15 years old when he was captured in Afghanistan. His lawyers had also retraced their way through the appeals process under the new law.

Whoa! Military Commissions Again Called to a Halt

Three detainees had been declared "unlawful enemy combatants" by Bush before his military order was struck down—Australian David Hicks, Yemini national Salim Achmed Hamdan and Canadian Omar Khadr. After Congress passed the Military Commissions Act of 2006 the military commissions resumed at Guantanamo. The first successful military commission convened with the arraignment of 31-year-old Australian David Hicks in March 2007.

A Plea Bargain for David Hicks

Hicks was charged with providing material support to terrorism, which the new military commissions act defined as a war crime. His defense team planned to challenge the law as being applied retroactively after Hicks had been detained 4½ years, so they had arrested him, held him and then passed a law making what he did a crime. Section 9 of Article I of the US Constitution states that "No Bill of Attainder or *ex post facto* Law shall be passed"—which is exactly what happened to Hicks.

In a special, late evening session of the commission, Hicks pleaded guilty. The US had agreed with Australia that Hicks would be returned there to serve his sentence. Accepting a plea bargain and pleading guilty was the quickest way out of Guantanamo and resulted in a lighter sentence. The plea bargain specified Hicks would be returned to Australia within 60 days of sentencing, that any proceeds from what he writes would be turned over to the Australian government, that he sign a statement saying he was never mistreated while in US custody (although he had complained about abuse), that he would not talk to the media for a year and that he would submit to US interrogation and testify at future military tribunals.

Hicks was sentenced to an additional 9 months – Bush had originally wanted life imprisonment. ACLU staff attorney Ben Wizner said he was told these were the world's most dangerous terrorists and then they give him a DUI sentence. With regard to renouncing any claims of mistreatment or unlawful detention, Wizner questioned why the US had to hide its conduct with a gag order.

"Case Dismissed" for Salim Achmed Hamdan and Omar Khadr

After being refused *certiorari* by the Supreme Court, Hamdan and Khadr were again scheduled for trial by military commission at Guantanamo with back-to-back arraignments in June 2007. Khadr was the first to face the military judge, Army Col. Peter Brownback, who said he had no alternative but to throw the case out because Khadr had been determined an "enemy combatant," not an "unlawful enemy combatant," by the combat status review tribunal. Bush had added the critical term "unlawful" under authority of his now defunct military order. The new procedures require this determination to be made by a "competent tribunal."

The judge dismissed the case "without prejudice," which means Khadr could be tried again for the same alleged war crimes if his combat status was properly deemed "unlawful." Khadr was not free to go, however, for he will be held until the combat status review tribunal decides he is no longer an enemy combatant. Shortly thereafter, charges against Hamdan were dropped for the same reason. The Khadr and Hamdan decisions apply to all detainees at Guantanamo, including the 14 high-value CIA prisoners.

Prosecutors for the Bush administration appealed to the new Court of Military Commission Review. In September 2007 a three-judge panel ruled that Col. Brownback could continue with the trial—not a surprising result since the judges are hand-picked by the administration—and that a military commission judge could hear evidence to make that decision and then proceed with the trial. As trial preparations began for Khadr in December 2007, the judge ordered that prosecution witnesses not be identified to defendant or anyone else. This grossly hinders determining credibility of witnesses and underscores the deviation from rights to a public trial and ability to confront witnesses against you.

More Court Setbacks for the Bush Administration

Both the Supreme Court and the US Court of Appeals for D.C. made mid-2007 rulings threatening Bush's policy of indefinite detentions at Guantanamo without *habeas corpus* rights.

The US Supreme Court Reconsiders

Lawyers for al-Odah and other detainees asked Army Lt. Col. Stephen Abraham, a member of the combat status review commissions, to sign an affidavit to help the detainees' cases. Abraham, a 26-year military intelligence veteran currently in the reserves, and also a California lawyer, readily agreed. He had run the central computer depository for evidence used for the CSRTs and saw documents for hundreds of the cases. He also served as chief liaison between CSRT panels and the intelligence community. In his seven-page affidavit, the first information to come from the CSRT process, Abraham said intelligence agencies capriciously held back information that would have helped one side or the other. Then with only vague and incomplete information available the panels were pressured to declare the detainees to be enemy combatants. Abraham said he was asked to serve on one of the panels that was pressured in that manner. When that panel decided in favor of a detainee it was ordered to reconvene and consider more evidence. The panel stood firm on its decision, but Abraham was never asked to serve again. Two months later the same detainee was put through the CSRT process again with a new panel which ruled he was an enemy combatant. In his affidavit Abraham said that what was supposed to be specific information lacked any resemblance of credible evidence.

Abraham's affidavit was released in June 2007 and submitted to the Supreme Court the same day to support the attorneys' petition to reconsider denial of *certiorari*. That court's April decision was a 6-3 split but two of the justices (Stevens and Kennedy) who voted for denial, indicated they might reconsider if the administration caused unreasonable delay or subjected detainees to other continuing injuries. Abraham's affidavit must have satisfied that "other and ongoing injury" because a week after its submission the Supreme Court made the rare decision to reverse itself and hear the case of *Boumediene v. Bush*. Two issues expected to be decided are the constitutionality of denying *habeas corpus* and the fairness of the CSRT.

Unexpected Ruling from the D.C. Circuit

When the Supreme Court denied *certiorari* to Guantanamo detainees in April 2007, it said the appellants had not exhausted all other legal channels. The court was referring to the Detainee Treatment Act of 2005 (attached to the Pentagon's authorization act for fiscal year 2006) which provided that Combat Status Review Tribunals would determine if detainees were enemy combatants. The act also said the determination of that tribunal could be appealed to the appeals court for DC. The first case appealed under that act involved eight detainees in two cases that came together—*Bismillah v. Gates* and *Parhat v. Gates*.

A three-judge panel of the D.C. circuit unanimously ruled in July 2007 the government must provide all records on Guantanamo detainees when they challenge their detention by combat status review tribunals, not just the records used during the tribunal proceedings. Further, it said a meaningful review of combat status review tribunals could not be made "without seeing all the evidence, any more than one can tell whether a fraction is more or less than half by looking only at the numerator and not the denominator."[31]

This issue remains unresolved. The records requested are the damning evidence of prejudice Lt. Col. Abraham described in his affidavit for the Supreme Court. The government says it is not possible to assemble all the records. There has even been discussion on convening new combat status review tribunals rather than turn the records over to the court. Unfortunately, there were also rulings in the decision which limited the appeals court review. The Detainee Treatment Act of 2005 only allowed determination on whether the Pentagon followed the rules and whether a preponderance of evidence showed the detainee to be an enemy combatant. The ruling also limited what lawyers can discuss with detainees and allowed the lawyers' mail to be censored by special Pentagon teams.

A Last Thought

In the case of *Boumediene v. Bush*, the one dissenting vote in the February 2007 appellate court decision was cast by Judge Judith W. Rogers. On the evening of the decision she commented: "The combined actions of the Bush administration, the previous Congress, and two of the three judges today have taken us back 900 years and granted the right of kings to the president."[32]

Those are sober words to ponder but there is more. New Jersey's Seton Hall University made a study of government documents on Guantanamo. Statistics from those documents show: 55% of the detainees had not even been accused of a crime, 40% were not alleged to have any connection with Al Qaeda, and only 8% were shown to have fought with a terrorist group. Then came the shocker: A whopping 86% were captured by bounty hunters–the Northern Alliance and Pakistan authorities–when the US was offering large sums for suspected terrorists.

Is the full significance of that percentage apparent? That

means as many as 666 of those 775 human beings that have been (and many still are) caged for years under atrocious and inhuman conditions were innocent people. They were just in the wrong place at the wrong time, with the ethnic and religious qualifications to lure greedy bounty hunters. We Americans pride ourselves with a heritage that started over 200 years ago with a document that expounds: "We hold these truths to be self-evident, that all men are created equal, that they are endowed by their Creator with certain unalienable Rights, that among these are Life, Liberty and the Pursuit of Happiness."

In juxtaposition to that phrase, the word "Guantanamo" will forever be a black mark in American history. How far has our country fallen and what will happen next? I will address one possible answer—the one to be avoided—in the next chapter. The final chapter will present an optimistic and desirable potential.

Notes for Chapter 9

1. Quotation cited by Nina Totenberg, NPR legal correspondent, transcript published in Raban, Jonathan; "Dictatorship is in Danger," *Guardian* (UK), from O'Connor speech at Georgetown Univ, 9 Mar 2006.

2. Lardner, George, Jr., "Legal Scholars Criticize Wording of Bush Order," *Washington Post*, 3 Dec 2001.

3. The Third Geneva Convention (adopted in 1929, revised in 1949) pertains to treatment of enemy soldiers as prisoners of war. The Fourth Geneva Convention (adopted in 1949) applies to the treatment of civilians in time of war. Under the laws of war, only a "lawful combatant" enjoys "combat immunity" or the "belligerent privilege" for the lawful conduct of hostilities during armed conflict. Thus a soldier cannot be tried for murder if he kills the enemy according to the laws of war.

4. Presidential memorandum, "Humane Treatment of al Qaeda and Taliban Detainees," signed by George W. Bush, 7 Feb 2002.

5. McCoy, Alfred W., "The US Has a History of Using Torture," History News Network, 4 Dec 2006, at http://hnn.us/articles/32497.html

6. A thorough history of the American style of torture is found in Alfred W. McCoy's *A Question of Torture: CIA Interrogation, from the Cold War to the War on Terror* (NY: Owl Book, 2006).

7. Haugaard, Lisa, "Textbook Repression: US Training Manuals Declassified," *Covert Action Quarterly*, n.d., at http://mediafilter.org/caq/caq61.CAQ61manual.html

8. Jay Bybee has since been appointed a federal appellate judge with the US Ninth Circuit Court of Appeals.

9. Torture Memo—for Alberto R. Gonzales, counsel to the president: *Re: Standards of Conduct for Interrogation under 18 U.S.C. §§ 2340-2340A*, 1 Aug 2002.

10. They are 3(b) of Category I; and 1, 2, 5, 6, 9, and 11 of Category II.

11. Savage, Charlie, "Military Lawyers See Limits on Trial Input," *Boston Globe*, 27 Aug 2006.

12. Lewis, Neil A., "Rules for Terror Tribunals May Deter Lawyers," *NY Times*, 13 Jul 2003.

13. Bravin, Jess, "Defense Lawyer at Guantanamo Questions Military Commissions," *Wall Street Journal*, 7 Apr 2006.

14. ABC News; "Leaked E-mails Claim Guantanamo Trials Rigged," 1 Aug 2005.

15. Gorman, H. Candice, "An Exchange on *Habeas Corpus*," Guantanamo Blog, 24 Jan 2007, at http://gtmoblog.blogspot.com/2007.01/exchange-on-habeas-corpus_24.html

16. *Rasul v. Bush*, 542 U.S. 466 (2004), pp. 1-2.

17. Marquis, Christopher, "Pentagon Will Permit Captives at Cuba Base to Appeal Status," *NY Times*, 8 Jul 2004.

18. AI press release; "USA: Administration Continues to Show Contempt for Guantanamo Detainees Rights," 8 Jul 2004.

19. "AP Gets Shocking New Report on Guantanamo," *Editor & Publisher*, 17 Nov 2006.

20. Leonnig, Carol D., "Guantanamo Bay Military Reviews Ruled Illegal," *Washington Post*, 31 Jan 2005.

21. "Addition to the Geneva Conventions of 12 Aug 1949, Relating to the Protection of Victims of International Armed Conflicts (Protocol 1)," adopted 8 Jun 1977 by the Diplomatic Conference on the Reaffirmation and Development of International Humanitarian Law Applicable to Armed Conflicts, entered into force 7 Dec 1979.

22. Falk, Richard A.; "Re: Guantanamo and Geneva Conventions," private e-mail to author, 24 Jan 2005.

23. Williams, Carol J., "Marine Corps Issues Gag Order in Detainee Abuse Case," *LA Times*, 15 Oct 2006.

24. Savage, op. cit.

25. Ibid.

26. Smith, R. Jeffrey, "Top Military Lawyers Oppose Plan for Special Courts," *Washington Post*, 3 Aug 2006.

27. Smith, R. Jeffrey, "Many Rights in US Legal System Absent in New Bill," *Washington Post*, 29 Sep 2006.

28. Shane, Scott and Adam Liptak, "Detainee Bill Shifts Power to President," *NY Times*, 30 Sep 2006.

29. Binion, Carla; "Bush's Absolute Power Grab," *Consortiumnews.com*, 21 Oct 2006.

30. *Manual for Military Commissions*, Department of Defense issue implementing the Military Commissions Act of 2006, signed by Secretary of Defense Robert M. Gates, 18 Jan 2007.

31. Glaberson, William, "Court Tells US to Reveal Data on Detainees at Guantanamo," *NY Times*, 21 Jul 2007.

32. Rosenberg, Carol, "Panel: Guantanamo Captives Can't Sue in US Courts," *Miami Herald*, 21 Feb 2007.

10

America in Denial Cannot Long Endure

*There is no greater mistake and no graver danger than not to see
that in our own [US] society we are faced with the same phenome-
non that is fertile soil for the rise of fascism anywhere, the insignificance and powerlessness of the individual.* – Erich Fromm, 1941[1]

The insignificance and powerlessness of the individual! Social psychologist Erich Fromm wrote that warning just before
the US entered World War II. He was born in Frankfurt, Germany, to Orthodox Jewish parents and moved to the US in
1934 as Hitler was coming into power. His studies on the irra-
tionality of mass behavior were influenced by Sigmund Freud's
ideas on character development through biological drives and
psychological factors plus Karl Marx's view that society, especially its economic systems, is more important to character
development. But Fromm added another aspect: he makes freedom the central aspect of human nature, thus as freedom dimin-
ishes in a democracy, human nature becomes lost and unfo-
cused. Fromm's description of the general attitude in Germany
during the rise of the Third Reich is a warning we Americans
should not ignore today. Fromm described it thus:

> The dark and diabolical forces of man's nature were relegated
> to the Middle Ages and to still earlier periods of history, and

they were explained by lack of knowledge or by the cunning schemes of deceitful kings and priests....When Fascism came into power, most people were unprepared, both theoretically and practically. They were unable to believe that man could exhibit such propensities to evil, such lust for power, such disregard for the rights of the weak, or such yearning for submission.[2]

American political scientist and historian Dr. Michael Parenti agrees with Fromm, adding that "there's a concern that we're tending toward fascism, or we're replicating fascism today." What ruthless leaders have "learned in the more than 80 years since its [fascism's] origin is that they can achieve many of the things...while retaining a democratic veneer." Parenti continues: "The essence of fascism, I believe, is its output. And its output is a system which systematically redistributes wealth from the many to the few, and ensures the domination of giant cartels over the whole political economy." Parenti sees the use of "plain old Americanism" as the "cloak around which people will rally and give the president these extraordinary powers, and surrender their own liberty and the like."[3]

With lip service of "Plain old Americanism" our democratic structure has indeed been reduced to a thin veneer. Like Germany in the 1930s, people in the United States today are unprepared to recognize fascism when it meets them here at home. They believe such an extreme is impossible in a democracy. The entire scenario is so unbelievable people turn their minds to other things—to sports, television, computer games, work or whatever—anything but politics.

That is the denial that is sounding the death knell for America as a democracy. I will show here where this denial will inevitably lead us if it continues.

How Dark Is the Cloud That Hovers?

Election 2000 put them in power and 9/11 kicked off their agenda. Since then the neoconservatives have persistently and effectively chipped away the structure of our country as a democracy. It started with the PATRIOT ACT and continues today with "executive orders," "signing statements," "state secrets privilege," and ordinary old deception enshrouded in all the secrecy people will tolerate. Democracy seems to have won a few battles by nipping in the bud such programs as TIPS, TIA, MATRIX, PATRIOT Act II, the VICTORY Act and National ID Cards, but those were only temporary victories. The essence of every one of those programs has reappeared in a different form buried in another department. Today we cannot make a phone call, send an e-mail, search the internet, check out a book, buy an airline ticket or open a bank account without the government watching. Over 100,000 of us have our travel rights restricted because of various watch lists. Our early warning mechanisms for incursions on our freedoms and rights have been dismantled with the restrictions and fears impressed on WHISTLEBLOWERS.

Even a new type of terrorism has been codified – "Domestic Terrorism." Any person committing any violation that threatens bodily harm can be charged as a domestic terrorist. Speeding tickets can provide the excuse for arrest and detention. Some of the most common state-law offenses can be transformed into a serious federal crime. This new form of terrorism can have grave consequences for anyone when this country experiences another serious emergency. All this and more has been outlined above.

The institutions of government have also experienced an alarming change as 22 existing agencies were conglomerated into the Department of Homeland Security and 16 intelligence agencies were gathered under the wing of one National Intelligence Director. Beyond this, the entire North American continent has been militarized and continental United States has been declared a battle zone. This reorganization provides tighter administrative control, less freedom and more authoritarianism. The neoconservative agenda has also politicized the judicial branch. Throughout US history appointments of judges and Supreme Court justices have been made along political lines. Appointments during the Nixon, Ford, Reagan and the two Bush administrations have, however, put the judicial branch in a political stance that supports the neoconservative agenda. Of the numerous decisions by the various US Courts of Appeal documented throughout this book, the judges appointed by these Republican presidents have, with few exceptions, upheld the neoconservative agenda.

With the addition of two appointees by George W. Bush, the US Supreme Court has become almost hopelessly skewed in favor of neoconservative issues. Four justices (John G. Roberts Jr., Samuel A. Alito Jr., Antonin Scalia and Clarence Thomas) are consistently "conservative." Three (Stephen G. Breyer, Ruth Bader Ginsburg, and David H. Souter) are consistently "liberal." Another (John Paul Stevens) usually votes "liberal." The swing justice (Anthony M. Kennedy) usually votes with the "conservatives." In issues of neoconservative interest the Supreme Court is often split 5-4 in favor of the neoconservatives, with Kennedy being the swing vote in virtually every case.

In essence, and in actual fact, the entire spectrum of our civil rights, and many human rights, has been overrun in the name of national security by an administration obsessed with secrecy and deception, which also possesses an absolute contempt for the rule of law. Fromm warned in 1941 that Americans would become insignificant and powerless. It is against this backdrop we must anticipate the future, especially martial law, because that will be the turning point where democracy completely dissolves and a dictatorship takes over.

The cloud hovering over America is indeed dark.

Preparing for Martial Law on Battlefield USA

A mere week after the 9/11 attack, Congress passed Special Joint Resolution 23,[4] known as the Authorization for the Use of Military Force authorizing the president to use "all necessary and appropriate force against those nations, organizations, or persons he determines planned, authorized, committed, or aided the terrorist attacks that occurred on September 11, 2001." That law opened the scope of forceful action to cover the entire planet and gave substance to the war on terrorism. Such enormous power was granted because Congress deemed it "both necessary and appropriate that the United States exercise its rights to self-defense and to protect United States citizens both *at home* and abroad" (emphasis added). It further legitimized the United States homeland as a battlefield. Bruce Fein, former associate deputy attorney general under Reagan, observed that "by declaring the US to be a battlefield, Bush [has] already made it possible for himself to declare martial law, because you can always declare martial law on a battlefield. All you would need would be a pretext, like another terrorist attack on the US."[5]

Section 1076 – Repeal of Posse Comitatus

In October 2006 Bush signed the National Defense Authorization Act for Fiscal Year 2007 (H.R. 5122).[6] Attached was Section 1076, rushed through passage during the waning months of the Republican-controlled Congress, which according to Senator Patrick Leahy was "slipped in as a rider with little study" while "other congressional committees with jurisdiction over these matters had no chance to comment, let alone hold hearings on, these proposals."[7] It was a de facto repeal of the *Posse Comitatus Act of 1878*. The legislation amended Section 333 of the Insurrection Act[8] to add conditions when the president can employ the national guard and/or the armed forces in major public emergencies, including "natural disaster, epidemic or serious public health emergency, terrorist attack or incident, or other condition in any state or possession of the United States, the president determines that domestic violence has occurred" to an extent justifying federal intervention. Note that familiar catchall phrase at the end – "or other condition... the president determines..."

Section 1076 also amended Section 334 of the Insurrection Act[9] to add "or those obstructing the enforcement of the laws" after "insurgents" to the paragraph authorizing the president to order disbursement within a limited time. It used to be only insurgents that could be forcibly disbursed. Now the law applies to legitimate peaceful protesters.

Bush's National Continuity Policy

The potential for martial law came much closer into focus on May 9, 2007, when Bush signed a dual executive order – National Security Presidential Directive No. 51 and Homeland Security Presidential Directive No. 20 to establish a new national continuity of government policy (NSPD-51/HSPD-20) which replaces all previous presidential orders and outlines the administration's policy for continuity of government in an extreme emergency.

This defines "Catastrophic Emergency" as "any incident, regardless of location, that results in extraordinary levels of mass casualties, damage, or disruption severely affecting the US population, infrastructure, environment, economy, or government functions." Should such an event occur, the Constitution would effectively be suspended under this directive and extraordinary powers would be conferred on the president and vice-president. This dovetails perfectly with Section 1076 of H.R. 5122 which gives the president strong discretionary powers to use the military to "restore public order and enforce the laws of the United States."

Although this directive gives lip service to guaranteeing constitutional democracy and the checks and balances of three branches of government, its one overriding theme is that during a catastrophic national emergency the power of the executive branch and the president is paramount. Bush's new National Continuity Policy opens the door to martial law.

Declaring national emergencies is not new. The Congressional Research Service (CRS) released a report in November 2006 titled "National Emergency Powers" which points out that these "delegations or grants of power authorize the President to meet the problems of governing effectively in times of crisis." It continues: "Under the powers delegated by such statutes, the President may seize property, organize and control the means of production, seize commodities, assign military forces abroad, institute martial law, seize and control all transportation and communication, regulate the operation of private enterprise, restrict travel, and in a variety of ways control the lives of United States citizens."[10]

That is a lot of power for one person to wield. But the operative phrase is "delegations or grants of power." It was not the intent of the Constitution or Congress to delegate or grant dictatorial power. The CRS report continues:

> There are, however, limits and restraints upon the President in his exercise of emergency powers. With the exception of the *habeas corpus* clause, the Constitution makes no allowance for the suspension of any of its provisions during a national emergency. Disputes over the constitutionality or legality of the exercise of emergency powers are judicially reviewable. Indeed, both the judiciary and Congress, as co-equal branches, can restrain the executive regarding emergency powers. So can public opinion. Furthermore, since 1976, the President has been subject to certain procedural formalities in utilizing some statutorily delegated emergency authority.

What happened in 1976? That year Congress passed the National Emergencies Act[11] to curtail the random manner in which emergencies were declared by executive order. This abolished some of the statutory authorizations for declaring a national emergency and modified others. It also mandated reporting the declaration and subsequent updates to Congress. Section 1621 of the Act states: "Such proclamation shall immediately be transmitted to the Congress and published in the Federal Register." Section 1641 requires the president to notify Congress immediately of any subsequent significant orders, executive orders, rules and regulations issued during the emergency.

Section 1076 of the Insurrection Act modification discussed above also requires the president to notify Congress as soon as practicable of his determination to use the military, and every 14 days thereafter as long as the emergency continues. However, Bush's NSPD-51/HSPD-20 leaves some doubt about the executive reporting to Congress in a national emergency. Section 20 of that directive reads very similar to his signing statements: "This directive shall be implemented in a manner that is consistent with, and facilitates effective implementation of, provisions of the Constitution concerning succession to the Presidency or the exercise of its powers." This echoes the unitary executive theory Bush is so fond of, as well as his reluctance to be responsible to Congress. In addition, nothing in the continuity of government planning initiated by Bush's presidential directive provides for notifying Congress of a national emergency, yet it would be a national emergency that triggered implementation of continuity of government planning.

The American public still doesn't know the full scope of NSPD-51/HSPD-20. Neither does Congress. The directive is unclassified except for certain continuity annexes and states that "except for Annex A, the Annexes attached to this directive are classified and shall be accorded appropriate handling, consistent with applicable Executive Orders." In response to numerous queries from constituents regarding a possible conspiracy in the classified annexes, Oregon Representative Peter DeFazio asked the White House to see them. Normally a congressperson can view classified material in a secure room at the Capitol. DeFazio had made the request numerous times. This time it was different. For the first time in his experience DeFazio got the answer "DENIED." The Bush administration declined to explain why. DeFazio stated: "We're talking about the continuity of the government of the United States of America. I would think that would be relevant to any member of Congress, let alone a member of the Homeland Security Committee. Maybe the people who think there's a conspiracy out there are right."[12]

What Will Trigger Martial Law?

Only a major event could be used to trigger martial law. The Bush administration has been studying what such an incident could be, under the label of disaster planning. The President's Homeland Security Council – composed of cabinet-level officials to coördinate homeland security-related activities among the administration's departments and agencies – has identified 15 scenarios to facilitate federal, state and local disaster planning. Here I will summarize only those that can be controlled or timed – which would enable a "false flag" terrorist attack – and not address conventional explosives used in parking lots or on public transit, as shown in the Homeland Security Council's scenarios, because they would not create the devastating consequences needed to justify martial law. Neither would a cyber attack although it could be used in conjunction with other scenarios. What are left are nuclear, biological and chemical attacks.

Nuclear Attacks

The Homeland Security Council outlines two scenarios under a nuclear attack: The first is a 10-kiloton bomb exploded in a major city (the Hiroshima bomb is estimated at 14 kilotons) which would result in an unknown number of fatalities, 450,000 evacuations, 3,000 square miles contaminated, and hundreds of billions of dollars in economic impact. That is a big step up from 9/11 and, let us hope, too severe to consider. Nevertheless, in May 2007 a homeland security readiness test took place in Indiana – at the Muscatatuck Urban Training Center (Jennings County) and Camp Atterbury (Johnson County) with more than 2,000 active duty and 1,000 national guard troops, plus local and state law enforcement agencies, responding to a simulated nuclear bomb attack. This was one of three simultaneous tests – another in Rhode Island simulated a hurricane and a third in Alaska replicated a terrorist attack. These disaster-response tests are held biannually under the joint sponsorship of the US Northern Command, the Department of Homeland Security and the Canadian Department of National Defense.

The second type of nuclear attack hypothesized by the Homeland Security Council is exploding a "dirty bomb" to spread radioactive contamination in three cities. A dirty radioactive bomb is a conventional nuclear explosive that spreads radioactive material over a wide area. Such an attack would result in some 540 fatalities, 60,000 detectable contaminations and billions of dollars in economic impact. This might be enough to justify martial law, especially if numerous attacks occurred simultaneously.

Biological Attacks

A bio-terrorism report published by the Department of Veteran's Affairs, pointed out that bio-terrorism has the greatest chance to harm large numbers of people.[13] It also has a greater potential for fear and anxiety – emotions that could help support martial law. Yet, protecting people after such an attack is easier than after chemical or nuclear attacks. The agent used in a biological attack could be a toxin, a virus or bacteria. Infectious disease experts have identified three specific agents as the ones most likely to be used:

- The first is spraying anthrax spores in a large city which could produce 13,000 fatalities, extensive contamination, and billions in economic impact.
- Second is pneumonic plague bacteria which would result in 2,500 fatalities, 7,000 injuries with the economic impact only in the millions. This could be the most likely scenario to expect because of the low impact on economy. Antibiotics started within 24 hours can successfully treat pneumonic plague. Nevertheless, the possibility of evacuations and quarantines would better justify use of the military for control.
- The third type of biological attack most likely for terrorists to use is to spread the smallpox *variola* virus to contaminate large

areas. Smallpox, being a virus, is difficult to treat. Most of the population under 35 have not been vaccinated for this and so would be susceptible because vaccinations were discontinued when smallpox was declared globally eradicated. An epidemic would also result in quarantines which would justify military control.

Chemical Attacks

Four scenarios using chemical agents are identified in the Homeland Security Council's list of possible catastrophes to prepare for. They are:

- Spraying blister agents, such as mustard gas, into a crowded football stadium. This is estimated to cause 150 fatalities, 70,000 hospitalized with 100,000 evacuated. Because this scenario would be so localized, it probably isn't sufficient to justify martial law unless numerous attacks occurred throughout the land.
- Spraying a nerve gas such as Sarin into the heating/air conditioning system of three office buildings in a city would result in 6,000 fatalities, 350 injuries of building occupants and $300 million economic impact. An unknown number of people downwind would be evacuated. Again, multiple incidents of this kind are possible.
- Spreading toxic industrial chemicals by using conventional explosives to destroy petroleum and petrochemical facilities 350 people would be killed and 1,000 hospitalized. Up to 700,000 people would be evacuated.
- Spreading chlorine gas by using conventional explosives to blow up large chlorine tanks or a chlorine plant. This is similar to the previous scenario except it would be more devastating. This could result in 17,500 fatalities, 100,000 hospitalizations, and up to 70,000 people evacuated. It would also contaminate the immediate area and the waterways.

Of course the foregoing scenarios are not comprehensive. There are many more agents that could be employed and numerous combinations that could be used; however, these examples are sufficient to illustrate the variety of disasters that could be orchestrated. The federal government is actually planning for these events. In fact, it is secretly rewriting a national response plan from which state governments feel excluded.

State and local officials question why their input is being ignored regarding federal disaster planning. After all, they are the first responders and a national plan is supposed to show how federal, state and local agencies will work with the federal government. A 71-page draft of the plan released to the states in early August 2007 was renamed the "National Response Framework." Bruce Baughman, Alabama's emergency management chief and a 32-year veteran of FEMA, said the draft was "a step backwards because its authors did not set requirements or consult with field operators nationwide who will use it to request federal aid, adjust state and county plans, and train workers." Homeland Security spokesperson Laura Keehner responded, "State and local officials were included earlier in the decision-making process, but an initial draft they produced along with FEMA- and DHS-preparedness officials in May [2007] 'did not meet expectations'."[14] The existence of this early August draft was not publicly known until it was leaked to the *Congressional Quarterly*.[15]

This operation in secrecy has a familiar ring. It is all the more ominous in light of NSPD-51/HSPD-20 which was also released in May when the earlier National Response Plan "did not meet expectations." Since Bush's directive gives him sole power in major public emergencies, the administration sees no need to involve state and local officials in the planning. A November 2007 budget document obtained by Associated Press confirms White House intentions to cut allocations to local police, firefighters and rescue department. The dhs proposal of $3.2 billion for that purpose in fiscal 2009 was more than halved to $1.4 billion. The National Response Framework flows in logical progression after Section 1076 of H.R. 5122 and NSPD-51/HSPD-20.

The Martial Law Enforcers

Martial law would be the beginning of fascist rule. As

events unfold to reveal the nature of this rule one might question if US troops would continue to follow orders. Let me explain some training exercises that conditions troops and law enforcement officials to support martial law, at least initially.

Training the Enforcers

NORTHCOM, which has effectively absorbed NORAD, has been training to counter the effects of a terrorist attack ever since its formation. Two major exercises – Ardent Sentry and Vigilant Shield – take place annually but NORTHCOM also participates in up to a couple dozen smaller exercises each year which take place on a lower tier. The National Exercise Program outlines all military exercises worldwide for all commands. Where applicable it also includes state and local law enforcement. The exercises are divided into four tiers:

- Tier I is directed by the White House with a focus on strategy and policy. It requires full government-wide participation with two levels of exercises – the national level exercise is higher and involves all applicable government departments and agencies, the other is a principle level exercise involving one or more cabinet departments such as DOD and DHS.
- Tier II has a federal strategy and policy focus with significant simulation of a disaster or terrorist attack.
- Tier III involves other federal exercises of operational, tactical, or organizational focus and simulation.
- Tier IV has a state, territorial, local, tribal or private sector focus.

Ardent Sentry is always part of a national level exercise in Tier I. Its primary focus is to support civil authorities. Other commands with their own code-names also participate in national level exercises as applicable. The other annual exercise is Vigilant Shield which is variously scheduled in Tiers I, II and III. Its primary focus is homeland defense.

There are two other NORTHCOM exercises which take place biennially. Amalgam Phantom (formerly Amalgam Warrior) is a live-air exercise that occurs on even years in conjunction with

Ardent Sentry and typically involves two or more NORAD defense regions.[16] It was something like Amalgam Warrior that was taking place on 9/11 and caused a lot of the confusion. In odd years, Northern Edge takes place with Ardent Sentry in Alaska to support civil aviation. The exercises described above in Indiana, Rhode Island and Alaska involved Ardent Sentry and Northern Edge.

DHS announced in May 2007 that the first national level exercise for fiscal year 2008 is scheduled for 15-24 October 2007. It was the fourth Top Officers (TopOff-4)[17] exercise involving 15,000 federal, state, territorial and local participants in an all-out response to a coördinated and multi-faceted attack. The scenario started with three coördinated attacks on Guam with simulated detonations of radiological dirty bombs. Following were similar attacks in Portland, Oregon and Phoenix, Arizona. Besides NORTHCOM and DHS, participants included the European Command, Southern Command, Strategic Command and presumable the Pacific Command since Guam was involved.

These counterterrorist exercises are advertised as necessary to deal with the aftermath of another terrorist attack, not as a preventive drill, and they involve all law enforcement and first-responder agencies at all levels, as well as military troops. They condition the public to expect government control when a major incident occurs and develop the manner in which various terrorist tools and agents can be used to provide the desired level of devastation. All of this sounds like the right thing to do and thus avoids close scrutiny; however, as good as all this may appear, these exercises also manipulate the physical and psychological capabilities of everyone involved to support the government if another false flag attack is perpetrated.

So active duty military and the national guard can be mobilized to take control in a national emergency—and counted on to follow orders pertaining to normal operations such as conducting evacuations and enforcing quarantines and curfews. But what about the real dirty work? Soldiers in Iraq are now balking at the atrocities they are forced to commit. Who would conduct such operations under martial law? Who would disarm the estimated 90 million gun owners in this country? Who would conduct the urban warfare here in the US, with all the expected "collateral damage," when some of those gun owners decide to defend their rights and property? It's hard to envision many US troops shooting up the streets in American cities and killing civilians, if that should become necessary. So this is where hired guns enter the picture.

The White House Republican Guard

Many people are not aware of what Jeremy Scahill calls the "often-overlooked subplot of the wars of the post-9/11 period," along with "the outsourcing and privatization they have entailed."[18] By July 2007 there were 180,000 private contractors from 630 companies working for the US in Iraq – cynically called the "coalition of the billing." It is estimated that 118,000 of those are Iraqis. Hundreds of others are from Chile, some trained during the coercive Augusto Pinochet regime. The remainder come from over 100 countries including Fiji, Brazil, Scotland, Croatia, Hungary, New Zealand, Pakistan, South Africa, the Philippines, Nepal, Colombia, Ecuador, El Salvador, Honduras, Panama, Peru and Australia. Most of them perform mundane jobs that used to be done by service personnel such as cooking, KP, laundry and truck driving. Sometimes the drivers do run into hostile situations.

A 2006 government report said 48,000 of the total are private contractors working for 170 companies who engage in armed combat as "security guards;" equipped with automatic rifles, body armor, helicopters, and armored trucks. They have guarded the highest officials, including the commanding general in Iraq and civilian American VIPs. How many armed mercenaries are there today is unknown. Estimates place the figure between 60,000 and 100,000. Of the war-contracting companies, Blackwater USA is the largest. Others include DynCorp International, Triple Canopy, Erinys, ArmorGroup, Hart Group Ltd., Control Risks Group and Aegis Defense Services. The latter three are British and some firms send mercenaries to countries other than Iraq, as DynCorp does to Latin America to fight the drug lords.

Former US Ambassador to Iraq, Joseph C. Wilson thinks it's very dangerous to contract for violence to support foreign policy, since the billions of dollars these companies get paid makes them a powerful, well-armed lobby group with questionable loyalties. They seem exempt from both civil and military law and have almost no congressional oversight. (Watch for cosmetic changes since the September 2007 Blackwater scandal.)

Being unaccountable brings out the most unscrupulous behavior. One 54-year-old man said they "kill innocent people in the street....They are frenzied dogs." A housewife added: "They simply kill." An Iraqi policeman said "They bump other people's cars to frighten them....Two weeks ago, guards of a convoy opened fire randomly that led to the killing of two policemen." Even other foreign contractors say Blackwater guards smudge all their reputations: "I and others have had Blackwater aggressively try to run us off the road and point guns at us at checkpoints," and "They ride around in their vehicles pointing their weapons at people in the street and in cars."[19]

Will these mercenaries contract to enforce martial law on US soil? No problem. Blackwater gained domestic experience when 150 of their armed mercenaries in full battle dress rushed to New Orleans after Hurricane Katrina in August 2005. Their number continued to grow as they were officially hired by the DHS to patrol streets in unmarked vehicles and protect banks, hotels, large businesses and rich individuals. Mercenary contractors from other companies, including an Israeli company,[20] also rushed to Louisiana to guard businesses and expensive homes from looters.

That first deployment of Blackwater mercenaries on US soil opened a new and lucrative market for the company's services.

Blackwater representatives have met with state and local officials to solicit potential business following future natural disasters. Michael Ratner of the Center for Constitutional Rights sees this domestic deployment as a dangerous trend:

> Unlike police officers, they are not trained in protecting constitutional rights. These kind of paramilitary groups bring to mind Nazi Party brownshirts, functioning as an extrajudicial enforcement mechanism that can and does operate outside the law.[21]

It is not difficult to envision how Blackwater and the other "security contracting" companies would be used if martial law were declared. Blackwater alone is reported to have 21,000 former special forces troops, ex-soldiers and retired law- enforcement officials on call to train and lead mercenary soldiers with 20 aircraft and helicopter gunships. Its 7,000 acre base in North Carolina, considered the world's largest private military-training facility, trains tens of thousands of law enforcement officers and friendly-nation troops annually. Blackwater is building additional facilities in California and Illinois as well as a jungle training base in the Philippines. The paramilitaries for martial law are ready and waiting.

Where Will the Dissidents Go?

Precedents abound for detaining suspicious people. Most renown, perhaps, is President Franklin Roosevelt's Executive Order 9066 which confined people of Japanese, German and Italian ancestry from designated geographical areas, even if they were American citizens. The entire west coast was one such zone and some 120,000 Japanese and Japanese-Americans were sent to ten "relocation camps" for the duration of World War II.[22] The justification for relocating these people was based exclusively on their Japanese ancestry. They had a deadline to liquidate their holdings, invariably at a sacrifice, and relocate before being forcibly moved.

Less well-known are Roosevelt's Presidential Proclamations 2525, 2526 and 2527 which authorized detention of any "enemy alien" alleged to be potentially dangerous. Ensuing action rounded up some 11,000 Germans, 3,200 Italians, over 10,000 Japanese (some reports say 18,000) and scores of other Europeans – US citizens and legal residents, single adults and entire families – and interned them in at least eleven detention camps or stations.[23] Some detainees were not released until three years after the war's end. Incarceration was based on race along with other evidence, frequently questionable – hearsay, unsubstantiated allegations, neighbors voicing suspicions and even for just keeping contact with relatives in their homeland. Those detained were never told why and could not refute whatever it might be. Immigrants would not fare well under martial law today.

Readiness Exercise 1984

A more recent precedent for mass incarcerations was Readiness Exercise 1984 (REX-84) during the Reagan administration. It was not the first readiness exercise, and it was only an exercise, but its procedure is still applicable. The scenario was FEMA having to detain a huge influx of 400,000 refugees crossing the Mexican border resulting from war in Central America. This was the time of the Iran-Contra Scandal and US hostilities toward Nicaragua. Reagan's order authorized this test of FEMA's ability to assume military authority and also provided for closing ten military bases for conversion to detention camps. According to Professor Carl Jensen, founder of Project Censored at California's Sonoma State University, "REX-84 coördinated 34 federal departments and agencies to conduct a civil readiness exercise during April 5-13, 1984,...The training exercise included the use of the military to control civil disturbances, major demonstrations, and strikes, which would affect government operations and resource mobilization."[24] Jensen said fighting terrorism, relocating large populations and imposing martial law were also part of the exercise.

United States Civil Disturbance Plan 55-2 – called Operation Garden Plot – was employed as part of REX-84. It is ostensibly a plan for giving military assistance to state and local law enforcement agencies during times of extreme civil unrest.[25] It would target what is considered "disruptive elements" such as protest and resistance groups and other types of nonconformists. Garden Plot is activated when state and local authorities cannot handle the situation. Deadly force is permitted. When federal troops were ordered into Los Angeles in May 1992 to assist the national guard and local police to control the riot following the acquittal of the officers involved in the Rodney King beating, they followed Operation Garden Plot.

Another program employed during REX-84 was Cable Splicer, a plan to take over state and local governments systematically. Some analysts think Cable Splicer is part of Garden Plot. Cable Splicer started in California when Ronald Reagan, as governor, enlisted help from the state national guard to configure a program to help the federal government should President Nixon declare martial law. Its purpose at that time "was to legitimize the arrest and detainment of anti-war protesters and political troublemakers during the Vietnam era."[26] Information about Garden Plot and Cable Splicer was first published by the alternative press in 1975, but the planning did not become widely known until the mid-1980s when REX-84 became public knowledge. They are still believed to exist today, probably in a more refined form.

According to Carl Jensen there were between 160 and 190 active internment camps in the US by late 1999, most of which were on active or closed military bases. Each is capable on housing 10,000 to 300,000 detainees. The Texas State University website claims there are currently "over 600 prison camps in the United States, all fully operational and ready to receive prisoners,...The camps all have railroad facilities as well as roads leading to and from the detention facilities. Many have an airport nearby"[27] There have been many articles published on the web giving locations by state, pictures, maps – even aerial photographs. Is this all paranoia – a set of conspiracy theories – or is there some substance to the allegations of hundreds of detention camps existing today? Let me do a little analysis of various programs to put this subject in context so you can reach your own conclusion.

Civilian Augmentation of Military Operations

Today with an all-volunteer military the trained soldiers or sailors are too specialized and too valuable to stretch over all the tasks necessary to support an army or navy, so contracted civilian help – augmentation – is being used to perform mundane tasks such as food services, supply, laundry, cleaning, transportation and more. These support functions need to be planned in advance, so each military branch grants contingency contracts for a civilian augmentation program if it is ever needed – the army's Logistics Civil Augmentation Program (LOGCAP), the navy's Construction Capabilities (CONCAP) and the air force's Air Force Contract Augmentation Program (AFCAP). They are all similar in function but tasks differ according to needs. For this discussion I will address the army's program.

LOGCAP was put in place in December 1985 and first used in 1987 when the army corps of engineers had to plan, construct and maintain two oil pipelines to support potential operations in Southwest Asia. When the 1991 Gulf War began the ratio of civilian contractors to military personnel was 1:100. For a longer conflict that ratio would have strained logistics. Eventuality prompted the concept of an "umbrella" LOGCAP contract, described as "an indefinite-delivery/indefinite-quantity cost-plus award-fee, on-call provider service contract with actual costs depending on specific requirements."[28] That mouthful means when it is activated, the contractor will be reimbursed for legitimate expenses and awarded an additional fee based on performance. LOGCAP contracts are global in scope in order to cover contingencies worldwide. They can also be activated for work in the US.

The first of these "umbrella" contingency contracts – LOG-CAP I – was awarded to Kellogg, Brown & Root (KBR – a subsidiary of Halliburton until 2007) in August 1992 and in force for five years. LOGCAP II was awarded to DynCorp International and expired in February 2002. LOGCAP III went back to KBR in December 2004 to be in effect for ten years. It is to provide needed *construction* and services globally. KBR helped construct 14 enduring bases in Iraq and it also worked with the army corps of engineers and the navy seabees (construction battalion) to build Camp X-Ray, Camp Delta, Camp Five and Camp Six at Guantanamo. KBR is experienced in building camps, but it also has another type of contingency contract.

KBR's $385 Million Contingency Support Program

KBR announced in January 2006 it had "been awarded an Indefinite Deliver/Indefinite Quantity contract to support the Department of Homeland Security's US Immigration and Customs Enforcement (ICE) facilities in the event of an emergency" for $385 million over a five-year period which "will be executed by the US Army Corps of Engineers, Fort Worth District."[29]

ICE is Homeland Security's largest investigation agency and is composed of four law enforcement divisions and several support divisions. The KBR contingency contract would augment ICE's detention and removal operations by supporting the army corps of engineers to build temporary detention and processing capabilities which could also be used by other government organizations as well – the FBI, CIA, Secret Service, Treasury Department, or any federal agency that would be instructed to detain people.

Publicity about this contract focuses attention on immigration, but again, watch the wording carefully. One part of KBR's press release discusses possible needs for detention camps "in the event of an immigration emergency, as well as the development of a plan to react to a national emergency, such as a natural disaster." Then it discusses a natural disaster but evades what other type of national emergency might occur. Another part is even more worrisome for it admits these quickly built camps might be required "in the event of an emergency influx of immigrants into the US, or *to support the rapid development of new programs*" (emphasis added). That phrase didn't go unnoticed. Many commentators have speculated on what other new programs might be in the pipeline.

The next question is where these emergency detention centers would be built. Clayton Church, a spokesperson for the army corps of engineers said they "could be at unused military sites or temporary structures and that each one would hold up to 5,000 people."[30] This requires a deeper look.

The Army's Civilian Prison Camps

Army Regulation 210-35,[31] first drafted in December 1997 went through a "rapid action revision" in January 2005. It provides policy and guidance for two separate, distinct activities: 1) establishing and managing civilian inmate labor programs on army installations, and 2) establishing prison camps on army installations. Only the latter is relevant to this topic. Ostensibly this program provides on-base housing for the prison labor program, but according to the regulation this is not the exclusive purpose. It specifically states: "Establishing civilian inmate prison camps on army installations is separate from establishing civilian inmate labor programs." It concedes "correctional systems" may approach the army to build or lease unoccupied facilities. Presumably any federal law enforcement agency would qualify. If that seems to stretch the policy too much, it is provided in the regulation that the army's "Assistant Chief of Staff for Installation Management may modify chapters and policies contained in this regulation." The groundwork is laid for KBR to build detention camps on army property.

Does the Army have enough unused facilities to accommodate a large prison camp program under martial law? Most certainly. During the recent round of military-base closures in 2005 the Department of Defense recommended 33 major closures—which was the fifth round of base closures since 1988. So Carl Jensen's claim of 160-190 detention camps already existing may not be far off the mark.

Even active military bases are so large that a prison camp could be constructed almost unnoticed. I recently drove through the sprawling Hunter Liggett Military Reservation in California and saw some construction in the foothills and realized it could be a civilian prison camp with no one aware of it. The military controls a lot of land and they have the authority to quarantine large blocks of it from public access.

Restoring World War II Internment Camps

A December 2006 AP report said: "Notorious internment camps where Japanese-Americans were kept behind barbed wire during World War II will be preserved as stark reminders of how the United States turned on some of its citizens in a time of fear."[32] This story mentioned that the national park service was authorized $38 million to restore the ten camps where people of Japanese ancestry were confined. Additional grants, requiring 50% matching funds, were authorized for non-federal organizations to research and restore the ten camps. Wouldn't it be ironic if these camps, restored for the purpose of memorializing America's folly, were commandeered under martial law for emergency internment of another 120,000 people? Such is possible and KBR could be assigned to manage them.

A Final Word

This chapter plays out the drama of what will likely happen if American citizens allow denial of reality to continue. Everything is in place for martial law. Section 1076 of H.R. 5122 abolished *Posse Comitatus* and set the stage for military control within the US. NSPD-51/HSPD-20 established the procedures for taking over the country. REX-84, Garden Plot and Cable Splicer tell how it will be done.

Today FEMA doesn't have to coördinate 34 separate federal departments and agencies, Homeland Security has already absorbed 22 of them including FEMA itself. To identify who should be rounded up, the Pentagon's Counterintelligence Field Activity has at least 13,000 dissidents on its database and the FBI's Terrorist Screening Center has another 800,000 on its watch list. The government already knows who they want to take off the streets and the military is prepared to do that.

There is no shortage of troops to enforce martial law who will follow orders well. The national guard can be nationalized at the president's beck and call, and over the objections of state governors. An ample supply of mercenary contractors is available for the real dirty work. There will be no lack of martial law enforcers.

KBR's contingency contract ensures experienced capabilities to build and run detention facilities. The army's civilian prison camp program assures enough real estate on which to build them. Even refurbished World War II detention camps can meet an immediate need,

All that is needed is a "catastrophic emergency" to set the wheels of martial law in motion. 9/11 illustrates how easily such an emergency can be orchestrated.

Psychologist R.D. Laing believes people develop a "pseudo sanity" and adapt to "pseudo realities" and thus live in a "social fantasy system." Dr. Daniel Burston adds that people "embedded within social-fantasy systems like these function effectively within the framework of these groups. But their sense of reality regarding the world outside of their reference group is profoundly impoverished as a consequence....[W]e are seeing a growing threat to the viability of democratic decision-making systems across the board, around the world."[33]

Dr. Michael Parenti warned: "In spite of a veneer of optimism and initiative, modern man is overcome by a profound feeling of powerlessness which makes him gaze toward approaching catastrophes as though he were paralyzed" – like the deer in the headlights. Erich Fromm gave the same warning decades earlier, but added the empowering observation that "for everybody who is powerless, justice and truth are the most important weapons in the fight for his freedom and growth." Fromm narrowed it down further, saying "truth is one of the strongest weapons of those who have no power."[34]

Truth is a force that can unmask the phantom democracy – the pseudo patriotism – so many of us are fixated on. It can penetrate and explain the motives of our leaders who are sending us astray. It can help us recognize the evil that our country is perpetrating throughout the world – endowing us with the vision America could and should hold. But how do we recognize it – how do we make it work? That is the subject of the next and final chapter.

Notes for Chapter 10

1. *Escape from Freedom* (NY: Owl Book, 1941), pp, 239-240.
2. ² Ibid, p. 6.
3. Goldstein, Ritt, "US: Patriotic Pride and Fear," *Asia Times*, 8 Jul 2004.
4. S.J. Resolution 23 (Public Law 107-40); "Authorization for Use of Military Force," passed 18 Sep 2001.
5. Lindorff, Dave, "Martial Law Is Now a Real Threat," *Counterpunch*, 27 Jul 2007 at http://www.counterpunch.org/lindorff07272007.html
6. H.R. 5122 (109th Congress) to become Public Law 109-364.
7. Morales, Frank, "Bush Moves Toward Martial Law," *Toward Freedom*, 26 Oct 2006 at http://towardfreedom.com/home/content/view/911
8. 10 U.S.C. 333; "Interference with State and Federal Law."
9. 10 U.S.C. 334; "Proclamation to Disburse."
10. "National Emergency Powers," Congressional Research Service report to Congress by Harold C. Relyea, updated 13 Nov 2006.
11. 50 U.S.C. 1601-1651; "National Emergencies Act."
12. Kosseff, Jeff, "Congressman Denied Access to Post-attack Continuity Plans," *Newhouse News Service*, n.d. 2007.
13. *Bioterrorism: What You Need to Know*, Dept. of Veterans Affairs, 2006.
14. Hsu, Spencer S., "States Feel Left out of Disaster Planning," *Washington Post*, 8 Aug 2007.
15. Sullivan, Eileen, "DHS Achieves Target Weight for National Response Guidelines," *Congressional Quarterly*, 1 Aug 2007.
16. Some sources say Amalgam Phantom takes place twice a year – in the fall for the east coast and in the spring for the west coast – but both couldn't happen in conjunction with Ardent Sentry.

17. These are congressionally mandated biennially to involve top officers in counter terrorism activities.

18. Scahill, Jeremy, *Blackwater: The Rise of the World's Most Powerful Mercenary Army* (NY: Nation Books, 2007), p. xvii.

19. Agence France Presse; "Iraqis Round on Blackwater 'Dogs' after Shooting," 18 Sep 2007.

20. The Israeli company, Instinctive Shooting International, is now an approved vendor for the US Department of Homeland Security.

21. Scahill; op. cit., pp. xxv and 332.

22. The ten Japanese-American "relocation camps" are Gila River and Poston in AZ, Jerome and Rohwer in AR, Manzanar and Tule Lake in CA, Granada in CO, Minidoka in ID, Topaz in UT and Heart Mountain in WY.

23. Detention camps included Kooskia in ID, Fort Missoula in MT, Fort Stanton and Santa Fe in NM, Fort Lincoln in ND, Fort Forrest in TN, and Crystal City, Kenedy and Seagoville in TX. Detention stations included Sharp Point in CA and Ellis Island in NY.

24. Jensen, Carl; "Civilian Detention Camps," PBN News website, n.d.

25. Operation Garden Plot was also called Oplan Garden Plot (Operations Plan Garden Plot), MACDIS (Military Assistance to Civil Disturbances),and Garden MACDIS. It may have a different name today.

26. Jensen, op. cit.

27. "FEMA and REX-84," Texas State University website, n.d.

28. Bowen, Stuart W., Jr., (insp. gen.), "Memorandum for Commander, US Army Matériel Command; Deputy Assistant Secretary of the Army for Policy and Procurement; Director, Defense contract Audit Agency," Report No. 05-003 for Iraq Reconstruction, 23 Nov 2004.

29. KBR press release; "KBR Awarded US Department of Homeland Security Contingency Support Project for Emergency Support Services," KBR website, 24 Jan 2006.

30. Swarns, Rachel L., "KBR-Halliburton Get $385 Million Contract to Build Detention Centers Just in Case They Are Needed," *NY Times*, 4 Feb 2006.

31. AR210-35 – Army Regulation 210-35; *Civilian Inmate Labor Program*, 14 Jan 2005.

32. Werner, Erica, "Congress Funds Restoration of W.W. II Internment Camps," *San Jose Mercury News*, 6 Dec 2006.

33. Goldstein, op. cit.

34. Fromm; op. cit., p. 286, 248.

11

Beyond Democracy

The world we have made, as a result of the level of thinking we have done so far, creates problems we cannot solve at the same level of thinking at which we created them. — Albert Einstein[1]

I have been agonizing over how to write this concluding chapter. What can I write that will change the direction of my country? I have searched for information to inspire my readers. There are volumes of inspiring words—words written, not years or centuries ago, but some reaching back 4,000 years—and the message is still the same. But I don't know how to paraphrase or rephrase all that wisdom in a single chapter.

Yet this chapter must be written. As I pondered my dilemma, it seemed that I should just tell my experiences. Something brought my life to the point where I wanted to write this book. Why not share that? Perhaps I should start with the quotation above.

I became aware of Einstein in my pre-nuclear-age high school years as someone regarded as a world-class scientist. After World War II he became better known as a pioneer nuclear physicist whom I considered a genius, but still in the scientific arena. Then in the 1970s I came upon the philosophical side of

America in Peril

Einstein which were revealed in statements he made in his sunset years of the second thoughts he had about helping humanity acquire such a monstrous responsibility: "Our world faces a crisis as yet unperceived by those possessing power to make great decisions for good or evil. The unleashed power of the atom has changed everything save our modes of thinking, and thus we drift toward unparalleled catastrophe...a new type of thinking is essential if mankind is to survive and move to higher levels."[2]

Those words impressed me. It was refreshing to hear a genius who had devoted his life to the unbending laws of science show such concern. This thought bite gnawed at my consciousness. The problem is, does it require generations for a more enlightened thinking to appear? I truly believe not that much time is needed for human thought to be transformed individually and collectively. My hope is that it can be achieved within one generation—because if it can't, as Einstein warned, we drift toward unparalleled catastrophe.

My Thought-Bite Philosophy

A composer/musician friend, Tom Rawson, recently sent me a CD with his song "Coloring Outside the Lines"[3] about a little girl scrupulously staying within the lines in her coloring book. Suddenly a mischievous grin crosses her face and she looks up and says: "Gonna color outside of the lines this time."

What a break from a stinted lifestyle it is to be a little daring. I envision America waking up and saying that exact thing. Leo Tolstoy did his bit of borderless coloring in the 19th century with his book *The Kingdom of God is Within You* which explored an individual's view of life. Tolstoy tried to publish it in his homeland in 1893 but the Russian government squashed it saying it was too dangerous to church and state—too much scribbling outside the lines. Then it was translated into English and published in London in 1894.

Tolstoy defined three philosophies of life and claimed humanity has already passed through two of them. He felt it was impossible to view life in other ways than through one of these three. I think he may be correct.

The first viewpoint is a focus on oneself, what Tolstoy refers to as the *individual conception of life*. This is epitomized by primitive humanity where the struggle for survival predominates. There are still self-centered people in the world today, but we tend to hope this viewpoint is diminishing, although there are those who are abused to the point where survival takes first priority in their environment. Dr. Viktor Frankl tells of the sheer fight for survival and the "unrelenting struggle for daily bread and for life itself" while in a German concentration camp during World War II. He wrote "with the majority of prisoners, the primitive life and the effort of having to concentrate on just saving one's skin led to a total disregard of anything not serving that purpose." Frankl relates his experience as a doctor trying to help another prisoner, but the man died and was dragged outside the prison hut and left in a snow bank. Frankl's next words stayed with me for decades: "While my cold hands clasped a bowl of hot soup which I sipped greedily, I happened to look out the window. The corpse which had just been removed stared at me with glazed eyes. Two hours before I had spoken to that man. Now I continued sipping my soup."[4]

Tolstoy second viewpoint is the *social conception of life* where humans extend their love and dedication to others. It was fairly easy to care about the closest relationships of family and clan, but to move one's concern beyond that—to the tribe and nation—was more difficult and took special training. According to Tolstoy's theory, *it is not possible to move beyond the nation state with only the social conception of life*. That is an important point—we will continue to have the conflict among nation states unless we transcend the social conception of life. A global government, even global harmony, can never be achieved while the majority of humanity is stagnated at the social level. International treaties and diplomacy all stem from the social conception.

That idea caught my attention. The limitations of the social outlook are illustrated in today's futile struggle for harmony while each nation is elbowing for its own special interests. The attitudes of nationalism and patriotism seem definitely to be the ultimate limit of the social conception of life. This must be what Einstein had in mind when he warned we can never solve our global problems with the thinking we possess today.

Instead, a worldview that transcends national boundaries and border fences is desperately needed – which brings us to Tolstoy's last conception: "In the third theory of life a man's life is limited not to society and classes of individuals, but extends to the principle and source of life – God."[5] This view embraces the entire planet and is what Tolstoy calls the divine conception of life – or what we might refer to as the *spiritual perception of life.*

For Tolstoy, the transition from a social viewpoint to the spiritual perception began sometime during the Roman Empire and continues today. That seems consistent with a movement toward the new way of thinking Einstein said we needed. It all sounds good, but we get back to the same question – do we have to wait centuries for this advanced awareness to develop? If so, the world could be in pretty sad shape by then – if it even remains part of the planetoid system.

I prefer to hope that thought processes of the mind advance in a different dimension than time. The Buddhist monk Thich Nhat Hahn provides a useful model – the concept of "mindfulness" which basically says that paying attention and being aware of our tasks involves taking control of our minds rather than being controlled by them. This is not easy. We are all spoiled and our attention wanders. Extraneous thoughts sneak in and we go into rote behavior and then we find ourselves following the crowd. That is not control of thinking. "When you are washing dishes think about washing dishes" is the thought bite Thich Nhat Hahn gives us. It takes conscious effort to keep our minds focussed. Yet it makes sense that doing a task mindfully is an important step toward a spiritual perception of life.

What about wisdom? Does control of thoughts—mindfulness, paying attention and awareness—lead to greater wisdom? The *Bhagavad Gita*, one of the most respected books of Indian spiritual literature, defines three divisions of wisdom:

> • There is wisdom which knows when to go and when to return, what is to be done and what is not to be done, what is fear and what is courage, what is bondage and what is liberation—that is pure wisdom.
> • Impure wisdom has no clear vision of what is right and what is wrong, what should be done and what should not be done.
> • Wisdom obscured by darkness occurs when wrong is thought to be right and things are thought to be that which they are not.

It is the pure wisdom we seek. The last two can be summed up as uninformed and confused. Mindfulness and awareness can lead to greater wisdom and help us sort out confusion and lead to true information. Mohandas Gandhi provided another insight about truth—the knowledge leading to wisdom. He equated truth to God and dedicated his life to seeking it. It was his belief that everyone has a little bit of the truth, so if we could all get together and communicate with open minds we would assemble the true picture.

Which makes me remember the bumper sticker of the 1970s that admonished us to "Question Authority." This provoking thought can easily be misunderstood. Perhaps the essential message here is that we need to have confidence in our own ability to think clearly and not depend on authorities to make all the major decisions. If we have made some progress in taking control of our mind and thinking we should be able to reason most things out for ourselves. Then when our thinking differs from the authorities, we must seek the correct answer, the correct action, or the correct whatever. We seek the truth.

To sum up these thought bites, I would posit:

My thought process is evolving.
A spiritual perception of life is the next step.
Mindfulness and awareness lead to greater wisdom.
Seeking the truth of all things should be a lifestyle.
I can be daring and "color outside the lines."
Develop confidence in my own judgment and follow it.
I-Thou

What a list! This sums up my spirituality and how I have tried to address Einstein's call for a new level of thinking as I steer toward the goal I am trying to reach in my life. You might have noticed I slipped in an extra item not yet discussed. The "I-Thou" concept is what seems to be the first and most important step toward developing a spiritual perception of life, although we might not at first realize that.

Compassion

I was raised a Protestant and became a Catholic shortly after Janet and I were married. We followed that tradition for a while but then along came Pope John XXIII with his wandering crayon and opened a window of the church for a little fresh air. Renewal came amid much controversy and the word "ecumenism" became popular. I started looking into the message from other denominations, and then other religions—not that I wanted to convert, I was just curious. My curiosity brought me a fresh feeling of spirituality. Thought bites I had accumulated over years congealed into a concept and confidence in my own ability to search for the truth. I started straying beyond the boundaries of dogma and colored a little outside the institutional lines. What I discovered was the core message is the same in all religions. Only superficial ideologies constructed by humans keep people apart.

One evening I went to a talk given by a respected friend who discussed an encounter described by Jewish philosopher Martin Buber. Once on a bus Buber noticed a man across the aisle. The usual attitude in public places is to keep to one's self, eyes deflected, silent, but Buber observed this person and contemplated his personality. Suddenly the man happened to look up. When their eyes met there was mutual warmth. He could see Buber's compassion and returned it. This was my introduction to Buber's "I-Thou" concept.

I was fascinated and found a copy of Buber's book *I and Thou*[6] which turned out to be a masterful treatise on what our relationship with others is and could be. He also introduces the "I-It" attitude with which we look upon another as an object. Objects have value only insofar as they are useful to us. In "I-It" we see others for their value or usefulness in fulfilling our personal agenda. The "I-Thou," on the other hand, embraces others for their value. In thinking back over memories of past incidents, I realized I had experienced the I-Thou a few times.

Once when I was in the third grade, my parents went to significant effort and sacrifice to provide me with new school clothes during the depression years. Some of my classmates were not as fortunate. I always felt a little superior to those more shoddily dressed and shaggy headed. One lunch hour I watched one poorly-dressed girl unwrap her lunch and noticed how carefully the sandwiches were packaged, albeit with bread wrappers. My mother took special care to make my lunch appealing and I realized the same loving attention was put into preparing the lunch for that girl. I thought to myself that she is really loved by her parents, which gave her new value in my eyes. That is my first-remembered "I-Thou" experience. In years afterward I wasn't always so observant, or so compassionate, but that first "I-Thou" incident hibernated within me.

Years later when I was at work, I attended an inter-departmental working group meeting. Usually with such combinations of people, there tends to be competition and vying for authority. One particular person seemed singularly annoying to me. I found my mind wandering outside the agenda as I contemplated this individual and wondered what he was like away from work. Did he have a family and what did they think of him? Was he loved by wife and children? Did he barbecue hot dogs for the kids after work? What other things did they do together? My imagination rolled on. Aside from being a little overzealous, he wasn't such a bad guy. I didn't realize it, but I was entertaining an "I-Thou" encounter.

After that, that fellow and I enjoyed a more congenial relationship and I slowly came to realize that a wholesome interaction with others depends primarily on my own attitude. It made a difference when I started recognizing others as fellow human beings with problems and pleasures just like mine, instead of objects with value only in proportion to their usefulness to me.

For me, adapting the "I-Thou" relationship globally is the final critical step toward a spiritual perception of life—to say nothing of addressing the problems we have created on this planet. When I begin to feel a little jaded about the troubles in Darfur, or Ethiopia, or dozens of overwhelming other places, I pull myself up short and look at one of my grandchildren trying to imagine them in one of those places—which makes me shudder. There are parents and grandparents who have to live under those circumstances. How would I cope if I were a parent in extreme destitution and had to decide which child most needs the only scrap of food available? These thoughts sound morbid—and they are—but they are reality for some people. Just being aware of them helps me to put the big picture in focus.

A Benevolent World Order

Call it a benevolent world order, a spiritual perception of life or simply global peace and justice—achieving it should be a desire for all of us, but we often don't know where to start. It's been a dilemma for me for years. After lowering my sights from seeking earth-shaking enlightenment to something more manageable I have a suggestion. In this chapter, as I conceptualized my thought-bite philosophy it made me more aware—

mindful, if you will—of my everyday activities, revealing a pattern I vaguely knew was there but did not see in its full significance. This exercise has outlined the direction I want to steer my life. Let me share this with you.

All of us have thought bites that lurk in our subconscious. Gandhi talks of the "small, inner voice" that spoke to him. We all experience that voice. Call it conscience, God speaking to us, or whatever, it is there. When we pay attention to this voice, we often have an experience that sticks or a new insight. Perhaps we should make more of an effort to recall these happenings that impressed us during our lifetimes. They don't all come at once, but we can keep adding to the list as they come to mind. In my experience, as my list grew, a pattern took shape which helped me think and study these concepts. Which led to discussing it with others and experimenting with actions that fit that pattern. Trying to live a far mellower, less competitive or consumer-driven routine made me find my lifestyle to be much more wholesome and fulfilling. I think this might be approaching the spiritual perception of life.

If you join me in this process, I am convinced it will influence your actions, as it did mine. At first it might be easier just to share your feelings—which is a good way to communicate. People are interested in exchanging feelings that aren't too confrontational. When others begin to perceive that we really care, they will respond and our hopes and dreams will propagate. This is something we can do anytime and anywhere. Perhaps this is the surest way to arrive at that new way of thinking.

I believe a spiritual perception of life is within everyone's reach if we set our mind to it and become more caring. Just by observing another person and trying to understand what life is like for them can develop more sympathetic attitudes in us. How would we feel in that person's skin? When others see that we care, it spreads, and when enough people look on others with concern and compassion, a unified desire to turn this country around is certain to emerge. Jim Douglass called it the nonviolent equivalent of a nuclear critical mass. That is the only solution I see to the peril America, and the world, now faces. The time has come when we must seriously consider moving beyond democracy.

One more thought bite comes to mind. I was disgusted when the atom bombing of Nagasaki was described as a Catholic chaplain blessing a Catholic pilot who then bombed Nagasaki's Urakami Cathedral—the center of Catholicism in Japan. Ironic? It soured me on religion. Then one day I met that chaplain. Father George Zabelka visited our home one evening before speaking at an FOR potluck where he admitted he had done wrong as a chaplain in not preaching against bombing civilians. His repentance caused him to spend the rest of his life teaching peace. He also was disturbed along his pilgrimage to reflect on his history. Martin Luther King Jr.'s words from the Montgomery jail was one impetus: "Blood may flow in the streets" but "We must not harm a single hair on the head of our white brothers." The Sermon on the Mount was another: "Love your enemies. Return good for evil." Which brought him to his peacemaking stance that evening. He left us with this thought bite: "Do something for peace. Do anything. But do something."

So I pass that along—just do something. It is imperative that every last one of us, no matter what our occupation or vocation, do something to accelerate the one process that will bring peace and justice to our country and our planet—something that will attain and spread a spiritual perception of life. Big rallies and marches have their place but I'm sure it will be the persistent day-to-day contact with others that will chip away the patriotic façade and transform this planet into a peaceful world. Talk about it. Discuss it. Live it. Demonstrate it. We can do it. Albert Einstein set the priority: "Our task must be to free ourselves from this prison by widening our circle of compassion to embrace all living creatures and the whole of nature and its beauty."[7]

Notes for Chapter 11

1. MacHale, Desmond, *Wisdom* (London, 2002).

2. Mattern, Douglas, "Albert Einstein: Scientist, Philosopher, World Citizen," *New Realities*, Jul/Aug 1984.

3. Rawson, Tom, *Outside the Lines* (Seattle, Ironwood Studios, Dec 1992).

4. Frankl, Viktor E., *Man's Search for Meaning* (NY: Washington Square Press, 1959).

5. Tolstoy, Leo, *The Kingdom of God is Within You* (Lincoln: Univ of Nebraska Press, 1894).

6. Buber, Martin, *I and Thou* (NY: Charles Scribner's Sons, 1958).

7. Albert Einstein letter dated 1950, in H. Eaves' *Mathematical Centers Adieu*, 1977.

Appendix A

Players in *Pax Americana*
(More prominent players are highlighted)

Abrams, Elliott – Assistant Secretary of State for Inter-American Affairs in the Reagan admin. Convicted in 1991 of two counts of lying to Congress but granted a Christmas Eve pardon by George Bush Sr. a year later. Formerly Senior Director of the White House Security Council's Office for Democracy, Human Rights and International Operations and Deputy National Security Adviser in the George W. Bush admin. Signed 1998 letter to President Clinton.

Armitage, Richard L. – Assistant Secretary of Defense for International Security Affairs in the Reagan admin, Presidential negotiator, ambassador and coördinator of emergency humanitarian assistance in the Bush Sr. admin, Deputy Secretary of State (#2 spot in state department) in George W. Bush admin. Member board of directors for the ConocoPhillips Oil Company. Signed 1998 letter to President Clinton.

Barnett, Roger – US Naval War College. Contributed to the 2000 Report.

Bennett, William J. – Secretary of Education in the Reagan admin. Director of the Office of National Drug Control Policy in the Bush Sr. admin. Former co-director of "Empower America" and distinguished fellow of Heritage Found. Signed 1998 letter to President Clinton.

Bergner, Jeffrey – Board member of Hudson Inst. Board member of Asia Foundation. Assistant Secretary of State for Legislative Affairs in George W. Bush admin. Signed 1998 letter to President Clinton.

Bernstein, Alvin – National Defense University professor. Contributed to the 2000 Report.

Bolton, John R. – Assistant Attorney General in Reagan admin. Assistant Secretary of State for International Organization Affairs in the Bush Sr. admin. On board of directors for Project for the New American Century. Under Secretary of State for Arms Control and International Security in George W. Bush admin. US Ambassador to the United Nations in George W. Bush admin. Signed 1998 letter to President Clinton.

Cambone, Stephen – In charge of strategic defense policy at Defense Department during Bush Sr. admin. Under Secretary of Defense for Intelligence in George W. Bush admin. Contributed to the 2000 Report.

Cheney, Dick – Secretary of Defense under the Bush Sr. admin. Headed Halliburton Corporation during the late 1990s. Vice President of the United States.

Cohen, Eliot – Member of Defense Department's policy planning staff during Bush Sr. admin. Founding member of the Project for the New American Century. Member of the Defense Policy Board in George W. Bush admin. Professor and director of Strategic Studies, Johns Hopkins University. Contributed to the 2000 Report

Cross, Devon Gaffney – On board of directors for Project for the New American Century. Contributed to the 2000 Report.

Dobriansky, Paula J. – Deputy Assistant Secretary of State for Human Rights and Humanitarian Affairs in the Bush Sr. admin. Member of Project for the New American Century. Under Secretary of State for Global Affairs in George W. Bush admin. Signed 1998 letter to President Clinton.

Donnelly, Thomas – Former Deputy Director of Project for the New American Century. Research fellow for American Enterprise Inst. Principle Author of The 2000 Report.

Epstein, David – Associated with Office of Secretary of Defense. Contributed to the 2000 Report.

Fautua, David – Lt. Col. US Army. History professor at West Point. Contributed to the 2000 Report.

Feith, Douglas J. – Under Secretary of Defense for Policy in George W. Bush admin.

Fukuyama, Francis – Member Project for the New American Century. Advisory board member of Endowment for Democracy. Advisory board member of the New America Foundation. Signed 1998 letter to President Clinton. Later drifted from neoconservative agenda and opposed the war upon Iraq.

Goure, Dan – Center for Strategic and International Studies. Contributed to the 2000 Report.

Jackson, Bruce P. – Former chair of Project for the New American Century, now on its board of directors.

Kagan, Donald – Former co-chair of Project for the New American Century. Contributed to The 2000 Report. Father of Fred and Robert Kagan.

Kagen, Fred – Former professor at West Point Military Academy. Resident scholar at American Enterprise Inst. Contributed to the 2000 Report.

Kagan, Robert – Co-founder of Project for the New American Century, now on its board of directors. Signed 1998 letter to President Clinton. Contributed to the 2000 Report.

Khalizad, Zalmay – Former UNOCAL advisor. Former US Ambassador to Afghanistan and Iraq. Signed 1998 letter to President Clinton.

Killebrew, Robert – Colonel, US Army (ret), contributed to the 2000 Report.

Kristol, Irving – Considered founder of American neoconservatism, founder and editor of many conservative magazines, distinguished senior fellow of the American Enterprise Inst. Lifetime member of the Council on Foreign Relations. Awarded Presidential Medal of Freedom by George W. Bush. Father of William Kristol.

Kristol, William – Former chief of staff to Vice President Dan Quayle. Co-Founder of Project for the New American Century. Signed 1998 letter to President Clinton. Contributed to the 2000 Report.

Lagon, Mark – Deputy assistant secretary of state for international organization affairs in George W. Bush admin. Contributed to the 2000 Report.

Lasswell, James GAMA Corporation – Contributed to the 2000 Report.

Libby, I. Lewis – Advisor to State Department during Reagan admin. Deputy Undersecretary of Defense for Bush Sr. Formerly chief of staff for Vice President Dick Cheney until forced to resign over the Valerie Plame scandal. Contributed to the 2000 Report.

Martinage, Robert – Senior Analyst, Center for Strategic and Budgetary Assessment. Contributed to the 2000 Report.

Meilinger, Phil – US Naval War College. Contributed to the 2000 Report.

Owens, Mackubin – Professor of Strategy and Force Planning, US Naval War College. Contributed to the 2000 Report.

Perle, Richard – Assistant Secretary of Defense in Reagan admin. Member, American Enterprise Inst. for Public Policy Research, the Project for the New American Century and the Hudson Inst. Patron of the Henry Jackson Society. Served on the Defense Policy Board (1987-2004). Signed 1998 letter to President Clinton.

Rodman, Peter W. – Member of National Security council staff in Nixon and Ford admins. Director of State Department Policy Planning Staff in Reagan admin. Special assistant to the president on national security affairs in the Bush Sr. admin. Assistant secretary of defense for International Security Affairs in George W. Bush admin. Signed 1998 letter to President Clinton.

Rosen, Steve – Harvard University. Former director of foreign policy issues for the American Israel Public Affairs Committee. Fired from that position in April 2004 and awaiting trial for espionage in April 2006. Contributed to the 2000 Report.

Rumsfeld, Donald – Ambassador to NATO in Nixon admin. White House chief of staff in Ford admin. Secretary of Defense in Ford admin. Secretary of Defense in George W. Bush admin. Signed 1998 letter to President Clinton.

Schmitt, Gary – Senior fellow for Project for the New American Century. Contributed to the 2000 Report.

Schneider, William, Jr. – Under secretary of state for security assistance, science, and technology in Reagan admin. Chair of President's General Advisory Committee for Arms Control and Disarmament in Bush Sr. admin. President of International Planning Services, Inc (an international trade and finance advisory firm). Adjunct Fellow of the Hudson Inst. Chair of Defense Science Board in George W. Bush admin. Signed 1998 letter to President Clinton.

Sheehan, Jack – Retired Marine Corps Gen. Senior Vice President of the Bechtel Group. Member of Henry Jackson Society. Member of the Defense Policy Board in George W. Bush admin.

Shulsky, Abram – The RAND Corporation. Member, Project for the New American Century. Director, Pentagon's Office of Special Plans. Contributed to the 2000 Report.

Vickers, Michael – Former Army Special Forces officer and CIA operative. Director of Strategic Studies at the Center for Strategic and Budgetary Assessment. Contributed to the 2000 Report.

Watts, Barry – Former Air Force officer. Headed the 1991 Gulf War Air Power Survey's work on operations and effectiveness. Former director of Northrop Grumman Analysis Center. Former director of program analysis and evaluation in the Office of the Secretary of Defense in the George W. Bush admin. Contributed to the 2000 Report

Weber, Vin – Vice chair of Empower America. Member, Project for the New American Century. Signed 1998 letter to President Clinton.

Wolfowitz, Paul – Served in state department during Reagan admin. Undersecretary of Defense for Policy during Bush Sr. admin. Dean, international relations program at Johns Hopkins Univ. during 1990s, Deputy Defense Secretary (#2 spot in Defense Department) in the George W. Bush admin. President, World Bank until forced to resign effective 30 June 2007. Signed 1998 letter to President Clinton. Contributed to The 2000 Report. In December 2007 Secretary of State Condoleeza Rice offered him the chairpersonship of the International Security Advisory Board.

Woolsey, R. James – Under Secretary of Navy in Carter admin. Ambassador for negotiating the conventional forces in Europe treaty in Bush Sr. admin. CIA Director in Clinton admin. Trustee, Center for Strategic and International Studies. Chair of advisory committee of the Clean Fuels Foundation. Member, Project for the New American Century. Signed 1998 letter to President Clinton.

Zakheim, Dov – Deputy Undersecretary of Defense for Planning and Resources in Reagan admin. Served on "Vulcans" to advise Gov. George W. Bush on international affairs. Member, Project for the New American Century. Former Under Secretary of Defense (Comptroller) and Chief Financial Officer in George W. Bush admin. Vice President of Booz Allen Hamilton. Contributed to the 2000 Report.

Zoellick, Robert B. – Deputy Secretary of Treasury for Financial Institutions in Reagan admin. Under Secretary of State for Economic and Agricultural Affairs in Bush Sr. admin. US Trade Representative (2001-2005). Deputy Secretary of State (# 2 job in state department) (2005-2006). Signed 1998 letter to President Clinton.

Appendix B

Highlights of the USA PATRIOT Act

Title I – Enhancing Domestic Security Against Terrorism
Section 101 – Established counterterrorism fund for Justice Department – unnamed amount and no fiscal year limits.

Section 103 – Re-energizes the Justice Department's "Technical Support Center" (established in 1996) with more funds.

Section 105 – Established "national network of electronic crimes task forces" under the Secret Service which will prevent, detect and investigate a wide variety of electronic and computer crimes.

Title II – Enhancing Surveillance Procedures
(This Title is the vehicle that makes radical changes in criminal and intelligence laws. It grants authorities more freedom to surveil, monitor and investigate citizens with fewer checks on abuse. These provisions can be used for any intelligence or law enforcement cases, not just international terrorism.)

Section 201 – Authority to accept wire, oral and electronic communication relating to terrorism. (Expands the list of federal offenses in which wiretaps may be used.)

Section 202 – Authority to accept wire, oral and electronic communication relating to computer fraud and abuse offenses. (Establishes new wiretap authority regarding computer crimes.)

Section 203(a) – Authority to share grand jury information.

Section 203(b) – Authority to share electronic, wire and oral interception information.

Section 203(c) – Procedures.

Section 203(d) – Foreign intelligence information. (Allows sharing of all "foreign intelligence" information among any/all federal agencies, including previously secret grand jury testimony. "Foreign intelligence" is defined as outlined in the FISA.[1] This sharing can be done without a court review or involvement.)

Section 204 – Clarification of intelligence exceptions from limitations on interception and disclosure of wire, oral and electronic communication.

Section 205 – Employment of translators by the FBI.

Section 206 – Roving surveillance authority under the Foreign Intelligence Surveillance Act of 1978. (Creates a roving wiretap authority where the court order follows the target rather than the phone.)

Section 207 – Duration of FISA surveillance of non-United States persons who are agents of a foreign power. (Lengthens the duration of FISA warrants to one year and lengthens the duration of physical search orders.)

Section 208 – Designation of judges: (Increases the number of FISA judges.)

Section 209 – Seizure of voice-mail messages pursuant to warrants. (Removes voice mail from wiretap reqmts.)

Section 211 – Clarification of scope.

Section 212 – Emergency disclosure of electronic communications to protect life and limb. (Requires release of information to federal investigators from firms such as internet service providers. Consent, notice and judicial review not required in an emergency.)

Section 213 – Allows secret "nonphysical search and search warrants" (sneak and peek searches where investigators can enter a suspect's home without a warrant and without informing the suspect they have done so or have seized property).

Section 214 – Pen register and trap and trace authority under FISA. (Allows investigators to obtain telephone numbers dialed to and from a particular phone as well as internet routing information with minimal judicial review under FISA.)

Section 215 – Access to records and other items under FISA. (Allows investigators to seize "any tangible thing"–information and belongings–in FISA-type investigations using secret intelligence tools, under weak judicial review standards.)

Section 216 – Modification of authorities relating to use of pen registers and trap and trace devices. (Permits seizure of internet routing information–website links and addressing information–under a low standard of proof with no protection against possible seizure of message content.)

Section 217 – Interception of computer trespasser communications. (Allows interception without a judge's consent.)

Section 218 – Foreign intelligence information. (Lowers the standard for obtaining FISA warrants. Scope of foreign intelligence only has to be a "significant purpose" of the investigation, rather than the more demanding "primary purpose.")

Section 219 – Single-jurisdiction search warrants for terrorism. (Establishes single-jurisdiction search warrants and nationwide service of warrants for physical evidence–roving warrants which can follow suspects from place-to-place on a single warrant.)

Section 220 – Nationwide service of search warrants for electronic evidence. (Establishes single-jurisdiction search warrants and nationwide service of warrants for electronic evidence–roving warrants which can follow suspects from place-to-place on a single warrant.)

Section 221 – Trade sanctions.

Section 222 – Assistance to law enforcement agencies.

Section 223 – Civil liability for certain unauthorized disclosures.

Section 224 – Provides that all of Title II will expire on 31 December 2005; with the exception of Sections 203(a), 203(c), 205, 208, 210,

America in Peril

211, 213, 216, 219, 221, and 222 which are permanent, unless Congress renews them before that date.

Section 225 – Immunity for compliance with FISA wiretap.

Title III: International Money Laundering Abatement and Anti-terrorist Financing Act of 2001

(This title, with three sub-titles, is the longest of the ten and takes up most of the 342 pages.)

Section 303 – Provides that the entire Title III expire on 1 October 2005 unless Congress passes a joint resolution to make it permanent. (Congress repealed this section instead.)

Section 311 – Outlines the conditions when a federal investigator can impose extreme "special measures" upon domestic banks and financial institutions when seeking terrorist financing information.

Section 312 – Imposes new requirements on domestic banks and financial institutions for monitoring certain accounts to detect possible terrorist financing.

Sections 316 & 319 – Set up formerly unheard of provisions for forfeiting an account upon conviction of a terrorist crime, especially money laundering.

Section 319 – Creates 120-hour deadline for financial institutions to respond to certain information requests involving a wide spectrum of accounts; also requires financial institutions to provide information on certain "correspondent" accounts with foreign banks.

Section 326 – Adds and expands means of tracking new bank account owners; also commissions a study to use identity numbers for tracking aliens and foreign nationals.

Section 358 – Authorizes secret accessibility for federal investigator to consumer records without legal liability.

Section 361 – Establishes/expands treasury department's FinCEN office, spelling out additional duties and increasing funding.

Title IV: Protecting the Border

Section 403 – Mandates system to allow state department to access certain FBI criminal files; also sets up new-technology standards for visas and checkpoints.

Section 411 – Re-defines terrorism to three types of "terrorist organizations" with wide latitude for federal investigators to identify them. This expands grounds for deportation for alleged support of terrorist groups of causes.

Section 412 – Allows detention of suspected aliens for seven days without charges – a suspect not deported or charged with a crime during that period must be released. Allows for indefinite detention for aliens deemed not removable with a review of their detention every six months. Mandates biannual reports to Congress on aliens detained (name, when and where detained and nature of charges not required).

Sections 414, 415, 416 & 417 — Establishes new standards/studies for border entry and exit systems employing data bases and machine-readable passports. Increases personnel for guarding the borders.

Section 416 — Expands foreign student monitoring and increases funding.

Unknown Sections — Noncitizens (including lawful permanent residents) can be arrested or detained on mere suspicion of a crime, or they can be denied re-admittance to the US for engaging in free speech protected by the First Amendment.

Title V: Removing Obstacles to Investigating Terrorism

Section 503 — Greatly expands DNA information bank, including all violent criminals and terrorists.

Section 504 — Removes barriers so that information from criminal investigations and intelligence can be cross-shared.

Sections 505 — Lowers the requirements for issuing "national security letters" (which are used instead of warrants and at the sole discretion of the justice department), imposes a gag order on recipients and require no judicial review. Provides federal investigators secret access to information and reports without civil liability.

Sections 507 & 508 — Federal investigators can access educational records without a court order.

Title VI: Providing for Victims of Terrorism, Public Safety Officers and Their Families

Section 605 — The Uniformed Division, US Secret Service. (This section added by the USA PATRIOT Act Improvement and Re-authorization Act of 2005 established a national police force under the Department of Homeland Security.)

Title VII: Increased Information Sharing for Critical Infrastructure Protection

Section 701 — Provides way for a "secure information sharing system" among all law enforcement agencies including state and local to pursue and prosecute multi-jurisdictional terrorist activities and conspiracies.

Title VIII: Strengthening the Criminal Laws Against Terrorism

Section 802 — Creates new crime of domestic terrorism—an act which is 1) a federal or state crime, 2) is dangerous or harmful to human life, 3) is intended to affect policy by coercion or intimidation, and 4) must occur in the United States. This federalizes all activity which meet the four requirements under the crime of "domestic terrorism."

Section 803 — Expands and redefines crime of harboring, concealing, or providing material support to terrorists and terrorist organizations and imposes stronger penalties.

Section 808 — Expands definition of "federal crime of terrorism" to include some computer crimes.

America in Peril

Sections 809, 810, 811 & 812 – Eliminates statute of limitations for certain terrorist crimes. Increases penalties for terrorism.

Unknown Sections – Allows attorney general or secretary of state to designate a domestic group as a terrorist organization and deport any noncitizen that belongs to it. Makes an act of terrorism against a mass transit system a federal crime. Criminalizes possession of substances that can be used in a chemical or biological attack or for any purposes except "peaceful" purposes. Noncitizens can be deported for paying membership dues to a political organization.

Title IX: Improved Surveillance

Section 901 – Requires CIA to share information with justice department (FBI).

Section 903 – Deputizes all "officers and employees" in all 13 agencies of the "intelligence community" as a mini-CIA to investigate terrorism.

Section 905 – Requires justice department and similar law-enforcement agencies to share information with the CIA.

Section 908 – Establishes a cross agency training program for all law enforcement officers and agencies, including state and local, to help them better recognize "foreign intelligence" material, information or evidence in the course of their work.

Title X: Miscellaneous

Section 1005 – Provides for grants to state and local fire departments and first responders under the "First Responders Assistance Act." Grants can include equipment and technology for gathering and analyzing intelligence information.

Section 1016 – Establishes new programs for critical infrastructure protection.

Note for Appendix B

1. The broad definition of "foreign intelligence" set forth in the FISA includes "information, whether or not concerning a United States person, with respect to a foreign power or foreign territory that relates to the national defense or the security of the United States or the conduct of the foreign affairs of the United States."

Appendix C

Examples of Civil Rights Violations
from the TSA's Watch Lists

(This list is made up from just ten hits, out of 100,
when the internet was searched for "no-fly list.")

Adams, Jan – Age 55. Co-founder of *War Times* print and internet publication. Delayed at San Francisco Airport on 7 August 2002. Boarding pass was marked with red "S" for additional scrutiny at San Francisco and at layover in Chicago. Eventually allowed to fly both times.

Chang, Nancy – Senior litigation attorney at Center for Constitutional Rights. Has been singled out for searches and questioning at the airport.

Dear, John – Age 43. Jesuit priest, member of Catholic peace group Pax Christi and former executive director of Fellowship of Reconciliation. Says that since 9/11 he's been taken aside at the boarding gate every single time, searched and questioned.

Fathi, David C. – Age 41. US citizen of Iranian descent. Resides in Wash., DC. Civil liberties lawyer and senior staff counsel for ACLU's National Prison Project. Two arrests for peaceful civil disobedience in 1988 and 1991. Has been delayed, detained, interrogated and searched at airports seven or eight times.

Gordon, Rebecca – Age 50. San Francisco human rights advocate and co-founder of *War Times* print and internet publication. Delayed at San Francisco Airport on 7 August 2002. Boarding pass was marked with red "S" for additional scrutiny at San Francisco and at layover in Chicago. Eventually allowed to fly both times.

Green, Michelle D. – Age 36. Active duty US Air Force master sergeant based in Alaska. Since early January 2004, while flying on official business, has been unable to board flight without significant delays.

Hay, Alexandra – Age 22. Middlebury College, VT, student studying abroad in Paris. She was delayed in getting on plane twice in late 2003. Worried about getting on flight to Paris, she had prior arrangement by ACLU that got her walked through. Having no problems in the future could not be guaranteed, however.

Ibrahim, Mohamed – Age 51. US citizen. Lives in Philadelphia, works as project voice coördinator for American Friends Service Committee. Since November 2003 has been repeatedly delayed, detained, interrogated, embarrassed and subject to enhanced screening procedures at airports.

Johnson, Robert – Physician & surgeon. Former army lt. col. A critic of the Iraq war, running on Democratic ticket against Republican Congressperson John McHugh, told in 2006 he is on the no-fly list.

Kennedy, Edward M. "Ted" – US senator (D-MA). Stopped and questioned

5 times in March 2004 at Reagan National and Boston Logan airports. Got off list in 3 weeks because of personal contact with the Homeland Security Secretary Tom Ridge. Was told "T Kennedy" was on the list, later discovered there are 7,000 men in the US named "T. Kennedy."

Lawinger, Virgine – Age 74. Member of Peace Action in Milwaukee. She and 20 other members of her group were stopped at Milwaukee airport and missed their flight to Wash. DC to lobby the Wisconsin delegation. Was told by sheriff deputies that one or several of them were "on a list."

Lewis, John – US Congressperson (D-GA). Well-known civil rights advocate. Stopped several times by no-fly list.

Moore, James – Television news correspondent (Emmy winner) and author. Co-author of *Bush's Brain: How Karl Rove Made George W. Bush President*. Critic of Bush. Has been on no-fly list since January 2005.

Nelson, David C. – Age 34. Attorney in Belleville, IL. Has been stopped at the airport more than 40 times. Learned that other "David Nelson"s across country – including the David Nelson of "Ozzie and Harriet" fame – have had the same experiences.

Oden, Nancy – Green Party USA official in ME. Prevented from flying out of Bangor, ME airport to Chicago in November 2001.

Olshansky, Barbara – Assistant legal director for Center on Constitutional Rights. Stopped and searched every time she flew since 9/11.

Radack, Jesselyn – Former department of justice ethics adviser. Argued that John Walker Lindh was entitled to an attorney. Believed to have been put on list as retribution for whistleblowing.

Rodriguez, William – Maintains official 9/11 story is a coverup, campaigning for new and independent investigation. Claims to be on no-fly list.

Several children too young to be a threat – One a 4-year-old and another was 9 months old generated "false positives."

Shaw, John – Age 74. Retired Presbyterian minister. Lives in Sammamish, WA. Has been on the airport watch list.

Stevens, Cat (Yusuf Islam) – Former pop singer. Converted to Islam in 1978 and changed his name. Was denied entry into US in September 2004 when his name was found on the no-fly list.

Stuber, Doug – Art dealer, leader of Green Party USA. Has been questioned by secret service agents and given a retina scan at airports. In most cases he was allowed to fly but sometimes missed the flight.

Syed, Sarosh – Age 26. Immigrated from Pakistan in 1995. Became a US citizen in 2001. Special projects coördinator for ACLU in Seattle, WA. Delayed at airport half-a-dozen times since fall of 2002.

Walter, James W. – Maintains official 9/11 story is a coverup and is campaigning for a new and independent investigation. Claims he is on the no-fly list.

Young, Donald E. – US congressperson (R-AK). Third-most senior Republican in House of Representatives. Was flagged in 2004 at airport check-in, mistaken for "Donald Lee Young."

Appendix D

Coercive Techniques Outlined in the CIA's *Kubark Handbook*

- **Arrest** – Manner and timing are critical. Catch the subject off balance and maintain the initiative. Early hours of the morning when they least expect it is best. That is a time their mental and physical resistance is lowest.
- **Detention** – Make subject feel isolated in a strange environment. Remove familiar clothes and give them an outfit that doesn't fit and feels uncomfortable. Control their diet, sleep patterns and other fundamentals. Manipulate irregularities so the prisoner feels disoriented. Other techniques used are to keep the prisoner naked in a windowless, soundproof cell with no toilet; also to put rats and cockroaches in the cell and serve the prisoner inedible and disgusting food.
- **Deprivation of Sensory Stimuli** – Make subject feel isolated. Being cut off from external stimuli causes their awareness to turn inward. Many examples are given on how to do this. The more well-adjusted and normal a subject is, the more they are affected by deprivation of the senses.
- **Threats and Fear** – The threat of torture is usually more effective than torture itself. A threat can trigger fears more damaging than actual physical coercion. Fear of the unknown induces regression. One technique practiced during the Vietnam war was to take detainees up in a helicopter, throw one out, and tell the next in line he goes too if he doesn't talk.
- **Debility** – Physical weakness is induced by various methods: prolonged constraint; prolonged exertion; extremes of heat, cold or moisture; and deprivation or drastic reduction of food or sleep. This technique was deemed counter-productive but the threat of debility – stress positions for a short time or a brief deprivation of food or sleep – seem to produce the anxiety necessary to extract information.
- **Pain** – Pain introduced by the interrogator is likely to increase noncoöperation and resistance by the subject; also, extreme pain might cause false confessions just to alleviate the pain. Pain that is self-induced is more successful. For instance, a person told to stand at attention under threat of something worse is more likely to become less resistant to questioning.
- **Heightened Suggestibility and Hypnosis** – This should be done by someone trained in the field, not the interrogator. Although most theories regarding hypnotism work against success in this approach, the individual practitioner is encouraged to judge the circumstances for themselves. If subject is tricked into believing they are talking to a friend, it might work.
- **Narcosis or Drugs** – Using an inert substance (placebo) to make a subject think they have been drugged may be more effective than actually drugging them. A person thinking "I am drugged" may alleviate a guilt complex about revealing information; also, a drug administered without subjects'

America in Peril

knowledge may make them more susceptible to hypnosis. Drugs are tricky and can cause hallucinations, illusions, delusions and disorientation that affects the information divulged.

Appendix E

US Reservations Regarding the Convention Against Torture and Other Cruel, Inhuman or Degrading Treatment or Punishment

Upon signature:
Declaration:
"The Government of the United States of America reserves the right to communicate, upon ratification, such reservations, interpretive understandings, or declarations as are deemed necessary."

Upon ratification:
Reservations:

I. The Senate's advice and consent is subject to the following reservations:

(1) That the United States considers itself bound by the obligation under article 16 to prevent 'cruel, inhuman or degrading treatment or punishment,' only insofar as the term 'cruel, inhuman or degrading treatment or punishment' means the cruel, unusual and inhumane treatment or punishment prohibited by the Fifth, Eighth, and/or Fourteenth Amendments to the Constitution of the United States.

(2) That pursuant to article 30(2) the United States declares that it does not consider itself bound by Article 30(1), but reserves the right specifically to agree to follow this or any other procedure for arbitration in a particular case.

II. The Senate's advice and consent is subject to the following understandings, which shall apply to the obligations of the United States under this Convention:

(1)(a) That with reference to article 1, the United States understands that, in order to constitute torture, an act must be specifically intended to inflict severe physical or mental pain or suffering and that mental pain or suffering refers to prolonged mental harm caused by or resulting from (1) the intentional infliction or threatened infliction of severe physical pain or suffering; (2) the admin. or application, or threatened admin. or application, of mind-altering substances or other procedures calculated to disrupt profoundly the senses or the personality; (3) the threat of imminent death; or (4) the threat that another person will imminently be subjected to death, severe physical pain or suffering, or the admin. or application of mind-altering substances or other procedures calculated to disrupt profoundly the senses or personality.

(b) That the United States understands that the definition of torture in article 1 is intended to apply only to acts directed against persons in the offender's custody or physical control.

America in Peril

(c) That with reference to article 1 of the Convention, the United States understands that 'sanctions' includes judicially-imposed sanctions and other enforcement actions authorized by United States law or by judicial interpretation of such law. Nonetheless, the United States understands that a state party could not through its domestic sanctions defeat the object and purpose of the Convention to prohibit torture.

(d) That with reference to article 1 of the Convention, the United States understands that the term 'acquiescence' requires that the public official, prior to the activity constituting torture, have awareness of such activity and thereafter breach their legal responsibility to intervene to prevent such activity.

(e) That with reference to article 1 of the Convention, the Unites States understands that noncompliance with applicable legal procedural standards does not *per se* constitute torture.

(2) That the United States understands the phrase, 'where there are substantial grounds for believing that he would be in danger of being subjected to torture,' as used in article 3 of the Convention, to mean 'if it is more likely than not that he would be tortured.'

(3) That it is the understanding of the United States that article 14 requires a state party to provide a private right of action for damages only for acts of torture committed in territory under the jurisdiction of that state party.

(4) That the United States understands that international law does not prohibit the death penalty, and does not consider this Convention to restrict or prohibit the United States from applying the death penalty consistent with the Fifth, Eighth and/ or Fourteenth Amendments to the Constitution of the United States, including any constitutional period of confinement prior to the imposition of the death penalty.

(5) That the United States understands that this Convention shall be implemented by the United States government to the extent that it exercises legislative and judicial jurisdiction over the matters covered by the Convention and otherwise by the state and local governments. Accordingly, in implementing articles 10-14 and 16, the United States government shall take measures appropriate to the federal system to the end that the competent authorities of the constituent units of the United States of America may take appropriate measures for the fulfillment of the Convention.

III. The Senate's advice and consent is subject to the following declarations:

(1) That the United States declares that the provisions of articles 1 through 16 of the Convention are not self-executing.

Appendix F

Fifth, Eighth and Fourteenth Amendments to the US Constitution

Amendment V

No person shall be held to answer for a capital, or otherwise infamous crime, unless on a presentment or indictment of a grand jury, except in cases arising in the land or naval forces, or in the militia, when in actual service in time of war or public danger; nor shall any person be subject for the same offense to be twice put in jeopardy of life or limb; nor shall be compelled in any criminal case to be a witness against himself, nor be deprived of life, liberty, or property, without due process of law; nor shall private property be taken for public use, without just compensation.

Amendment VIII

Excessive bail shall not be required, nor excessive fines imposed, nor cruel and unusual punishments inflicted.

Amendment XIV

Section 1. All persons born or naturalized in the United States, and subject to the jurisdiction thereof, are citizens of the United States and of the state wherein they reside. No state shall make or enforce any law which shall abridge the privileges or immunities of citizens of the United States; nor shall any state deprive any person of life, liberty, or property, without due process of law; nor deny to any person within its jurisdiction the equal protection of the laws.

Section 2. Representatives shall be apportioned among the several states according to their respective numbers, counting the whole number of persons in each state, excluding Indians not taxed. But when the right to vote at any election for the choice of electors for President and Vice President of the United States, Representatives in Congress, the executive and judicial officers of a state, or the members of the legislature thereof, is denied to any of the male inhabitants of such state, being twenty-one years of age, and citizens of the United States, or in any way abridged, except for participation in rebellion, or other crime, the basis of representation therein shall be reduced in the proportion which the number of such male citizens shall bear to the whole number of male citizens twenty-one years of age in such state.

Section 3. No person shall be a Senator or Representative in Congress, or elector of President and Vice President, or hold any office, civil or military, under the United States, or under any state, who, having previously taken an

America in Peril

oath, as a member of Congress, or as an officer of the United States, or as a member of any state legislature, or as an executive or judicial officer of any state, to support the Constitution of the United States, shall have engaged in insurrection or rebellion against the same, or given aid or comfort to the enemies thereof. But Congress may by a vote of two-thirds of each House, remove such disability.

Section 4. The validity of the public debt of the United States, authorized by law, including debts incurred for payment of pensions and bounties for services in suppressing insurrection or rebellion, shall not be questioned. But neither the United States nor any state shall assume or pay any debt or obligation incurred in aid of insurrection or rebellion against the United States, or any claim for the loss or emancipation of any slave; but all such debts, obligations and claims shall be held illegal and void.

Section 5. The Congress shall have power to enforce, by appropriate legislation, the provisions of this article.

Appendix G

Interrogation Techniques

Category I
1. Gagging with gauze
2. Yelling at detainee
3. Deception
   a. Multiple interrogators
   b. Interrogator posing as an interrogator from a foreign nation with a reputation for harsh treatment of detainees

Category II
1. Use of stress positions (such as standing) for a maximum of 4 hours
2. Use of falsified documents or reports
3. Isolation facility for 30-day increments.
4. Nonstandard interrogation environment/booth
5. Hooding detainees
6. Use of 20-hour interrogation segments
7. Removal of all comfort items (including religious items)
8. Switching detainees from hot rations to MREs (Meals Ready to Eat—army field rations)
9. Removal of all clothing
10. Forced grooming (shaving of facial hair, etc.)
11. Use of individual phobias (such as fear of dogs) to induce stress

Category III
1. Use of scenarios designed to convince detainee that death or severe pain is imminent for him or his family
2. Exposure to cold weather or water (with medical monitoring)
3. Use of wet towel and dripping water to induce the misperception of drowning
4. Use of mild physical contact such as grabbing, light pushing, and poking with finger

Category IV
1. Detainee will be sent from Guantanamo, either temporarily or permanently, to Jordan, Egypt or another country to allow those countries to employ interrogation techniques that will enable them to obtain the requisite information (called extraordinary rendition).

Appendix H

Protocol Additional to the Geneva Conventions of 1949 Relating to the Protection of Victims of International Armed Conflicts (Protocol 1)

Adopted on 8 June 1977 by the Diplomatic Conference
on the Reaffirmation and Development of International
Humanitarian Law applicable in Armed Conflicts

Entry into force 7 December 1979, in accordance with Article 95

Article 75.-Fundamental guarantees

1. In so far as they are affected by a situation referred to in Article 1 of this Protocol, persons who are in the power of a Party to the conflict and who do not benefit from more favourable treatment under the Conventions or under this Protocol shall be treated humanely in all circumstances and shall enjoy, as a minimum, the protection provided by this Article without any adverse distinction based upon race, colour, sex, language, religion or belief, political or other opinion, national or social origin, wealth, birth or other status, or on any other similar criteria. Each Party shall respect the person, honour, convictions and religious practices of all such persons.

2. The following acts are and shall remain prohibited at any time and in any place whatsoever, whether committed by civilian or by military agents:
   (a) Violence to the life, health, or physical or mental well-being of persons, in particular:
      (i) Murder;
      (ii) Torture of all kinds, whether physical or mental;
      (iii) Corporal punishment; and
      (iv) Mutilation;
   (b) Outrages upon personal dignity, in particular humiliating and degrading treatment, enforced prostitution and any form of indecent assault;
   (c) The taking of hostages;
   (d) Collective punishments; and
   (e) Threats to commit any of the foregoing acts.

3. Any person arrested, detained or interned for actions related to the armed conflict shall be informed promptly, in a language he understands, of the reasons why these measures have been taken. Except in cases of arrest or detention for penal offences, such persons shall be released with the minimum delay possible and in any event as soon as the circumstances justifying the arrest, detention or internment have ceased to exist.

4. No sentence may be passed and no penalty may be executed on a person found guilty of a penal offence related to the armed conflict except pursuant to a conviction pronounced by an impartial and regularly constituted court respecting the generally recognized principles of regular judicial procedure, which include the following:

(a) The procedure shall provide for an accused to be informed without delay of the particulars of the offence alleged against him and shall afford the accused before and during his trial all necessary rights and means of defence;

(b) No one shall be convicted of an offence except on the basis of individual penal responsibility;

(c) No one shall be accused or convicted of a criminal offence on account of any act or omission which did not constitute a criminal offence under the national or international law to which he was subject at the time when it was committed; nor shall a heavier penalty be imposed than that which was applicable at the time when the criminal offence was committed; if, after the commission of the offence, provision is made by law for the imposition of a lighter penalty, the offender shall benefit thereby;

(d) Anyone charged with an offence is presumed innocent until proved guilt according to law;

(e) Anyone charged with an offence shall have the right to be tried in his presence;

(f) No one shall be compelled to testify against himself or to confess guilt;

(g) Anyone charged with an offence shall have the right to examine, or have examined, the witnesses against him and to obtain the attendance and examination of witnesses on his behalf under the same conditions as witnesses against him;

(h) No one shall be prosecuted or punished by the same Party for an offence in respect of which a final judgement acquitting or convicting that person has been previously pronounced under the same law and judicial procedure;

(i) Anyone prosecuted for an offence shall have the right to have the judgement pronounced publicly; and

(j) A convicted person shall be advised on conviction of his judicial and other remedies and of the time-limits within which they may be exercised.

5. Women whose liberty has been restricted for reasons related to the armed conflict shall be held in quarters separated from men's quarters. They shall be under the immediate supervision of women. Nevertheless, in cases where families are detained or interned, they shall, whenever possible, be held in the same place and accommodated as family units.

6. Persons who are arrested, detained or interned for reasons related to the armed conflict shall enjoy the protection provided by this Article until

their final release, repatriation or re-establishment, even after the end of the armed conflict.

7. In order to avoid any doubt concerning the prosecution and trial of persons accused of war crimes or crimes against humanity, the following principles shall apply:

(a) Persons who are accused of such crimes should be submitted for the purpose of prosecution and trial in accordance with the applicable rules of international law; and

(b) Any such persons who do not benefit from more favourable treatment under the Conventions or this Protocol shall be accorded the treatment provided by this Article, whether or not the crimes of which they are accused constitute grave breaches of the Conventions or of this Protocol.

8. No provision of this Article may be construed as limiting or infringing any other more favourable provision granting greater protection, under any applicable rules of international law, to persons covered by paragraph 1.

Glossary

AAMVA – American Association of Motor Vehicle Administrators
ABA – American Bar Association
ABC – American Broadcasting Corp
ACLU – American Civil Liberties Union
AFCAP – Air Force Contract Augmentation Program
AID – Agency for International Development
a.k.a – Also known as
ALA – American Library Association
AOL – America On-Line
AP – Associated Press
AR210-35 – Army Regulation 210-35
ATM – Automatic Teller Machine
ATS – Automated Targeting System
AM – Amplitude Modulation
ARDA – Advanced Research and Development Activity
AT&T – American Telephone & Telegraph Co.
BBC – British Broadcasting Corporation
BPG – Bi-national Planning Group
CAPPS – Computer-Assisted Passenger Prescreening System
CBP – Customs and Border Patrol Agency
CBS – Columbia Broadcasting System
CDC – Center for Disease Control
CEO – Chief Executive Officer
CI – Counterintelligence
CIA – Central Intelligence Agency
CIFA – Counterintelligence Field Activity
CMS – Center for Medicare and Medicaid Services
CNN – Cable News Network
CNO – Chief of Naval Operations
COINTELPRO – COunterINTELligencePROgrams
CONCAP – Construction Capabilities (Navy Civil Augmentation Program)
CRS – Congressional Research Service
CTC – CounterTerrorism Center
DCI – Director of Central Intelligence (head of the CIA)
DCSNet – Digital Collections Systems Network
DHS – Department of Homeland Security
DIA – Defense Intelligence Agency
DNI – Director of National Intelligence
DOD – Department of Defense
DOJ – Department of Justice
DPG – Defense Planning Guidance, or Defense Policy Guidance

DSS –	Defense Security Service
DUI –	Driving Under the Infuence
EFF –	Electronic Frontier Foundation
EPA –	Environmental Protection Agency
EPIC –	Electronic Privacy Information Center
EPW –	Enemy Prisoner of War
EU –	European Union
FAA –	Federal Aviation Administration
FACA –	Federal Advisory Committee Act
FBI –	Federal Bureau of Investigation
FCC –	Federal Communications Commission
FDA –	Food and Drug Administration
FDIC –	Federal Deposit Insurance Corporation
FEMA –	Federal Emergency Management Agency
FEPP –	Free Expression Policy Project (of the Brennan Center at NY Univ. School of Law)
FISA –	Foreign Intelligence Surveillance Act
FOIA –	Freedom of Information Act
FOI/PA –	Freedom of Information/Privacy Acts
FOX –	Fox News
G-2 –	Army Intelligence
GAO –	Government Accountability Office (formerly General Accounting Office)
GE –	General Electric
GNP –	Gross National Product
GOP –	Grand Old Party (Republican party)
HHS –	Department of Health and Human Services
HSPD –	Homeland Security Presidential Directive
HUMINT –	Human Intelligence
IC –	Intelligence Community
ICE –	Immigration and Customs Enforcement
ICRC –	International Committee of the Red Cross
ID –	Identification
IED –	Improvised Explosive Device
IEEE –	Inst. of Electrical and Electronics Engineers
IMINT –	Imaging Intelligence
INS –	Immigration and Naturalization Service
INSCOM –	Information and Security Command
IRS –	Internal Revenue Service
ISOO –	Information Security Oversight Office (under National Archives)
JAG –	Judge Advocate General
JRIES –	Joint Regional Information Exchange System
KBR –	Kellogg, Brown & Root
LOGCAP –	Logistics Civil Augmentation Program (Army)
MASINT –	Measurements And Signature Intelligence

MATRIX – Multistate Anti-Terrorism Information Exchange
MDAC – Microsoft Data Access Components
MRE – Meal Ready to Eat
NAFTA – North American Free Trade Agreement
NASA – National Aeronautics and Space Admin.
NATO – North Atlantic Treaty Organization
NAU – North American Union
NBC – National Broadcasting Company
NCTC – National Counterterrorism Center
Neocon – Neoconservative
NGA – National Geospatial-Intelligence Agency
NHTSA – National Highway Transportation Safety Admin.
NIMA – National Imagery and Mapping Agency, now called National Geospatial-Intelligence Agency
NIST – National Inst. of Standards and Technology
NORAD – North American Aerospace Defense Command
NORTHCOM – Northern Command
NRO – National Reconnaissance Office
NSA – National Security Agency
NSC – National Security Council
NSPD – National Security Presidential Directive
NY – New York
OFAC – Office of Foreign Assets Control (under OMB)
OIRA – Office of Information and Regulatory Affairs
OMB – Office of Management and Budget
ONDCP – Office of National Drug Control Policy
ONI – Office of Naval Intelligence
OPR – Office of Professional Responsibility (US Justice Dept)
OSS – Office of Strategic Services
OVP – Office of the Vice President
PBS – Public Broadcasting System
PENTTBOM – Pentagon/Twin Towers Bombing
PIN – Personal Identification Number
PNAC – Project for the New American Century
POW – Prisoner of War
PR – Public Relations
PUC – Public Utilities Commission
REX-84 – Readiness Exercise 1984
RNC – Republican National Committee
RISS – Regional Information Sharing System
SAIC – Science Applications International Corporation
SBU – Sensitive But Unclassified
SEC – Securities and Exchange Commission
SIGINT – Signals Intelligence
SOA – School of the Americas

SPP –	Security and Prosperity Partnership of North America
SS –	Steam Ship
SWAT –	Special Weapons And Tactics
SWIFT –	Society for Worldwide Interbank Financial Telecommunication
TALON –	Threat And Local Observation Notice
TGDC –	Technical Guidance Development Committee
TIA –	Total Information Awareness. Later renamed Terrorist Information Awareness
TIPS –	Terrorism Information and Prevention System
TopOff –	Top Officers
TRAC –	Transactional Records Access Clearinghouse
TSA –	Transportation Security Admin
TV –	Television
UAE –	United Arab Emirates
UCMJ –	Uniform Code of Military Justice
UK –	United Kingdom
UN –	United Nations
UPI –	United Press International
US –	United States
USA PATRIOT –	Uniting and Strengthening America by Providing Appropriate Tools Required to Intercept and Obstruct Terrorism
USCCR –	United States Commission on Civil Rights
USN –	United States Navy
USS –	United States Ship
USSOUTHCOM –	US Southern Command
US-VISIT –	US Visitor and Immigrant Status Indicator Technology
VA –	Veterans Affairs (Department of Veterans Affairs), formerly Veterans Admin.
VICTORY –	Vital Interdiction of Criminal Terrorist Organizations
VNR –	Video News Release
WMD –	Weapons of Mass Destruction
WTC –	World Trade Center

Additional copies of this book may be obtained
from your bookstore
or by contacting
Hope Publishing House
P.O. Box 60008
Pasadena, CA 91116 - U.S.A.
(626) 792-6123 / (800) 326-2671
Fax (626) 792-2121
E-mail: hopepub@sbcglobal.net
www.hope-pub.com